Nietzsche and Dostoevsky

SRLT

Nietzsche and Dostoevsky

Philosophy, Morality, Tragedy

Edited by Jeff Love and Jeffrey Metzger

NORTHWESTERN UNIVERSITY PRESS / EVANSTON, ILLINOIS

Northwestern University Press
www.nupress.northwestern.edu

Printed in the United States of America

10 9 8 7 6 5 4 3 2 1

Library of Congress Cataloging-in-Publication Data
Names: Love, Jeff (G. Jeffrey), editor. | Metzger, Jeffrey (Jeffrey Patrick), editor.
Title: Nietzsche and Dostoevsky : philosophy, morality, tragedy / edited by Jeff Love
    and Jeffrey Metzger.
Other titles: Studies in Russian literature and theory.
Description: Evanston, Illinois : Northwestern University Press, 2016. | Series:
    Northwestern University Press studies in Russian literature and theory | Includes
    bibliographical references and index.
Identifiers: LCCN 2016024109| ISBN 9780810133945 (pbk. : alk. paper) | ISBN
    9780810133952 (cloth : alk. paper) | ISBN 9780810133969 (e-book)
Subjects: LCSH: Dostoyevsky, Fyodor, 1821–1881—Criticism and interpretation.
    Nietzsche, Friedrich Wilhelm, 1844–1900. | Philosophy in literature. |
    Literature—Philosophy.
Classification: LCC PG3328.Z7 P573 2016 | DDC 891.733—dc23
LC record available at https://lccn.loc.gov/2016024109

To the memory of J. Michael Holquist, exemplary thinker, teacher and friend

Contents

Jeff Love and Jeffrey Metzger

Introduction

FRIEDRICH NIETZSCHE and Fyodor Dostoevsky stand at the threshold of what we might call the long twentieth century. This is of course not a question of chronology: Dostoevsky died in 1881, and Nietzsche's lucid and productive life ended in January of 1889. But in a fundamental sense they are the heralds and perhaps the creators of a particular dispensation—spiritual, moral, philosophical—that defined the twentieth century and that endures to this day, one that we may still consider to be most our own even as it continues to recede in some areas. More elusive, expansive, and enduring than Marx or Freud, Dostoevsky and Nietzsche remain keenly alive today because they have wounded modern humanity not, as Freud said of Copernicus, Darwin, and himself, with an insight or truth, but with an ever deepening and widening attitude of urgent, merciless questioning. They return to the fundamental inquiring attitude of the Greeks, but having come through two millennia of Christianity their questioning is born not of wonder but of the pain and terror of lost certainty and solace, and is sharpened and driven not by the discovery of reason but by the psychological and moral asceticism born of the Christian belief in—or invention of—evil.

Before the larger world even knew Nietzsche's name (or after it had forgotten it), he himself was aware of his profound and singular bond with Dostoevsky, reading several of his works and famously recognizing both deep kinship and troubling antagonism. It is Nietzsche, after all, who claimed famously that Dostoevsky was the only psychologist from whom he had anything to learn. While Dostoevsky did not seem aware of Nietzsche, it was not long until those immersed in Dostoevsky's fiction began to recognize an affinity with Nietzsche, and it can be argued with some justice that Dostoevsky's works played a determinative role in establishing the framework within which Nietzsche's texts entered into Russian culture at the end of the nineteenth and the beginning of the twentieth centuries. This remarkable, autumnal period of Russian culture, a period of decline and transformation, of brilliant religio-philosophic speculation that fell into silence with the extreme historical dislocation brought about by the revolution of 1917, provided an extraordinarily fecund proving ground for Nietzschean thought. Almost all the major figures of that era, from Vladimir Soloviev to Dmitry Merezhkovsky and Nikolay Berdyayev, debated the impact of Nietzsche's ideas, and, in particular, that of the Overman (*Übermensch*), in the most intense way, with some attempting to reconcile Christianity with Nietzsche, others denying the possibility of this reconciliation, and still others moving in their own directions with a singular question in mind: to what extent may man become God?[1]

This immense, complicated program (perhaps the latter term is too grandiose) of self-deification is characteristic of this period. Self-deification had in fact become an issue of considerable moment in Russia, a variety of different positions being taken, ranging from the god-man (*bogochelovek*) of Vladimir Soloviev to the man-god (*chelovekobog*) of Dostoevsky, that peculiar creature which emerges as the great advocate of suicide, Alexei Nilych Kirillov, in *Demons*. The terminology may well seem precious unless we consider its significance more carefully, for it reveals two positions deeply related by their mutual opposition. The god-man reflects what one might call a finitist position, that is, a position predicated upon becoming like God that falls short of complete self-deification. The man-god seems to be a somewhat curious attempt to explore a nonfinitist position or one that is not conditioned by the most fundamental conditioning factor of the finite being, its ineradicable dependence, its sustained failure ever to attain to autonomy, to use a Kantian term, as reflected by the simple fact that it remains mortal. Both these tendencies sought to adapt Nietzsche to their own purposes, and both failed. But the closeness of Nietzsche to a distinctively Russian concern with self-deification and to the incisive articulation of reservations about that purpose in Dostoevsky had a tremendous impact on Russian thought that has not yet been fully recovered or understood.

A second—perhaps the only other—significant moment in the reception of both Nietzsche and Dostoevsky emerges most dramatically in the interest that the so-called existentialists lavished on both as precursors to their own thinking. The hard core of existentialism, the thought of Martin Heidegger, has many affinities with Nietzsche and Dostoevsky that the master himself was wont to acknowledge. One need only mention his enormous book on Nietzsche published in 1961 that collects some of the many lecture courses he gave on Nietzsche in the latter half of the 1930s as well as other texts. There is also a somewhat apocryphal tradition of commentary from former students such as Karl Löwith and Hans-Georg Gadamer attesting to Heidegger's avid interest in Dostoevsky as both a fellow traveler of and possible counter to Nietzsche.[2] These affinities were developed explicitly almost wholly within France, largely in the traumatic post-war period. Albert Camus, for example, was deeply impressed by Dostoevsky and, in particular, by *Demons*, a work that features prominently in *The Rebel*. The popularity existentialism subsequently achieved in the United States seems to have contributed to the production of a whole series of monographs that place Dostoevsky and Nietzsche alongside Søren Kierkegaard and various others (even Kafka) as the spiritual fathers of existentialism. In this regard, one wonders how much influence Russian thinkers living in France, like Nikolay Berdyayev, had on existentialism, projecting their own pairing of Dostoevsky and Nietzsche onto the young movement. Be that as it may, the story of this second, French efflorescence of interest in Nietzsche and Dostoevsky as a dialogic pair remains to be told.

In light of the foregoing we might venture a brief comment on the common concerns that seem to bind these two rather astonishing moments of reception, one in prerevolutionary Russia, the other primarily in post-war France. Both moments have in common an intense concern with the question of human finitude. If for the Russians of the prerevolutionary period finitude might well have been something to overcome, the occasionally theatrical display of despair characteristic of the habitus of post-war existentialism reflects the conviction that we must come to terms with the ineluctability of finitude. Remarkable is that in both these cases, with quite different attitudes to finitude in mind, the significance of Dostoevsky and Nietzsche and, especially, of the relation of the one to the other, was recognized and accorded the highest significance. More than that, a fundamental ambiguity regarding finitude, whether we should come to terms with or attempt to overcome it, seems to have been discerned as a crucially distinctive aspect of the writings of both figures—the Russian attitude apparently having survived, albeit in different forms, into the French context, arguably as a result of direct influence combined with an apprehension of the inherent logic of the comparison.

The concerns with finitude animating this rather conjectural *Rezeptions-geschichte* (history of reception) have lost none of their urgency, and they open out onto a series of questions that shape and move the essays presented here. What is morality, if it is not commanded and secured by God? What is philosophy, if humanity is not defined by reason as our sole connection to the eternal and infinite—and what is reason if humanity is not defined by philosophy as its highest activity? What can tragedy be when it is staged for a bourgeois audience, but also what is bourgeois or even Socratic rationality when seen in the light of a genuinely tragic sensibility? Perhaps most fundamentally, how is suffering justified, if not through an ultimate reconciliation and union with God?

Francesca Cernia Slovin and Geoff Waite begin our collection with a fascinating synopsis of both Nietzsche's experience with Dostoevsky and of the fateful milieu in which those encounters took place. It is a landscape populated with philosophers and artists and aristocrats, but also with revolutionaries and assassins (and the occasional individual who combined almost all these things in one person, like Vera Zasulich). Their attention to the often violent and lawless figures in this story leads them to focus on one central concern, one might almost say obsession, common to both Dostoevsky and Nietzsche: crime and the criminal. The first consequence of this focus is to transform nihilism itself, from a philosophical or psychological-spiritual abyss into a stance of active negation, a revolutionary and so criminal dispensation of the will. Cernia Slovin and Waite, in other words, approach the question of crime (with or without punishment, with or without repentance and redemption) not as a question of abnormal psychology, but in order to understand a form of criminality for which the revolutionary and the philosopher are archetypes. The Russian nihilists are of course the paradigms of this type of nihilism, but, the authors argue, in his own way so is Nietzsche. But this, then, raises the more fundamental question, who is Nietzsche? The imperfectly understood mask and image who roamed in the minds of his contemporaries (and their successors) like Georg Brandes? A nihilist-revolutionary and philosopher-criminal whose writings are "propaganda by deed"? An always unrequited yet always seeking lover? "Every name in history"? And what, then, is his relationship to his "hostile brother," Dostoevsky, with whom Nietzsche seems to blend in his notebook entries on *Demons*?

The dissolution of boundaries and identities is also central to Jeff Love's chapter, which approaches Dostoevsky and Nietzsche by considering the forces that give rise to narrative. Thucydides would call these forces motion and rest, cosmic principles that manifest themselves in human beings as in the rest of nature. For modern consciousness, however, the forces are determinacy and indeterminacy, human intellectual experiences of the external (human and natural) world. Determinacy is the human attempt to gain mastery over the violent confusion of the world by fixing it with names and, ultimately, with a narrative. Indeterminacy is the terrifying loss of that sense of certainty and mastery. The crisis of meaning and justification that commands the attention of both Dostoevsky and Nietzsche is thus primarily a crisis of narrative; the old narratives no longer make sense of the world, so what is the way forward?

For Love, both urge us forward to new ways of living after narrative. Nietzsche, according to Love, advocates a parody of narrative, a kind of playing in the otherwise gruesome shadow of the dead God. Dostoevsky, in Love's reading, is the much more radical figure, proposing a way of life that dispenses with narrative altogether. There are two crucial moments in this proposal: the first when the Underground Man indicates to us that will is as much of a sickness as consciousness, and the second when Christ presents us with a life without will and struggle, and thus without narrative, in the legend of the Grand Inquisitor. The difference between the prisoner and the Inquisitor—or indeed between Dostoevsky and Nietzsche—can therefore not be reduced to any simple opposition, not even the opposition between acceptance of indeterminacy and the will to determinacy. "[T]he novelty of the prisoner is that he represents an overcoming of [the opposition between will and relinquishment of will], thus an overcoming of opposition."

Questions concerning the will and truth also animate Jeffrey Metzger's chapter, which considers the relationship between truth and reactivity by asking the more basic question of whether truth is perceived as an independent reality or produced by the will and desires of the perceiver. Focusing on the First Essay of *On the Genealogy of Morals*, Metzger argues that for Nietzsche, the truth is produced in the case of those "healthy" individuals who are able to incorporate and interpret the world to suit themselves. Those who are somehow "unhealthy" (the priests and the slaves of the *Genealogy of Morals*) are unable to create fictions in this hale, organic way, due either to external violence or internal inhibition. The violent intrusion of truth most often issues in *ressentiment*, a rancorous negation of that truth (e.g., the truth of another's superiority). At this point, one shifts from healthy, instinctive fictions to poisonous, destructive lies.

In addressing these questions to Dostoevsky, Metzger concentrates on the first few sections of *Notes from Underground*, contending that the Underground Man presents something close to the contrary view, that truth is primary but can be obscured by falsehoods or fictions believed because they promise greater power, over the natural world and ultimately over human beings and human nature itself. Though this puts Dostoevsky at odds with Nietzsche, the picture set forth by the Underground Man suggests that truth is ultimately apprehended by something other than reason or rationality, and thus by something other than the traditional Western philosophical conception of the will. The disagreement over the primacy of truth thus takes place on the field of a broader common rejection of the notion that human beings are defined by a rational will.

Michael Allen Gillespie next turns our attention directly to the problem of nihilism, never long out of sight for either Nietzsche or Dostoevsky. Gillespie argues that although the two shared a common understanding of the nihilism haunting their contemporaries, its specter called forth sharply divergent responses from each. Nietzsche recognized Raskolnikov, Kirillov, and especially the Underground Man as examples of "higher men" struggling to make sense of the world in the terms of the acutely self-conscious rationality and residual Christian moralism of their time. For Dostoevsky, the failures of these characters pointed backward, to the need for a return to and embrace of Christianity. For Nietzsche, their failures pointed forward, to the need for a complete overcoming of modern rationalism and Christian morality. One must then either find one's way to God or become a God oneself.

The same massive obstacle blocks both paths. The problem of senseless human suffering, or more simply the problem of evil, is as powerful an argument against the possibility of self-deification as it is against the existence of God. How can the reality of meaningless suffering be reconciled with any notion of providence, divine or human? Paying particular attention to the tormented arguments of Ivan Karamazov, Gillespie maintains that Dostoevsky uses Ivan to show that the same doubting rationalism that undermines faith in God also undermines any sense or concept of goodness beyond the rational egotism of the utilitarians, thus issuing in an intellectual and spiritual world in which higher types like Ivan cannot survive. Having seen in Dostoevsky's work how these higher types are crushed by the thought of a godless universe, Nietzsche makes the demand that they not merely accept the suffering of the innocent but themselves become the God who chooses it—this is the only path to self-deification left open, and so the only way to make sense of a godless universe.

Joshua Foa Dienstag continues this emphasis on the fundamental question of justifying existence, but frames it in terms of pessimism rather than nihilism. Like Gillespie, Dienstag notes that Nietzsche first read Dostoevsky in the same period that he wrote the "new prefaces" of 1886 for his early works, and thus was engaged in reflecting on and reappraising his philosophical project as a whole. For Dienstag the crucial identity adopted by Nietzsche in the course of this self-reflection was that of pessimist, though he was keen to distinguish his form of pessimism—a "Dionysian pessimism" or a "pessimism of strength"—from Schopenhauer's pessimism. It is in this context that Nietzsche's reading of *Notes from Underground* resonated so profoundly for him, for he found in Dostoevsky a bracing and incisive kindred spirit. Though Nietzsche ultimately (and emphatically) parts ways with Dostoevsky on the subject of Christianity, he recognizes in him a pessimism similar to his own and to that of Greek tragedy. Dostoevsky's work, like classical Greek tragedy, evinces a will to display and take pleasure in the ugly. Yet these things appear ugly only from a certain perspective, for what Dostoevsky and tragedy foreground is not ugliness in the sense of deformity or decay but rather the violent and chaotic features of existence, and the moments when those realities break through the illusions in which human beings usually live. True tragedy, and thus Dostoevsky, is defined not by a taste for the perverse or grotesque but by great honesty, a willingness and an ability to look squarely at "the hard, gruesome, evil, problematic aspect of existence," as Nietzsche says in the new preface to *The Birth of Tragedy*. The great enemy of tragedy, of course, is in Nietzsche's telling Socratic rationalism, and Dienstag traces the ways in which Dostoevsky's Underground

Man offers his own penetrating critique of that rationalism—its belief in the rational and predictable order of the world, its facile understanding of human motivation, and the crippling and humiliating inertia in which it necessarily eventuates for those unfortunate enough to fully absorb it.

Edith Clowes also stresses the similarities between Dostoevsky and Nietzsche, focusing on the spatial and architectural metaphors used by both to represent consciousness and the unconscious, often violent wellsprings of morality. She begins by noting that for both Dostoevsky and Nietzsche, the sources of consciousness and moral agency are represented as dwelling underground, not, as in traditional philosophic and religious imagery, in the open sunlight or in the highest, brightest part of a structure. This inverts not only the established moral valences of the metaphor but the basic idea of whether consciousness and morality are visible and susceptible of being signified by rational, descriptive speech. It also suggests that morality is the product of purely human, often irrational and immoral unconscious drives, not contact with or illumination by the divine. In the work of Dostoevsky and Nietzsche, Clowes argues, we have the paradox of this wordless, irrational unconscious becoming conscious of itself and speaking to us, though always imperfectly and indirectly. After discussing various subterranean images used in European literature before Dostoevsky, Clowes identifies the notion or symbol of the underground as an example of what Mikhail Bakhtin called a chronotope, or an "image of human nature." She then goes on to sketch the differences in this chronotope as it is used by Dostoevsky and Nietzsche, chiefly in *Notes from Underground* and in *On the Genealogy of Morals*. Among the various subtle but significant differences Clowes discerns, one crucial similarity emerges, the belief that the underground is a universal reality in each of us, and the only possible ground for authentic moral action and autonomy in a world without divinely ordained ethics. Only by acknowledging, contemplating, and redirecting the elemental drives previously buried in the underground can we achieve these hitherto elusive goals of modern thought. In Clowes's reading, then, Dostoevsky as well as Nietzsche pursues or advances the ends of modernity, largely by radicalizing previous modern self-understandings.

Ilya Kliger continues this examination of both writers' concern with the deficiencies of modern rationalism as well as their attempts to overcome them by glimpsing a fundamental reality usually hidden or suppressed. Framing his essay as an inquiry into the "historiographic imaginaries" of Dostoevsky and Nietzsche, Kliger reads both not only in the context of modern thought as a whole but in their specific historical moment. Kliger notes a striking similarity between Dostoevsky and the Nietzsche of the late 1860s and early 1870s. Both embrace a historiographic imaginary Kliger calls "tragic-nationalist," meaning that both see tragedy as the necessary salve or corrective to a deeply defective modern ethos, but further, that both also see the people, the Russian *narod* or the German *Volk*, as essential to the success and indeed the very existence of tragedy properly understood. It is not simply that the people are to be educated and transformed by tragedy—even more, for both writers the purpose of true tragedy is to provide an insight into the Dionysian and destructive essence of the *Volk* or *narod*, the elemental ground of existence that has not yet been extirpated or suffocated by the stultifying rationality of modern rationalism and bourgeois life. This glimpse into the true depths of the people, and so of reality and being itself, will be powerful enough to dissolve the individual, sparring egos comprising the audience, heal the ruptures in social life, and restore all members of the nation (Russian or German) to a primal fraternity. Tragedy here is thus not a matter of private aesthetic experience or contemplation, but a return to the immediacy of union with one's fellow man. Kliger spends the rest of the essay exploring how these concerns inform both writers' views on education and art, and in particular how they are given form in Dostoevsky's fiction, chiefly the major novels *Crime and Punishment* and *The Idiot*, centering on questions of the character of the tragic hero and of what it means for tragedy to have a plot.

Dmitri Nikulin's essay shares several key features with Kliger's: Both are concerned with the way in which Greek antiquity is represented in modernity, and the way that representation helps to define modernity. Both also concentrate on how the major philosophical problems with which each writer deals are articulated and worked through in concrete individuals. For Kliger, the first question is more specifically Nietzsche's, the second Dostoevsky's, but Nikulin tends to see both questions as central for each thinker, arguing that many of Nietzsche's ideas are embodied in his discussions of particular mythological figures, and that Dostoevsky was occupied with many of the same aspects of the Greek legacy as Nietzsche, specifically the notions of the Apollonian and Dionysian. Unlike the other chapters in our collection, Nikulin's argues for the clear superiority of one writer over the other, claiming that Dostoevsky's approach to these categories is more supple and accurate than Nietzsche's because it recognizes the duality inherent in each category. The young Nietzsche, for Nikulin, deploys a "rigid schematism" in his treatment of Dionysus and Apollo that "deprives them of their complex mythological and often contradictory traits and thus turns them into rational constructions necessary for a rather arbitrary reconstruction of the history of ancient literature." In Dostoevsky, by contrast, Nikulin finds a more subtle and illuminating account not only of the concepts of the Apollonian and Dionysian but of more fundamental ideas dealing with the self-destructiveness of a reflective consciousness that cannot relate to the other, or more basically with the human need to love.

In the end, we return to the questions that unite these "hostile broth-ers," questions that remain fundamental in the context of the long, brutal twentieth century and that reverberate with immense force and richness in the passionate investigations of Nietzsche and Dostoevsky. Perhaps their sig-nal virtue and menace for the present time resides in their openness to such questions. For can we say that we are open to them as well? Or, indeed, has the wonder of a new complacency not dissimilar to that of the waning nineteenth century closed our eyes—do we accept or evade the challenge of their fer-vent, searching demands that we give an account of ourselves?

NOTES

1. Nietzsche's reception in Russia has been the subject of many works. Of these one might consult: Bernice Glatzer Rosenthal, ed., *Nietzsche in Russia* (Princeton: Princeton University Press, 1986); Edith W. Clowes, *The Revolution of Moral Consciousness: Nietzsche in Russian Literature, 1890–1914* (DeKalb: Northern Illinois University Press, 1988), and *Fiction's Overcoat: Russian Lit-erary Culture and the Question of Philosophy* (Ithaca: Cornell University Press, 2004); Nel Grillaert, *What the God-Seekers Found in Nietzsche* (New York–Amsterdam: Rodopi, 2008).

2. Löwith notes that Heidegger had a portrait of Dostoevsky on his work desk in his *Life in Germany Before and After 1933*. Gadamer described Heidegger's interest in Dostoevsky to the important American Dostoevsky scholar Robert Louis Jackson as having been intense and sustained. Gadamer also made the enig-matic comment to Jackson that Heidegger suspected that Dostoevsky moved somewhat beyond the impasse of Nietzsche, who, according to Otto Pöggeler, an-other one of Heidegger's famuli, brought him to a standstill—"*Nietzsche hat mich kaput gemacht.*"

Nietzsche and Dostoevsky

Geoff Waite with Francesca Cernia Slovin

Nietzsche with Dostoevsky: Unrequited Collaborators in Crime without Punishment

Nietzsche and Dostoevsky can without exaggeration be called brothers, even twins. I think that if they had lived together, they would have hated each other with the peculiar hatred that Kirillov and Shatov in *Demons* felt for each other after their American trip during which time they had to spend four months together, half-starving in a shed.
—Lev Shestov, *Dostoevsky and Nietzsche*

It seems impossible to speak of Dostoevsky's genius without thinking of the word "criminal." . . . "Criminal": I repeat the word, in order to indicate the psychological similarity between the case of Nietzsche and Dostoevsky.
—Thomas Mann, "Dostoevsky"

The greatest homage we can pay them is to say that we would not be able . . . to ask them one question which they themselves had not asked and which, in their life, or by their death, they had not partially answered.
—Camus, *The Rebel*

Where violence and law had failed them, they had recourse to art.
—Carlo Levi, *Christ Stopped at Eboli*

In the language of the criminal is reflected the character of the criminal, his *Dasein*.
—Marx and Engels, *The Holy Family*

3

> How can we speak of terrorist activity without
> taking part in it?
> —Ivan Platonovich Kaliayev, at his assassination
> trial

THE COLLABORATION OF Friedrich Wilhelm Nietzsche (1844–1900; age 55) with Fyodor Mikhailovich Dostoevsky (1821–81; age 59) was so privately intense as to be not merely unpublished but simply unpublishable—as would have been Dostoevsky's collaboration with Nietzsche.[1] Had they had an alive collaboration, it would have hardly involved "communication" insofar as that is "the watchword of our liberal modernity," conveying "the most trivial and babbling thoughts."[2] Dostoevsky and Nietzsche both loathed liberal modernity and its linguistic usufruct (*servitutes personarum,* "personal servitude"). Their collaboration syncopates in a world wherein for, say, a novelist or a philosopher to think or write *about* crime—specifically terrorism against any possible authority—*can* be the same thing as to *be* criminal, terrorist. Tsarist Russia was not the same as Imperial Germany. However, their collaboratory and unrequited encounter perdures in our nearly global imperialist capitalism. When today there is return to them—to Nietzsche with Dostoevsky—it is not for the answers of their holy or unholy family but for its atonally symphonic *question of crime.*[3] Now ours.[4]

NIHILISM IN NICE, SAINT PETERSBURG, TURIN: 1873 TO 1888–89

In a letter posted from Nice on March 27, 1888, to Georg Brandes in Copenhagen, Nietzsche writes:

> I'm sorry for you in your now particularly wintry and gloomy North: how one keeps one's soul erect there! I admire almost everyone who does not lose faith in himself under an overcast sky, not to speak of "humanity," "marriage," "property," "the State" . . . Here I believe as a plant believes, in the sun. The sun of Nice—that is truly no prejudice. In Petersburg I would be a *Nihilist.*[5]

In Saint Petersburg, in *A Writer's Diary* entry for 1873, under the heading "One of Today's Falsehoods," Dostoevsky records:

> Let me say one thing about myself alone: a *Nechaev* I probably could never have become, but a *Nechaevist*—well, of that I can't be sure; perhaps I could have become one . . . in the days of my youth.[6]

4

Concerned with all varieties of nihilism since youth, when he wrote to Brandes Nietzsche was in the process of reading Dostoevsky's *Demons* (*The Possessed*). Almost exactly one year earlier, in February 1887, he had discovered, in a Nice bookshop, *Notes from the Underground*. Ever since, Nietzsche had attempted to read *everything* Dostoevsky wrote. Yet *Demons* is the only text to which he ever made extraordinarily detailed response.

Dostoevsky's diary entry addresses public response to *Demons*, recently published in 1871. This was the year of the Paris Commune and the year he stopped gambling all his money away. To write *Demons* was his *biggest* gamble, or so Nietzsche would have told him. Despite his financial woes, Nietzsche was not tempted by the casinos in Monaco, which he visited in 1882, calling them the "Paradise of Hell"[7]—a phrase Dostoevsky would have savored. In the casinos, just as outside them, police are omnipresent, Dostoevsky knew, and even though "dressed in plain clothes, mingling with the crowd, so that is *impossible* to recognize them," *he* could recognize them.[8]—Our twins may have hated each other, but both knew how to spot policemen in Heaven just as well as in Hell.

Reviewers in 1873 are exercised that Dostoevsky's use of "the well-known affair" around the nihilist Sergey Nechayev is not a "literal reproduction" and that nowadays "an idiotic fanatic such as Nechaev could find proselytes only among the idle and undeveloped and not among young people involved in studies." Dostoevsky responds: "*My* Nechaev character is, of course, unlike the actual Nechaev," and that "I also stood on the scaffold condemned to death, and I assure you that I stood in the company of educated people."[9]

On January 4, 1889, eight months after his letter to Brandes, Nietzsche writes to Malwida von Meysenbug in Rome from Turin. This was one of twenty-five letters written in five days: from New Year's Day to January 5, 1889, when he posted the final letter of his life and the longest and most intricate of the twenty-five—to Jakob Burckhardt in Basel. He informs the preeminent historian of the Renaissance and its *Übermenschen* that he, Nietzsche, is "all the names in history," including the just recently executed murderers of two women. Burckhardt barely glances at the letter before walking it over to Franz Overbeck and his wife Ida. Overbeck departs the next day for Turin, finding Nietzsche in his small flat revising manuscripts for publication, slashing at his rented piano, and dancing wildly naked. Overbeck is told that Nietzsche collapsed a few days earlier while throwing his arms around a horse being beaten in the adjoining piazza. Nietzsche has transformed Raskolnikov's nightmare of the same horse being beaten in *Crime and Punishment* into Dionysian ecstasy.[10] Forthwith, Overbeck transports Nietzsche back to Basel, this last time to its sanatorium, his first.

In all his letters from Turin, Nietzsche "settles accounts with his erstwhile philosophical conscience"—and (like Marx and Engels) not just *philosophical*.

This bevy of letter pigeons or bombs is released all over Europe to friends—some dating back to school days (Paul Deussen, Erwin Rohde), some more recent (Franz Overbeck, Malwida von Meysenbug, Heinrich Köselitz, Cosima Wagner). Each letter is tailored to a specific aspect of their relationship, or rather lack thereof. Except for his last letter, all are short, but all equally dense in allusion. In the same laconic manner Nietzsche settles accounts also with influential acquaintances (Jean Bourdeau, Hans von Bülow), with famous correspondents (Georg Brandes, August Strindberg), with his publisher (Georg Naumann), as well as with important, powerful strangers (Cardinal Mariani at the Vatican, King Umberto I of Italy, Heinrich Wiener, president of Germany). If these letters are "insane," then this may be the most *lucid* insanity ever recorded in history.[11] Nietzsche could well have addressed a letter to Dostoevsky, posthumously. Since that letter is not extant, *we* would have to write it.[12]

We cite in its entirety the letter of January 4, 1889, to Malwida von Meysenbug, addressed to her in the third person:

> Supplement to the "Memoirs of an Idealist Woman"
> Although Malwida is well known as Kundry, who laughed in a moment when the world was tottering, much is to be forgiven her, because she loved me very much: see the first volume of the "Memoirs" . . . I venerate all these select souls around Malwida[,] in Natalie [Herzen] lives her father and I was he, too.
> —The Crucified[13]

The allusion to Richard Wagner is predictable and therefore easy to unpack. In act 1 of *Parsifal*, Kundry laughs while reporting on Parsifal's lineage and while revealing his mother as "the Fool" (*die Törin*). Although Wagner's friend von Meysenbug has laughed at The Crucified's own mother, and thus also at her son's destiny, he forgives her because she said loving things in her published *Memoirs of an Idealist Woman* about him and their commune in Sorrento, where she had introduced Nietzsche to the world of Russian émigrés. Von Meysenbug translated Alexander Herzen's *Memoirs*, introduced Nietzsche to Lou Salomé, and was the tutor of Herzen's daughters, including Natalie. Nietzsche's allusion to Natalie is not predictable and therefore harder peripatetic luggage to unpack.

"I WOULD BE A NIHILIST, I AM NATALIE HERZEN"

We return to Nietzsche's letter in which he avers *"In Petersburg I would be a Nihilist."* The addressee in March 1888 is the Dane, Georg Brandes (1842–1927), influential literary critic and historian, staunch left-liberal and public atheist, defender of women's rights, and in the late 1880s by far the most important conduit back and forth among the Northern European, French, German, and especially the Russian intelligentsia, whom Brandes had met personally in Saint Petersburg in 1887. Brandes was about to promote (first in overflowing lecture halls in Copenhagen, then in writing) Nietzsche's work in Scandinavia, introducing Nietzsche and Strindberg in 1888 from a safe distance. Brandes would also introduce Nietzsche and Russia to each other at a time when Nietzsche's books and Brandes's own were officially banned by censors. The Russian intellectuals included Prince A. I. Urusov, an ardent fan of German philosophy and one of Russia's best-known lawyers, who was recused from cases, including ones involving terrorist assassins, as "a result of a secret order given to all court chairmen to remove lawyers who, for any reason, were disliked by the administration."[14] To Urusov, Brandes would send Nietzsche's latest book, *The Wagner Case: A Musicians-Problem*.[15] In its epilogue Nietzsche makes his first reference in print to Dostoevsky. Aesthetics, as goes without saying, replaces morality.

> Aesthetics is indissolubly bound . . . to biological presuppositions: there is a *décadence*-aesthetics, there is a *classical* aesthetics—"beauty-in-itself" is a fantasy in the brain, like all of idealism.—In the narrower sphere of so-called moral values, there is no greater contrast than between *master-morals* and the morals of *Christian* moral concepts: the latter having grown on a thoroughly morbid soil (—the Gospels present to us precisely the same physiological types depicted in Dostoevsky's novels), the master-morals ("Roman," "heathen," "classical," "Renaissance"), to the contrary, is the semiotics of sound constitution, of *ascending* life, of the will to power as the principle of life.[16]

Nietzsche also mailed a copy to a member of Urusov's circle, Princess Anna Ténicheff, presumably unnerved by the dedication to her signed, "The Antichrist."

When Nietzsche wrote the letter to him in March 1888, Brandes was planning to write the first monograph on Nietzsche, "Friedrich Nietzsche: A Treatise on Aristocratic Radicalism." In eager anticipation, Nietzsche thanked Brandes for the title, saying that it was among the cleverest anointings ever bestowed on him. Alas, he added, he could not read Danish. In November 1888, Brandes sent Nietzsche his most recent book (also published that year and which Nietzsche also could not read), *Indtryk fra Rusland* (Impressions of Russia), based on his visit in Saint Petersburg in 1887. It is unfortunate for the topic "Nietzsche with Dostoevsky" that Nietzsche could not have read *Impressions of Russia*, though he did get the gist from Brandes's letters, notwithstanding the fact that in the last part of 1888 Nietzsche had time and health to read little more than public media—and producing, under betimes horrific financial and physical conditions, *five* book manuscripts in *eight* months.

Not to mention hundreds of letters and far many more notebook pages. This remains among the greatest (intellectual) achievements recorded in history.

In *Impressions of Russia*, Nietzsche would have been intrigued by Brandes's detailed discussion (with many citations) of the shifting understanding in Russian nihilist fiction that occurred between the generations of Turgenev and Dostoevsky, and in the wake of the Paris Commune. Nietzsche had been introduced to specifically Russian nihilism no later than 1873, though he had been very familiar with anarchism already in the late 1860s, when he was editing Wagner's early manuscripts (including on Communism) that were written under Bakunin's powerful undertow. Together with other members of Malwida von Meysenbug's salon in 1873, Nietzsche was introduced to Turgenev's Basarov in *Fathers and Children*, first among the "literary nihilists."[17] It is virtually impossible that Dostoevsky's name did not come up in salon conversation. In 1875, in the park in Baden-Baden (where Dostoevsky in 1867 had had his first serious bout with gambling), Nietzsche and his sister Elisabeth, immersed in conversation, walked past Turgenev, who silently overheard them but did not speak. Like Malwida von Meysenbug, Lou Salomé knew Turgenev personally and she traveled to Paris for his funeral in 1883, just after her definitive breakup with Nietzsche.

When Nietzsche writes Brandes in March 1888, he is intently reading *Demons*, and so would likewise have been intrigued by Brandes's detailed descriptions of the sequence of not only fictional but very real terrorist assassinations up to the present day—but intrigued not merely because Nietzsche knew how deeply these had impacted Dostoevsky. In *Impressions of Russia*, Brandes vividly depicts one assassination attempt in particular—the one in 1878 on General Fedor Trepov, the governor and head of secret police in Saint Petersburg. This attempt was by the woman known as "The Angel of Vengeance." Vera Zasulich was "the most famous *terroristka*," "the most famous revolutionary in all of Europe"—more famous even than her erstwhile mentor, Sergei Nechayev.[18] Nietzsche did not know that Dostoevsky attended Zasulich's notorious trial and that this experience echoed profoundly in his *Demons*. Nietzsche *did* know that Nechayev was a main prototype for *Demons*. But there is more to it. Intriguing for Nietzsche, to say the least, would be to learn that he shared a mutual friend (not to say also lover) *both* with Nechayev *and* with "The Angel of Vengeance." In virtual effect, then, twins Nietzsche and Dostoevsky were incestuously related.

Natalie ("Tata") Herzen (1844–1936), to whom Nietzsche refers in his last letter to von Meysenbug in early 1889, was Alexander Herzen's eldest daughter, his hope to wrest the anarchist legacy away from Nechayev, and the tutee of the Malwida von Meysenbug to whom Nietzsche also proposed marriage. Nietzsche now regards Natalie as *himself*—since, in the implacable logic and genealogy of the Eternal Recurrence of the Same, Nietzsche *is* Alexander Herzen, Natalie's father, and so forth. Not only did Natalie and Vera Zasulich know one another but Natalie had been courted (in 1871) by Nechayev, who had earlier (in 1868) proposed marriage to Zasulich. Sergey Nechayev, like Nietzsche, was a man of many pseudonyms and masks; unlike Nietzsche he habitually carried with him Rousseau's *Confessions* as *un aide de seduction*—which sometimes was effective to that end, though not to the point of matrimony.[19] In 1877 it came to pass that Friedrich Nietzsche had also proposed to Natalie Herzen—if only also to be rejected.

Had some fool tried to force Natalie to choose between Nietzsche and Nechayev, this strong-willed and brilliant person would have simply refused both, and willingly suffered any consequences. Nietzsche was used to such rejection, as he would be again (a fortiori in 1882 by another Russian émigré, Lou Salomé). Nonetheless he was disappointed, having written his sister Elisabeth in 1877 that among all possible current candidates for marriage Natalie was the most "suited to me in her manner and *Geist*." He had hesitated only because he deemed her too old for him (i.e., exactly his age), wishing her "twelve years younger" (twenty-one).[20] In general, Nietzsche was attracted to a woman for her youth, beauty, intelligence, and linguistic ability, not for sex—even though, to the extent that he was a born-again Greek, all these would have been ultimately one and the same thing. Needless to say and above all, he desperately needed his wife to be a housewife, nurse, stenographer, and secretary.

Quite unmarried either to Nietzsche or to Nechayev, Vera and Natalie went on to make significant contributions to the communist and the anarchist traditions, respectively. (Vera helped Lenin found *Iskra*.) It was Russian émigrés who led Marx, nearing life's end, to view terrorist assassination as a legitimate, even laudable praxis. Although letters to Engels regarding Nechayev, beginning in 1870, had been consistently critical and derogatory about his "barracks communism," old Marx's letter to his daughter Jenny on April 11, 1881, refers differently to the assassination a month earlier of Tsar Alexander II by the Narodnaya Volya (People's Will or People's Freedom), with which Nietzsche's contemporary Nechayev (1857–82) was associated: "They are sterling people, through and through, *sans pose melodramatique*, simple, businesslike, heroic. Shouting and doing are irreconcilable opposites."[21] Marx likely never read Dostoevsky or Nietzsche, though it is unlikely that their names did not come up in conversation with the great polymath. Three months earlier, on January 28, 1881, Dostoevsky had died in Saint Petersburg, where Alexander II was to be exploded by a bomb on March 13—a latter-day gift of "propaganda by deed" from Dostoevsky's protagonists in *Demons* and indeed one facet of Dostoevsky the man's great complexity.[22] That same year, at the beginning of August 1881, Nietzsche experienced the Eternal Recurrence of the Same for the first time in Sils Maria.

In 1886, just months *before* he began reading Dostoevsky, Nietzsche would publish the following in *Beyond Good and Evil: Prelude to the Philosophy of the Future*:

> When today a philosopher makes it known that he is no skeptic . . . then all the world does not like to hear it; one looks at him with considerable timidity, wants to have many questions, questions . . . yes, among fearful listeners, and there is now a crowd of them, he is from then on called dangerous. To them, it is as if they could hear, in his rejection of skepticism, coming from far away, some evil, threatening sound, as if somewhere a new explosive were being tested, a dynamite of the spirit [*ein Dynamit des Geistes*], perhaps a newly discovered Russian Nihiline [*Nihilin*], a pessimism *bona voluntatis* [of goodwill] that does not simply say No, wills No, but instead—terrible to say! *does* No![23]

Nietzsche's neologism *Nihilin* or *Nihiline* is telling because this "quasi-feminization" points in the direction of women—not just as nihilists, but as *terrorists*, thus suggesting that it is also *they* with whom Nietzsche identifies in the propaganda by deed that is his published or exoteric writing. Nietzsche, like Herzen before him and Lenin after him, took deeply to heart the question posed by Chernyshevsky: What is to be done?[24] Paraphrasing Camus, the questions posed by Dostoevsky with Nietzsche to *us* are more important than *their* answers.

Brandes later wrote Nietzsche that, in *Indtryk fra Rusland*, he had acknowledged his debt to him.[25] Still linguistically inaccessible to Nietzsche, however, were the specifics:

> We are indebted to the philosopher Frederick Nietzsche for the establishment of the real and wide contrast between the morality of gentlemen and the morality of slaves . . . By the morality of gentlemen is meant all that morality which emanates from self-esteem, positive animal spirits: the morality of Rome, of Iceland, of the renaissance; but the morality of the slave, is all that morality which proceeds from unselfishness as the highest virtue, from the denial of life, from the hatred for the happy and the strong.[26]

And it is at this point, precisely, that Dostoevsky explodes into the picture, since he "developed into a colossal example of this type," that is, of the slave morality.[27]

Brandes was reading Dostoevsky through spectacles provided by Nietzsche, or so Brandes thought. Through the opaque lens of this now nearly blind man, Brandes initiated a long tradition of reading Nietzsche and Dostoevsky that focuses beyond their shared psychological acumen to see the *consequences* of the psychological type of the slave morality for criminality and crime. This focus, first calibrated by Brandes in 1888, was quickly recalibrated for "Dostoevsky with Nietzsche" in Russia no later than 1892 by Preobrazky and especially by the émigré Shestov, who was later to exert seminal influence on Georges Bataille's fascination (earlier than Thomas Mann), via Dostoevsky and Nietzsche, on crime and criminality—both theoretical and real. With Bataille's obsession the lens became sharp to the shattering point. For his part, Brandes had exhibited a remarkably detailed knowledge of Russian "nihilists of both sexes."[28] It is on the basis of this sociology that he refers to Raskolnikov's murders in *Crime and Punishment* and to the same theme in *Demons*. Brandes's conclusion reads:

> Even if it is not a political crime which Dostoevsky had represented, it is a crime which has this in common with the political, that it is not mean, was not committed for the vulgar, low object of procuring for the perpetrator greater personal profit, but was in a certain degree unselfish, and what is most important above all, it was committed by a person who at the moment of the crime does not harbor a doubt as to his right.[29]

Ecce Nietzsche, who would also have read in *Impressions of Russia* that, ever since the Paris Commune, "from all parts of Russia and Siberia young girls have streamed to Zürich to study medicine and socialism."[30] For Nietzsche, these women already included Lou Salomé and Natalie Herzen—the one on the "right wing" of these émigrés, as it were, the other on the "left."[31] Notwithstanding (or because of) the fact that both women had rejected his marriage proposals, Nietzsche remained "a Nihilist in Petersburg." Like *some* of Dostoevsky's protagonists, Nietzsche was spurred by Dostoevsky into willingness to take responsibility for his own way of killing by writing—and, more important, to do so with *joy*. In any case, Nietzsche absolutely rejected Dostoevskian redemption of any sort, regret for having committed any sort of crime.

In Nietzsche's last letter to Brandes (January 4, 1889) he applies Zarathustra's fundamental lesson in pedagogy to the Dane who was promoting him in Russia: "My Friend Georg, after you have discovered me, it was no great artistic achievement [*kein Künststück*] to find me: the difficulty now is to lose me . . ."[32] He would have said much the same thing in his last letter to Dostoevsky: "My Twin Brother Fyodor, after you have discovered me . . . lose me . . ."

CHRISTIAN KILLERS

Nietzsche knew from the introductions to the translations of Dostoevsky's novels quite little, but enough, about Dostoevsky's tumultuous relations with women (Marya Isaev, Polina Suslova, Anna Snitkina . . .), which however did not interest him in the least because so different from his own (asexual) experience. Similarly, he could not have known, but would hardly have been surprised to read, Dostoevsky's famous "personal Credo" against the Truth. As expressed to Natalya Fonvizina from the prison in Omsk:

> If someone proved to me that Christ is outside the Truth, and that *in reality* the Truth were outside of Christ, then I should prefer to remain with Christ rather than with the Truth.[33]

Actually, long before he himself became "The Crucified," Nietzsche had his response to Dostoevsky at the ready. As a twenty-one-year-old student of classical philology in Bonn *anno* 1865—the year Dostoevsky begins writing *Crime and Punishment*—Nietzsche writes his sister (on "Sunday after Whit-sun"): "As for your basic principle that Truth is always on the side of the more difficult, I agree." But only *partly*:

> If we had believed since youth that all salvation came not from Jesus but, say, from Mohammed is it not certain that we would enjoy the same blessings? To be sure, faith alone blesses, not the objective that stands behind the faith. This I write you, dear Lisbeth [or Fyodor], only in order to counter the most usual proofs of believing people, who invoke the evidence of their inner experience and then deduce from that the infallibility of their faith. Every true faith is also infallible, it performs what the believing person hopes to find in it, but it does not offer the slightest handhold to ground an objective Truth.
>
> Here the ways of men part. If you want to achieve peace of mind and happiness, then believe. If you want to be a disciple of Truth, then inquire [*forsche*]![34]

Philologist Nietzsche will remain supremely attuned to the fact that "Dostoevsky's Credo for Christ" is in explicit denial of the long secular tradition derived from Socrates: "But you, who follow me, concern yourselves less about Socrates, and far more about the truth [*aletheia*]."[35] Aristotle's version was applied to friendship: "It would appear desirable, and indeed it would seem to be obligatory, especially for a philosopher, to sacrifice even one's closest personal ties in defense of the truth [*aletheia*]. Both are dear to us, yet it is our duty to prefer the truth."[36] Variations of the phrase *amicus Plato, sed magis amica veritas* (I am a friend of Plato, but a greater friend of truth) later passed from Roger Bacon in the thirteenth century,[37] through hundreds of hands, secular and still religious. Dostoevsky's Christian credo *interrupts* this millennial flow from the philosophical, through the religious, to the atheistic and aesthetic. Nietzsche *maintains* this flow at least as undercurrent. At the end of *Thus Spoke Zarathustra I* (1882), Zarathustra takes leave from his first disciples, as Nietzsche would from Brandes: "Now I bid you to lose me and to find yourselves; and only when you have denied me will I return to you . . . *Dead are all gods: now we want the Overman to live.*"[38] Having embodied *all* of the Gospels, Zarathustra reverses Dostoevsky's Jesus: "But whosoever shall deny me before men, him will I also deny before my Father who is in heaven" (Matthew 10:3). And hereby does Nietzsche-Zarathustra reject Dostoevsky's Credo, of course. *But*, it turns out, *not all* of Dostoevsky's *Christian* protagonists.

What the man who would have been a "nihilist in Petersburg" could not have known—though this, too, he intuited—is the extraordinary conversation Dostoevsky had in early January 1881 in Saint Petersburg weeks before his death (February 9), with his close friend Aleksey Suvorin, who recalls this:

> Alyosha Karamazov would emerge as the hero of the novel's continuation, a hero from whom Dostoevsky wished to create a type of Russian Socialist, not the usual type we know and which sprouted out of European soil.[39]

But, Nietzsche retorts: "For a Christian to create Socialism is such a tired, hackneyed old story! Yet another Platonism for the masses . . . Why not, at the very least, turn your gentle monk, Alyosha Karamazov, into an anarchist, a terrorist!" So it then is that Nietzsche ("every name in history") ventriloquizes Dostoevsky through the voice of Suvorin's friend, a non-assassinated grand duke:

> It seems to you that in my last novel, *The Brothers Karamazov*, there was much that was prophetic. But wait for the continuation. In it Alyosha will leave the monastery and become an anarchist. And my pure Alyosha will kill the Tsar.[40]

Dostoevsky's magisterial biographer notes that "Dostoevsky spoke to Suvorin a month or so *before* Alexander II was assassinated [March 13, 1881], leading to the assumption that the Grand Duke had meant to speak of *an attempt* on the Tsar's life; but Dostoevsky could well have envisaged its *accomplishment.*"[41] In other words, as a truly decent liberal, this great biographer retreats immediately from what would have most delighted the self-described "decent criminal" Nietzsche.[42] One of the most astute historians of this entire Russian conjuncture is more than justified in speculating that this, Dostoevsky's "final testament" (our words, not hers) was "influenced by Vera Zasulich and his attendance at her famous trial."[43] And if Nietzsche knew of "The Angel of Vengeance," it would have only been through his unrequited lover Natalie Herzen.

Nearing the end of his life, Dostoevsky reaffirmed his Credo in more explicitly political terms:

> It is not in communism, not in mechanical forms that we find the socialism of the Russian People: they believe that salvation is ultimately to be found only in *worldwide union in the name of Christ*. That is our Russian socialism! So, you European gentlemen, you are laughing at the presence of this higher, unifying, "ecclesiastical" idea among the Russian People.[44]

But now Nietzsche, death also approaching, roars with laughter, for he certainly was a European gentleman behind one of his infinite masks—betimes signing off as "The Crucified One," betimes as "The Antichrist," betimes as "Dionysus." Depending on the situation, he has good reasons to reject Christ, Communism, Socialism—and certainly Christian Socialism or National Socialism.

Nietzsche had especially good reason to believe that his writing would bring him to the scaffold, assuming that his full exoteric and esoteric message would ever be grasped.[45] He could only hope to land in prison. Mock execution or not, he certainly was damned if he was going to repent or be redeemed. As he had learned from *The House of the Dead*, "The criminals with whom D[ostoevsky] lived together in prison were one and all unbroken creatures—are they not worth a hundred times more than a 'broken' Christ?"[46] In any event, as he writes unpublished in *The Antichrist: Curse on Christendom*: "The criminal of criminals is the *philosopher*."[47]

HERMIT IN WHITE NIGHTS

So it then is: "The violence of truth: Nietzsche with Dostoevsky," or, even "Nietzsche and Dostoevsky: philosophy, morality, tragedy." Yes, indeed. Yet for them also "the violence of love," because for these twin brothers truth and terrorism exist in an inextricable embrace with love. "Ah," Nietzsche writes beyond good and evil, "he who knows the heart can guess how impoverished, helpless, presumptuous, and mistaken even the best and deepest love really is—how it sooner *destroys* than rescues . . ."[48] "That is the problem of the Master [*des Herrschenden*]: *He sacrifices those he loves to his ideal*."[49] "I love life: I despise man. But for the sake of life I want to destroy him."[50] "What is done out of love, always happens beyond good and evil."[51] Finally: "The great epochs of our life are when we gain the courage to re-baptize our Evil as our Best."[52]

Now it is Dostoevsky's turn to respond to Nietzsche, a response we have to invent. In 1887 the self-described "hermit" had read "White Nights."

A year and a half later he vividly hallucinates its narrator-protagonist speaking about himself:

> A year before he had become obsessed with a young woman from Russia who had come to Switzerland to establish herself. They had met in Nice in the eerie chiaroscuro of early springtime in a bookstore where she had seen the dreamer leaning pensively over a book, *L'esprit souterrain*. Somehow aware that he was being watched, he fell obsessively in love with her. She was already betrothed to another man but he had disappeared. She promised to return in the same season to keep their rendezvous in Nice, but she never did because her betrothed had finally returned. So our friend leaves Nice and moves back into the underground atop a mountain.

"Good Lord, only a *moment* of bliss? Isn't such a moment sufficient for the whole of a man's life?"[53] This question is the answer to an earlier question posed to Nastenka *and* to Nietzsche (at *such* moments there is no difference between first and third person, female and male): "What have you done with your time, where have you buried the best years of your life? Have you lived or not?"[54] "Good Lord, only a *moment* of bliss? Isn't such a moment sufficient for the whole of a man's life?" This echo reverberates continually in Nietzsche's depopulated hermitage. This one moment ("*Verweile doch, Du bist so schön!*" "*Ich liebe Dich, o Ewigkeit!*"[55]) is what one needs to know about the Eternal Recurrence of the Same, no matter what the consequence will be: crime with or without punishment.

L'esprit souterrain discovered by Nietzsche in Nice consists of two parts or novellas. "Katia" or "*La logeuse*" (The Landlady) is followed by "Lisa."[56] Only the latter, subdivided into its still-familiar ten chapters, corresponds to what is now known as *Notes from the Underground*. In Nietzsche's French edition, however, the two texts are joined together by the two French "translators and editors" who also correctly admit that they are "adapters." But they also provide an unacknowledged intermezzo—the result being that "Lisa's" or "The Landlady's" protagonist, Ordynov in the third person, appears to be the first-person narrator of *Notes from the Underground*. Thus, the Dostoevsky first read by Nietzsche appears to focus on a response to two *women* (Katia and Lisa); the conflation of third and first person is constitutive of the style of both Dostoevsky and Nietzsche; and this focus (on women) and conflation (of narrative voices) preconditioned the response to *novelist* Dostoevsky by *philologist* Nietzsche. "The time of *nihilism*," writes Jean-Michel Rey, "is for Nietzsche the moment of an *intensified philology*, of a greater than ever attention to what language conceals, to what it expresses by hiding it, to what it veils by uttering it."[57]

Here is the very first sentence (now in English translation) by Dostoevsky that Nietzsche read when he flipped open "The Landlady" in the bookshop in Nice: "Ordynov had made up his mind at last to change his lodgings." And then, two pages later:

> Now he walked about the streets like a recluse, like a hermit who has suddenly come from his dumb wilderness into the noisy, roaring city. Everything seemed to him new and strange. But he was so remote from all the world that was surging and clattering around him that he did not wonder at his own strange sensation. He seemed unconscious of his own aloofness; on the contrary, there was springing up in his heart a joyful feeling, a sort of intoxication, like the ecstasy of a hungry man who has meat and drink set before him after a long fast; though, of course, it was strange that such a trivial novelty as a change of lodgings could exalt and thrill any inhabitant of Petersburg, even Ordynov; but the truth is that it had scarcely ever happened to him to go out without a practical objective.[58]

With the scant money he could spare—just enough for a small room, meager board, postage, and limited travel—Nietzsche did not hesitate to purchase *L'esprit souterrain*. This, to repeat, was February 1887 in Nice, where Nietzsche had arrived in October 1886. During 1886, the last great peripatetic philosopher had lived in seven locations; after his departure from Nice, on April 2, 1887, he would live in twelve—before arriving for his last repose in Sils Maria in 1888, from June to September, and finally on to his terminal hermitage in Turin, residing there until Overbeck transports him back to the Basel Sanitarium by train through the Gotthard Tunnel, with Nietzsche intoning his terrific poem about the bridge in Venice. Which is now to say the same bridge of the encounter and missed encounter in "White Nights." After the "Nerve-Clinic" in Basel, there follows the one in Jena, the one in his mother's house in Naumburg, and finally the one called Weimar . . .

After *Notes from the Underground*, Nietzsche's second book was *Humiliated and Insulted*:

> "After I left you, I went to see Katya," Alyosha rattled on . . . "She's such a serious, such a spirited girl! She spoke of our duty, of our mission in life, that we must serve mankind and, seeing that we had reached total agreement in a mere five or six hours of talking, we ended up vowing eternal friendship and that all our life we'd act as one."
>
> "Act in what?" the prince enquired in surprise.[59]

Nietzsche was supremely challenged by this question in his personal relationships *and* in his writing. *Act*, most certainly! But act in what, for what and whom? To what end? Friends recalled that Nietzsche wept when he first read and when he subsequently recalled reading *Humiliated and Insulted* and *Notes from the Underground*.

FROM THE MOST DANGEROUS BOOK IN 1886 TO THE SCAFFOLD

Beyond Good and Evil: Prelude to a Philosophy of the Future is published on August 4, 1886. Two days earlier, anticipating its publication, Nietzsche has provided his publisher a list of those twelve friends or acquaintances who are to receive personal copies, including Burckhardt and Overbeck. He adds a second list of editors of newspapers and journals (in Italy, Switzerland, Austria, and Germany) who are to receive copies for possible review. Thirty-one names he places on this list, most of them today swept into the dustbin of history.

We may regret that one name on Nietzsche's second list—Leopold, Knight of Sacher-Masoch—did not publicly review the copy he received of *Beyond Good and Evil*.[60] Yet we are compensated by one of the listed editors who did review his book. Indeed, we are richly compensated not merely because it was *this* review that introduced Nietzsche for the first time to Dostoevsky's writing, but also because in 1888 it eventually pushed Nietzsche to express in public what the consequences of his *own* thinking and writing were *intended* to be. So it is that we still attend to Joseph Viktor Widmann.

Widmann was on Nietzsche's list because he was an established writer, critic, friend of Brahms, and editor of the liberal Bern daily *Der Bund*. Widmann's feuilleton appeared six months after the publication of *Beyond Good and Evil* in two installments of *Der Bund*, on September 16 and 17.[61] Entitled "Nietzsche's Dangerous Book," Widmann's review began with a "motto" identified as coming from Dostoevsky's *Raw Youth* (1875; also *The Adolescent*), which had recently been translated into German as *Junger Nachwuchs* (young offspring, new blood, new recruits).[62]

Here in English translation is Widmann's epigraph from Dostoevsky to "Nietzsche's Dangerous Book":

> With your permission, sir: I had a friend, Lambert, who at the age of sixteen said to me that when he was rich, his greatest pleasure would be to feed dogs bread and meat, while the children of the poor were dying of hunger, and when they had no wood for their stoves, he would buy a whole lumberyard, stack it up in a field, and burn it there, and give not a stick to the poor. Those were his feelings! Tell me, what answer should I give this purebred scoundrel when he asks, "Why should I necessarily be noble?"[63]

After this motto—having implied that Nietzsche *cannot* answer Lambert's question, and *therefore* is dangerously inhuman—Widmann launches his review. For the liberal Widmann, any properly democratic society, notably "ours," is best tested by its capacity to tolerate even the most dangerous challenge to it, to defuse the most radical explosive implanted in it or hurled at it—assuming, however, that the bomber is at least being *Redlich* (upright and honest). Widmann adds: "This honesty Nietzsche has truly, sufficiently demonstrated in this book, which two hundred years ago would have infallibly brought the author to the *scaffold*."[64]

Nietzsche was profoundly moved by this last remark, as Carl Bernoulli, the former student and enduring friend of Overbeck, was naturally the first to recognize.[65] It was, Bernoulli wrote in 1908, as if a mirror had been held up—in public—to hermit Nietzsche, in which he, and now the public, saw an image that was simultaneously "unrecognizable and yet uncannily familiar." Specifically, Nietzsche was compelled to see that his published writing—if properly understood *and* as he ultimately intended—would lead him to the scaffold, or to some other site or kind of execution.[66] What Bernoulli did not see, as we must, is that the motto of Widmann's review was apparently the *first text* by Dostoevsky Nietzsche ever read. Prudently, as was his wont, Nietzsche never cited this motto in the many (extant) letters he wrote immediately and in the days to follow, in which he proudly informed his friends and editors of the review's existence. He did not *repress* this shibboleth. Nor did he even suppress it. Nietzsche *embodied* it.

EMBODYING DEMONS IN SPRING 1888

If *Notes from the Underground, Humiliated and Insulted, The House of the Dead*, and "White Nights" are the first texts in Nietzsche's Dostoevsky-bookcase, the last book he read was *Demons*, which in effect he never returned to the shelf. This is the sole text by Dostoevsky to which Nietzsche gave extensive and detailed response. This was just months before he had almost to stop reading altogether (save for journals and his own writing), in order to compose his own final books for publication in the halcyon days of Turin. It is here that Nietzsche first mentions Dostoevsky by name in the public sphere. This is first in the epilogue to *The Wagner Case: A Musicians-Problem*, wherein the Christian Gospels lead directly to the morbid physiological types depicted in Dostoevsky's novels; then in *Twilight of the Idols: How One Philosophizes with the Hammer*, when, in remarks on "The Criminal and What Is Related to Him," it is averred that "Dostoevsky is the only psychologist from whom I had Something to learn" (para. 45); and finally in *The Antichrist: Curse on Christendom*, when it is lamented that

Dostoevsky did not live in the proximity of Redeemer-Types, including the Messiah as "the most interesting decadent, so as to have known the gripping attraction of such an admixture of the sublime, the diseased, and the infantile" (para. 31). Which is now to say, the original Idiot in the Evangelium *and* his Second Coming via Dostoevsky *and*—perchance—in his Third Coming in Nietzsche Himself. Leaving the latter suggestion to its own devices, all these published mentions of Dostoevsky by Nietzsche are so well known, so much discussed, that they must miss the most important point, simply because Nietzsche always conceals the most important point of his pen, dueling saber, and dynamite wick. Just as did, Nietzsche knows, Dostoevsky's fellow inmates in Siberia.

In a large notebook (designated 11–W II 3), Nietzsche records the most unprecedented reading ever given *Demons*, calling it by its Russian title *Bési*.[67] Precise dating is impossible to determine, but it was sometime between November 1887 and March 1888. Standard attempts to reconstruct the sequence of any Nietzschean reflection in his notebooks confront the fact that Nietzsche often writes them from back to front, interspersing later remarks with earlier ones, and so forth. This technique is a stylistic equivalent of the Eternal Recurrence of the Same, understood as Identity in Difference. That caveat in mind, we will proceed to Nietzsche's most critical encounter and collaboration. Before doing so, however, a *basic* timeline (i.e., now excluding letters, allusions, recorded conversations, and reminiscences by others) of Nietzsche's encounter with Dostoevsky: (1) September 1886: reading Widmann's "Nietzsche's Dangerous Book"; (2) February 1887: the bookshop purchase in Nice; (3) February 1887 to March 1888: these notebook pages on *Demons*; (4) his published references, all written in 1888: in *The Wagner Case*, in *Twilight of the Idols*, and in *The Antichrist*; finally (5), we argue, his indirect yet clear reference to *Demons* in his letter from Nice to Georg Brandes on March 27, 1888: "In Petersburg I would be a *Nihilist*."—Which is also now to say: "I might be a *certain* Dostoevsky."[68]

Without taking account of notebook (11–W II 3), it is pointless to analyze Nietzsche's full encounter with Dostoevsky. Furthermore, Nietzsche's glosses on *Demons* are untranslatable, especially when taking to heart Nietzsche's view of translation: his conviction that it is impossible to translate *not* a text's content but instead its author's *presto* and *tempo*—his music. In *Beyond Good and Evil* the sharpest example given is Machiavelli's *Il principe*, in which what is impossible "to be performed [*vorzutragen*] is the most serious matters in untamed *allegrissimo*: perhaps not without a malicious, artist's sense for the conflict he risks—thoughts, long, hard, tough, dangerous, a gallop-tempo and the very best, most mischievous mood."[69]—The consequent musical *style* may have been Machiavellian Nietzsche's ambition throughout his late oeuvre, his style.[70] But nowhere was it better attuned than in his last letter—that to Jakob Burckhardt—prepared by his collaboration with Dostoevsky's *Demons*.

Years later, Lenin would begin to transform the Soviet reception of Dostoevsky from dismissively negative to more nuanced (positive, even) by deeming *Demons* "repulsive but great."[71] The trained philologist, capable of reading a tad more closely than Lenin, would not have disagreed, albeit for *perhaps* different reasons or aims.

Now, God knows (as is said) how, given all the constraints on his life, Nietzsche could have devoted such intensive attention to *Demons*: a full twenty-two notebook pages entitled "*Bési*." But devotion (like God) is hardly the mot juste to describe this great, eccentric philologist and would-be lover's manner of reading whatever he found most significant in any text. In the case of *Demons*, Nietzsche combined simultaneously: *citing* the original verbatim (in this case French) *with* translating it into his unique German less or more literally, in tandem *with* interpolating his own thoughts in propria persona. Quotation marks flicker in and out, often rendering it impossible *and* unnecessary to determine who or *what*, exactly, is speaking. Paratactically ventriloquized in the 1920s: "Quotations in my work are like wayside robbers who leap out armed, and relieve the idle stroller of his conviction. The killing of a criminal can be moral—but never its legitimation."[72]

Interpolated and interpellated into Nietzsche's notebook pages on Dostoevsky, other authors "come and go" (speaking with T. S. Eliot) though all here speaking Nietzschean: Tolstoy (*My Religion*), Renan (*The Life of Jesus*), Wellhausen (*Sketches* and *Prolegomena for a History of Israel*), Benjamin Constant (*Essays of Contemporary Psychology*), and Nietzsche himself. In short, a veritable Russian Formalist *heteroglossia ante litteram*. Nietzsche's version is one for which today's postmodern reader of Mikhail Bakhtin's works on Dostoevsky—or reader of *Ulysses* and *Finnegans Wake* or of the *Passagen-Werk*—will be prepared, perhaps. Nowhere else in Nietzsche's oeuvre is stylistic experimentation so intense, so pushed to the point of syntactic breakdown, stuttering, apparent silence.[73] Had he published these notebook pages verbatim as a monograph, his reputation as the first postmodernist would be validated. Yet, for Nietzsche, the sky is far higher, the abyss far deeper, than those of "fiction" or "literary theory" or "sociology."

The only author in this or *any* notebook given more (quantitative) attention than Dostoevsky is Baudelaire, to whose just recently published *Oeuvres posthumes et correspondances inédites* (1887) Nietzsche devotes, at the same time, circa eighty pages, containing not only expected glosses on nihilistic *décadence à la Wagner* but also unexpected glosses on political economy. This is small surprise to anyone aware of the influence that the "harmonizer," American economist Henry Charles Carey (a.k.a. Dostoevsky's crystal palace), exerted on Nietzsche's Eternal Recurrence of the Same.[74] While political economy has no choice but to *lie* (he would pun) at the base of all Nietzsche's thinking, it is far more explicit in his encounter with Baudelaire than political economy is in his encounter with Dostoevsky—because he is his more intimate collaborator in crime. "Because bourgeois society in and of itself breeds crime, originates in crime, and leads to crime . . . , bourgeois society is, when all is said and done, a criminal society."[75]

Through the lens of *Demons*, Nietzsche reflects (on) political events, including the Decembrist Revolt of 1825, which he knew Dostoevsky supported. For Nietzsche "its entire existence was in seeking danger: the feeling of danger intoxicated it and became its natural need."[76] Danger it had certainly encountered. Nietzsche appears to endorse the massacre of the Decembrists—who (as Trotsky was to remark) "under pressure from the European bourgeois development . . . , wished to combine their liberal régime with the security of their own caste domination."[77] Nietzsche's remarks on *Demons* sometimes have "chapter headings" (e.g., "On the Psychology of Nihilism," "The Logic of Atheism") but many are not indexed. Existentially, what stands out is Nietzsche's citation of passages in *Demons* that reinforce a deep problem for him: unrequited love aimed at some yet-undefined larger purpose. This psychological aspect of the problematic Nietzsche had identified in his initial reading of Dostoevsky in early 1887, that is, in *Notes from the Underground, Humiliated and Insulted*, and "White Nights." But now, about a year later, Nietzsche constructs a far less humanist quasi-narrative out of disparate sentences in *Demons* so as to read (partly in French, partly German):

> Accuse no one—My desires to do so have enough strength to guide me—One can cross a river on a log, but not on a chip of wood . . . Even against these *négateurs* [detractors, nihilists] jealous: jealous of their *hopes*—that they can take hatred so seriously! "To what end expend this strength!"[78]

A few pages later or sooner:

> One can discuss everything without end, but from *me* has issued forth only a *negation without greatness and without strength*. In the end I flatter myself by speaking this way. Everything is always *faible et mou* [feeble and limp].[79]

Ecce Homo, Ecce Nietzsche. Apparently in his own voice, he rejects suicide as a necessary consequence of this particular nihilism.[80] *On the Genealogy of Morals: A Polemic* (1887), in which Dostoevsky makes no appearance, cites for the first and last time for public consumption what Nietzsche calls the "shibboleth" (*Kerbholz-Wort*) "Nothing is true, Everything is permitted."[81]

He cites as source not Dostoevsky (who never quite said it) but instead "the invincible order of Assassins, the order of Free-Spirits par excellence": the secret sect of eleventh-century Nizari Ismailis in Syria or Persia, home to Zarathustra.[82] Likely Nietzsche had contemporary Russian terrorists equally in mind. If so, this free spirit was pledging transhistorical allegiance to both assassin branches.

In any event, Nietzsche's reincarnation of *Demons* veers away from any *individual* psychology of the isolated nihilist or suicide (who may know, if not also secretly desire, exclusively unrequited love) toward the consequences for *political rebellion* or *revolution*: in other words, the threat of the *scaffold*—as mentioned by Dostoevsky in "The Gambler," for example, and where he in 1849 had himself stood in Simonovsky Place—but also even more dramatically by Widmann as an opening salvo in his review of "Nietzsche's dangerous book." In the notebook pages under the rubric "The Nihilist," *It* is written (*Es spricht, die Sprache spricht, ça parle*):[83]

> In the background of the uprising [*Aufruhr*], the explosion of a damned-up [*aufgestauten*] antipathy against the "Masters," the instinct for how much happiness already could be, after such long pressure, in feeling-oneself-free . . .
>
> Mostly a symptom that our lower levels of society have been handled in too humane a way, that they already have a foretaste of a happiness that is forbidden them . . . Not hunger engenders revolutions, but instead the fact that the people has [*sic*] appetite *en mangeant* [*Nicht der Hunger erzeugt Revolutionen, sondern daß das Volk en mangeant Appetit bekommen hat*] . . .[84]

Here the crucial phrase, lifted from the French translation of *Demons*, is *en mangeant*. It derives from the common French expression *l'appétit vient en mangeant*, often translated as "eating whets the appetite," also in the sense "the more you have, the more you want." The proverb is attested no later than the sixteenth century (Rabelais's *Gargantua*, notably), and still used for a variety of situations, at once sexual, economic, and political (e.g., "Give 'em an inch, and they'll take a mile," "Give 'em a finger, and they'll take an arm," etc.). The point of Dostoevsky's "speaker"—and now, apparently, Nietzsche *in propria persona*—is that the root cause of revolutions is not hunger or starvation but instead that the starving masses are given the slightest amount of sustenance, only causing them to demand more—including, ultimately, revolutionary command of the means of production.[85] A "repulsive but great" theory and practice, indeed!

Recall now, as he terminates forever his reading of Dostoevsky's own words, the very first words by Dostoevsky that Nietzsche read, a year and a half earlier, in the review of his "most dangerous book," in effect condemning Nietzsche himself to the scaffold.

With your permission, sir: I had a friend, Lambert, who at the age of sixteen said to me that when he was rich, his greatest pleasure would be to feed dogs bread and meat, while the children of the poor were dying of hunger, and when they had no wood for their stoves, he would buy a whole lumberyard, stack it up in a field, and burn it there, and give not a stick to the poor. Those were his feelings! Tell me, what answer should I give this purebred scoundrel when he asks, "Why should I necessarily be noble?"

The *structure* of these two passages (the first from Nietzsche in his note-book, the second from Dostoevsky in *The Adolescent*) has remained the same, except that there is a slight difference—as there always is in the Eternal Recurrence of the Same. The lethal culinary metaphor or fact remains, but the explicit or implicit questions (What Is Noble? What Is To Be Done?) now embrace the individual in political arms. No longer merely *Man ist, was man ißt* or even *Qu'ils mangent de la brioche!* But now instead: *das Volk sollte sein, was das Volk nicht ißt.* Any potentially revolutionary people must ever *be* what they *never* eat, are not *given* to eat—and so let them perish by themselves and "we" don't have to do the job for them.

This is the house of the dead today known euphemistically as the hegemony of post-industrial, post-socialist global capitalism. Certainly, twins Dostoevsky and Nietzsche—only *half*-starving in our American shed—did not foresee all of it. But the germane question is whether—*while reading them—we* can see *our* house of the dead, within and beyond it.

In 1887 Nietzsche dubs *La maison des morts* "one of the 'most human' books that exists,"[86] and friends recall him sobbing whenever he mentioned it. Despite his deep Bolshevik ambivalence about *Bési*, Lenin was to describe *Memoirs from the House of the Dead* as "the unsurpassed work of Russian and world *belles lettres*."[87] And Nietzsche wept.

ONSET: WHICH HOUSE OF THE DEAD?

As part of surplus value, "the criminal produces crime, *belles lettres*, novels and even tragedies."[88] "The Criminal and What Is Related to Him"—in *Twilight of the Idols: How One Philosophizes with the Hammer*—contains Nietzsche's penultimate testament for public consumption regarding Dostoevsky, Nietzsche with Dostoevsky alive not "half-starving in a shed" in America (Shestov) but in their House of the Dead:

For the problem at hand, Dostoevsky's testimony is germane—Dostoevsky, the only psychologist, by the way, from whom I had something to learn: he belongs among the most beautiful strokes of luck in my life, more than even the discovery of Stendhal. This *profound* human, who was correct ten-fold in his low estimate of the superficial Germans, experienced the Siberian prisoners, in whose midst he lived a long time, very differently than even he had expected—criminals, all serious, hardened criminals for whom there was no way back into society, as if carved out of nearly the best, hardest, and most valuable wood growing anywhere on Russian soil.[89]

Months earlier, on February 23, 1887, he has written from Nice to confidant Franz Overbeck that there have been three kindred-spirit discoveries throughout his life: at age 21, Schopenhauer (*Die Welt als Wille und Vorstellung*); at age 35, Stendhal (*Le rouge et le noir*); and now, at age 43, Dostoevsky (*L'esprit souterrain*).[90] Referring to *Notes from the Underground* as "two novellas," Nietzsche writes from Nice to Overbeck:

The instinct of affinity (or what should I call it?) spoke immediately, my joy was extraordinary: I must go back to my acquaintance with Stendhal's Rouge et Noir to recall an equal joy. (There are two novellas, the first a piece of music, very foreign, very *un-German* music; the second a psychological stroke of genius, a kind of self-mockery of the *gnōthi seauton* [know thyself]). By the way, those *Greeks* have a lot on their conscience—falsification was their real handiwork, the entire European psychology is sickened on Greek *superficialities*; and without the touch of Judaism, etc., etc., etc.[91]

As he is writing this letter, a major earthquake rocks the Franco-Italian Riviera, transforming Nice into what Nietzsche calls a "madhouse." During which he, however, remains in "great spiritual calm," reading Dostoevsky in his intact flat.[92]

And what of his reference to Stendhal in 1887? In *Beyond Good and Evil*, Stendhal will remain (*pace* Dostoevsky) "the last great psychologist."[93] In *Ecce Homo* Nietzsche will flash back to the moment he threw down the gauntlet to David Friedrich Strauss in 1873: "Basically I had put into practice one of Stendhal's maxims: he advised entering society by provoking a *duel*."[94] In the same notebook recording his reading of Dostoevsky's *Demons*, Nietzsche cites Stendhal in French: "An almost instinctive belief for me is that every powerful man lies when he speaks, and for even greater reason when he writes" [*tout homme puissant ment, quand il parle, et à plus forte raison, quand il écrit*].[95] And of course Nietzsche knew the words of the Underground Man: "I lied about myself just now when I said I was a spiteful civil servant. I lied out of spite. I was simply being mischievous with these people and their enquiries and with the officer."[96] Nietzsche's style was combat and therefore never in principle opposed to lying, adept as this "master of truth" was in the ancient Greek and Latin praxis of *strategema*.[97]

When reading-by-glossing, appropriating-by-expropriating, and always by embodying Dostoevsky's *Demons*, Nietzsche discovers, in the months prior to his so-called breakdown, that the "prison house of language" he had felt himself—rightly—to have been dwelling in all his life was ultimately figurative and metaphysical.[98] But *only* in comparison with the eminently literal and concrete House of the Dead in which Dostoevsky had suffered, and from which he had emerged to write Nietzsche. *Yes,* Nietzsche's experiences of "prison" and "exile" were real enough from womb to tomb: from Röcken and Naumburg to Schulpforta and the University of Basel; from horse's neck in Turin and the "Nerve-Clinics" in Basel and Jena to Villa Silberblick in Weimar and the return to Röcken—all followed posthumously by the Nietzsche Archive and our current anthology. *And yet.* Even convict Nietzsche's prison house of language is parole on good behavior compared with Dostoevsky's Fortress of Peter and Paul and Omsk Prison Camp, with Gramsci's Casa Penale di Turi and David Gilbert's Auburn Correctional Facility.[99] Never *this* kind of convict, Nietzsche's experience of the punishment of crime is what political prisoners in Mussolini's Italy lived as *confino*—as Carlo Levi knew firsthand (not to mention cousin Primo Levi's Auschwitz). Whereas Nietzsche knew *about* Dostoevsky's "mock" or "civil execution" before confinement with hard labor in Siberia, Nietzsche's *own* terrifying encounter with armed men was confined to the oneiric and hallucinatory: his recurrent nightmare of a man standing at the window across from his writing desk with a rifle, once or twice realized as a vision when awake.

Dostoevsky *and* Nietzsche did suffer certain crimes committed against them: the eminently physical violence of Tsarist law; the near-deafening silence of contemporary reader response in the German-speaking conjuncture. Nietzsche *with* Dostoevsky bore the burden of well-nigh intolerable bodily and psychological distress—within and from which they created some of the greatest writing ever written: "Where violence and law had failed them, they had recourse to art" (Carlo Levi). It is only those crimes they might have *written* (not wrote *about*) that continue to capture us: "The greatest homage we can pay them is to say that we would not be able to ask them one question which they themselves had not asked and which, in their life, or by their death, they had not partially answered" (Camus). Any collaboratory crimes Dostoevsky or Nietzsche committed—or have somehow been responsible for committing—cannot be punished. "Defenders of criminals are rarely artistic enough to use the beautiful horror of the deed to the advantage of the doer."[100] One way or the other, we collaborate *with* our two Unabombers before the fact: "How can we speak of terrorist activity without taking part in it?" (Kaliayev). Certainly "the terroristic purpose [*der terroristische Zweck*] of punishment is neither essential nor primal . . . ; far more, it is only introduced under particular conditions and always as something additional, as something supplemental."[101] If "fear is the mother of morality,"[102] and whenever morality claims to justify either crime or its punishment, it remains imperative to be beyond good and evil, and unafraid.

How, then, can Nietzsche with Dostoevsky conclude? For these brothers in crime, twins in America, *real* questions or answers occur as untranslatable *moments*. We have attended to Nietzsche asking:

Are not the greatest moments of our life when we gain the courage to rebaptize our Evil as our Best?

And to Dostoevsky asking:

Good Lord, only a moment of bliss? But isn't such a moment sufficient for the whole of a person's life?

In *our* moment, we conclude with another onset. If, for Lenin, Dostoevsky's *Demons* is "repulsive but great," we respond in chess notation: Great *because* criminal, terrorist!?[103] Quite unrequited.

NOTES

1. Nietzsche's *relationship* to Dostoevsky has been meticulously documented, though prior to the appearance of the Colli-Montinari edition (begun in 1967, ongoing): see especially Wolfgang Gesemann, "Nietzsches Verhältnis zu Dostoevkij auf dem europäischen Hintergrund der 80er Jahre," *Die Welt der Slaven: Vierteljahrschrift für Slavistik* 6:2 (1961): 129–56. But a relationship is not necessarily *collaboration*, and Gesemann's understanding of "the 1880s" is anything but ours. Building on Gesemann's work, with some new data, is G. M. Fridlender, "Dostoevskii i Nitsshe," in *Dostoevskii i Mirovaya Literatura* (Moscow: Khudozh, 1979), 214–54. While their work must be deeply appreciated for what it is, our tactic here is to draw the strictest possible "line of demarcation" (Althusser following Lenin) between existing academic scholarship and our own intervention. (See further: Ana Siljak, *The Angel of Vengeance: The "Girl Assassin," The Governor of St. Petersburg, and Russia's Revolutionary World* (New York: St. Martin's Press, 2008)). By contrast, we situate "Nietzsche with Dostoevsky" within the context of 1880s Russian nihilism and terrorism as these were absorbed in Western Europe by Nietzsche.

2. Jean-Jacques Lecercle, *A Marxist Philosophy of Language* (2005), trans. Gregory Elliott (Chicago: Haymarket, 2009), 214. Compare "COMMUNICATION, n. A fair for the display of the minor mental commodities, each exhibitor being too intent upon the arrangement of his own wares to observe those of his neighbor." Ambrose Bierce, *The Unabridged Devil's Dictionary* (1881–1906) (n.p.: Feather Trail, 2009), 18.

3. As in the genitive metaphor "fear of the masses" or "fear of death"—
signifying fear of being killed *and* fear of killing others—our "question of crime"
is double-edged: questioning's crime and crime's question, neither of which does
Nietzsche fear. In his words: "Fear is the mother of morality . . . The imperative
of herd-timidity [*Herden-Furchtsamkeit*]: 'we want it sometime for once to be that
there is *Nothing more to fear!*'" (*KSA* 5:122–23). Several of Dostoevsky's protagonists
would have heartily agreed, if not Dostoevsky himself. Here and henceforth, *KSA*
is short for *Friedrich Nietzsche, Sämtliche Werke: Kritische Studienausgabe in 15
Bänden*, ed. Giorgio Colli and Mazzino Montinari (Berlin: Walter de Gruyter, 1980).

4. Dostoevsky, at least, *has* returned to America after "September 11" with
proverbial vengeance—at least according to André Glucksmann's CNN-inspired
Dostoïevski à Manhattan (Paris: Robert Laffont, 2002). Glucksmann asks: "D'où
sont les nihilistes? Mais de nulle part, ils ont été avec nous, en nous, à nos côtés
[From where did the nihilists come? But from nowhere, they have always been
with us, within us, at our side]." Glucksmann appears pleased to think that his
"us" means *us*. Responses to Glucksmann's book were quick to follow in print and
on websites, often with reference to Nietzsche, including from the Islamic world.
Among the important critiques: Andrew McKenna, "Scandal, Resentment, Idol-
atry: The Underground Psychology of Terrorism," *Anthropoetics: The Journal of
Generative Anthropology* 8:1 (Spring/Summer 2002): 20–41; and Albert Boro-
witz, *Terrorism for Self-Glorification: The Herostratos Syndrome* (Kent, Ohio:
Kent State University Press, 2005), 111–20. Herostratos was arguably "the first
terrorist," having committed arson on July 21, 356 B.C.E., by setting fire to the
Temple of Artemis in Ephesus, a Wonder of the World. In *Human, All Too
Human: A Book for Free Spirits*, vol. 2 (1886), Nietzsche reveals he is well aware
of this foundational act. See *KSA* 2:406.

With regard to these and other questions raised by our epigraphs, we are hi-
jacking for our "Nietzsche with Dostoevsky" Camus's remark in 1950 about the
generation of Russian terrorists around 1905, specifically Kaliayev, whose question is cited in Albert Camus, *The Rebel* (1951), trans. Anthony Bower (New
York: Penguin, 2000), 135. Ivan Platonovich Kaliayev (1877–1905) was a poet
and member of the Organization for Combat in the Socialist Revolutionary Party
(SR)—the SR later, in 1918, was responsible for the assassination attempt on
Lenin by Fanny Yelimovna Kaplan, leaving Lenin gravely wounded for years,
forever altering the history of Communism and hence the world. For his part,
Kaliayev was hanged for assassinating a grand duke. Having initially aborted his
mission because his target was accompanied by his wife and their young neph-
ews, Kaliayev waited two days until the grand duke was by himself. At his trial
he stated: "I do not repent. I must die for my deed and I will. My death will be
more useful to my cause than Sergei Alexandrovich's death. I am pleased with
your sentence. I hope that you will carry it out just as openly and publicly as I
carried out the sentence of the Socialist Revolutionary Party. Learn to look the

advancing revolution right in the face." Cited in Evard Radzinsky, *The Last Tsar: The Life and Death of Tsar Nicholas II* (New York: Doubleday, 1992), 82. If Dostoevsky admires those criminals who repent and thus are redeemed (like himself?), Nietzsche regarded such criminals as yet another example of slave morality, in opposition to the master morality of criminals who did not. Nietzsche did admire the latter, indeed regarded himself as a criminal in his unique sense.

5. *KSB* 8:278–79; syntax rearranged for emphasis. Here and henceforth *KSB* is short for Friedrich Nietzsche, *Sämtliche Briefe: Kritische Studienausgabe in 8 Bänden*, ed. Giorgio Colli and Mazzino Montinari (Berlin: Walter de Gruyter, 1986).

6. Fyodor Dostoevsky, *A Writer's Diary*, ed. Gary Saul Morson, trans. Kenneth Lantz (Evanston, Ill.: Northwestern University Press, 2009), 65.

7. *KSB* 6:175. Nietzsche wanted to visit Monte Carlo, one of Dostoevsky's haunts, but only in order to see a (nonlethal) bullfight on a date with Resa von Schirnhofer, about whom see note 10 this chapter.

8. Dostoevsky, "The Gambler" (1866), *Notes from the Underground; and, The Gambler*, trans. Jane Kentish (Oxford: Oxford University Press, 1991), 125–75; here 198.

9. Ibid., 60, 65.

10. This rein between Dostoevsky's and Nietzsche's horses was first drawn by Anacelto Verecchia, *La catastrofa di Nietzsche a Torino* (Turin: Einaudi, 1971), 55. See Dostoevsky, *Crime and Punishment*, trans. David McDuff, rev. ed. (London: Penguin, 2003), 67–77. How much, when, and even if Nietzsche read *Crime and Punishment* (also referred to at the time simply as *Raskolnikov*) is unclear, but he certainly heard it discussed and read about it. In spring of 1886, after writing Overbeck about his discovery of Dostoevsky, his friend lent him a copy of Carl Bleibtreu's bestseller *Revolution der Literatur*, which had just appeared in 1886, as had *Crime et châtiment*, the first translation of Dostoevsky's last novel. Nietzsche returned Bleibtreu's book to Overbeck immediately after reading it that week, remarking that Bleibtreu was "rooting around like a pig in the most common newspaper-manure," and so on (*KSB* 8:75). But, characteristically, this reaction only whetted Nietzsche's appetite to read more Dostoevsky. That same week Nietzsche was visited in Zurich by Resa von Schirnhofer, who brought him news from Paris about her friends Natalie Herzen, Turgenev, and an unspecified acquaintance who knew Dostoevsky personally. Immediately after their first words of greeting, von Schirnhofer and Nietzsche shared their great enthusiasm for Dostoevsky, in particular *Notes from the Underground* and *House of the Dead*.

11. For an account of Nietzsche's last letters from Turin, see Geoff Waite, "Nietzsche—Rhetoric—Nihilism: 'Every Name in History'—'Every Style'— 'Everything Permitted' (A Political Philology of the Last Letter)," in *Nietzsche, Nihilism, and the Philosophy of the Future*, ed. Jeffrey Metzger (New York: Continuum, 2009), 54–78 and 173–81.

12. In response to an unknown but appreciated reader, we respond: *Mit singen—was sonst?*

13. *KSB* 8:575. When part of this letter appears in *Ecce Homo*, Nietzsche suppresses Malwida's name. See *KSA* 6:364. Nietzsche had once proposed marriage to her.

14. See *Diary of a Russian Censor: Aleksandr Nikitenko*, ed. and trans. Helen Saltz Jacobson (Amherst: University of Massachusetts Press, 1975), 325.

15. Nietzsche's most recent writing on Wagner provided the context in which Nietzsche was initially received in Russia. His first book translated into a foreign language was *Richard Wagner in Bayreuth*, published in French in 1877. Officially banned by Russian censors, this French version was nonetheless available at the German-language bookshop in Saint Petersburg at 5 Nevsky Prospekt, as it was in the foreign-language equivalents in Turin, Florence, Rome, Paris, London, and later New York City.

16. *KSA* 6:50–51.

17. See *Die Briefe des Freiherrn Carl von Gersdorff und Friedrich Nietzsche*, vol. 4: *Ergäzungsband*, ed. Ehrhart Thierbach (Weimar: Ort Verlag/Nietzsche-Archiv, 1937), 63.

18. For a splendid account of Vera Zasulich, the contemporary importance of which exceeds its historical interest, see Siljak, *Angel of Vengeance*.

19. For reflections on the relationship among the topics Rousseau, seduction, and other kinds of revolution, see Francesca Cernia Slovin, *L'ultima passeggiata* (Venice: Marsilio, 1999), and its translation: *The Last Walk: Life and Death of Jean-Jacques Rousseau*, trans. Stephen Sartarelli (New York: Xlibris, 2009).

20. *KSB* 5:227.

21. *Karl Marx and Friedrich Engels Correspondence, 1846–1895*, ed. Marx-Engels Institute, Moscow (London: Martin Lawrence, 1934), 390. Compare Lenin's purported remark to a Bolshevik comrade about Nechayev and Dostoevsky's *Demons*: "Even the revolutionary milieu was hostile to Nechaev," and hence it forgot that Nechayev "possessed a special talent as an organizer, a conspirator, and a skill which he could wrap up in staggering formulations." According to the same source, Lenin affirmed with approval Nechayev's reply to the question as to which Romanov should be killed: "The entire House of Romanov!" Cited in Dmitri Volkogonov, *Lenin: A New Biography*, trans. and ed. Harold Shukman (New York: Free Press, 1994), 22. For a relevant historical backdrop to this period, see Walter G. Moss, *Russia in the Age of Alexander II, Tolstoy and Dostoevsky* (London: Wimbledon, 2002).

22. Weeks before his death in 1881, Dostoevsky's residence in Saint Petersburg was ransacked by Alexander II's police, suspecting him of some involvement with assassination plots by Narodnaya Volya and searching for copies of its literature, but evidently finding nothing of interest to them.

23. *KSA* 5:137.

24. Nietzsche made extensive markings in the copy he owned of Ferdinand Brunetière's *Le Roman Naturaliste*, 2nd printing (Paris: Calman Lévy, 1884), especially in the chapter "Le roman du nihilisme" (pp. 29–50), which is devoted to Chernyshevky's *What Is To Be Done?* as "une sorte d'évangile du nihilisme russe" (p. 47).

25. See Georg Brandes, *Impressions of Russia* [1888], trans. Samuel C. Eastman (London: Walter Scott, 1889).

26. Ibid., 308–9.

27. Ibid., 309.

28. Ibid., 49–63.

29. Ibid., 321–22.

30. Ibid., 126.

31. Nietzsche's complex impact on Salomé is as well known as is hers on him. These Russian émigré women later included the brilliant Sabine Spielrein (1885–1942), whose life was also powerfully impacted by Nietzsche, in her case indirectly through the equally brilliant "anarcho-Nietzschean-anti-psychoanalyst" Otto Gross. "A Dangerous Method," for sure!

32. *KSB* 8:573.

33. Cited in Joseph Frank, *Dostoevsky: The Years of Ordeal 1850–1859* (Princeton: Princeton University Press, 1990), 160.

34. *KSB* 2:61.

35. *Phædo* 91c.

36. *Nicomachean Ethics*, 1096a.

37. *Opus Majus*, pt. 1, ch. 5.

38. *KSA* 4:101.

39. Cited in Joseph Frank, *Dostoevsky: The Mantle of the Prophet 1871–1881* (Princeton: Princeton University Press, 2002), 727.

40. Cited ibid. To be sure, hotly contested are the questions of whether there was ever to be a sequel to *The Brothers Karamazov*, whether Dostoevsky's narrators ever speak for him, whether this particular statement implying some affirmation of terrorist assassination was a marketing ploy, etc.

41. Ibid.; emphasis added.

42. Ibid. "If there is any mistake in the testimony of the grand duke, it would be in characterizing Alyosha as an 'anarchist' rather than as the much more plausible 'Russian Socialist,' a term that receives some support from the *Diary*." No, we add, if there be any "mistake" here it is that of a certain liberal ideology. Nietzsche describes himself as "a decent criminal" like Chambige and Prado in his last letter to Jakob Burckhardt. Prado had been recently guillotined in Paris for murdering a prostitute, known to Oscar Wilde (see his poem "A Harlot's House").

43. Siljak, *The Angel of Vengeance*, 312.

44. Dostoevsky, *A Writer's Diary*, 525.

45. For a preliminary defense of this argument, see Geoff Waite, *Nietzsche's Corps(e): Aesthetics, Politics, Prophecy, or, The Spectacular Technoculture of Everyday Life* (Durham, NC: Duke University Press, 1996).

46. *KSA* 14:339.

47. *KSA* 6:254.

48. *KSA* 5:224–25.

49. *KSA* 10:517.

50. *KSA* 10:462.

51. *KSA* 5:99.

52. *KSA* 5:93.

53. This is the last *sentence* of "White Nights" (1848), which Nietzsche read in German translation in early 1887; we cite from *Great Short Works of Fyodor Dostoevsky*, trans. David Magarshack (New York: Perennial Classics, 2004), 201.

54. Ibid., 171.

55. These are two famous lines from Goethe's *Faust* and from one of Nietzsche's last poems, respectively. In English: "Tarry awhile, you are so beautiful!" and "I love you, O Eternity!"

56. The first English translation of "The Landlady" was by Constance Garnett (1861–1946), a fascinating person indeed, whose influential translations were aided by the (former) terrorist known as "Stepniak," also mentioned in Brandes's *Impressions of Russia*.

57. Jean-Michel Rey, "Nihilism and Autobiography," in *Nietzsche and the Rhetoric of Nihilism: Essays on Interpretation, Language, and Politics*, ed. Tom Darby, Béla Egyed, and Ben Jones (Ottawa: Carleton University Press, 1989), 23–36; here 33; emphasis altered.

58. Fyodor Dostoevsky, "The Landlady," *The Gambler and Other Stories*, trans. Constance Garnett (New York: Macmillan, 1923), 245–312; here 245, 247; translation slightly modified.

59. Fyodor Dostoevsky, *Humiliated and Insulted: From the Notes of an Unsuccessful Author* (1861), trans. Ignat Avsey (Richmond, Surrey: Oneworld, 2008), 181.

60. Sacher-Masoch's best-known work, *Venus in Furs*, was published in 1869 or '70, but Nietzsche had only heard of it. He put Sacher-Masoch (1835–95) on his list because he was editor-in-chief of the Leipzig-based monthly literary magazine *Auf der Höhe*, which advertised itself as the "cosmopolitan, international revue." It was regarded as progressive for its philo-Semitism and its promotion of women's suffrage. Nietzsche did not know that the journal, begun in 1881, had just ceased publication in 1885. But 1886 did find Sacher-Masoch at the height of his fame, celebrated in Paris by *Le Figaro* and by another of Nietzsche's favorite journals, *La Revue des Deux Mondes*.

61. Jos[ef] V[iktor] Widmann, "Nietzsche's gefährliches Buch," feuilleton in *Der Bund* [Bern], September 16 and 17, 1886. Reprinted in *KGB* III 7/2:520–25.

Here and henceforth, *KGB* is short for Friedrich Nietzsche, *Briefwechsel: Kritische Gesamtausgabe*, ed. Giorgio Colli and Mazzino Montinari (Berlin: Walter de Gruyter, 1984).

62. Widmann cites from F. M. Dostojewskji, *Junger Nachwuchs*, trans. W. Stein, 2 vols. (Leipzig: W. Friedrich, 1886), 1:81.

63. See, by way of comparison, Dostoevsky, *The Adolescent* (1875), trans. Richard Pevear and Larissa Volokhonsky (New York: Random House, 2003), 56–57; in Russian the word here translated as "noble" also signifies "magnanimous" or "noble-minded." But in the German translation, now read by Nietzsche, the word is *"anständig,"* "decent" or "respectable"—which has nothing to do with what he associates with "noble" in his genealogy of morals. The voice speaking is that of the narrator (Dostoevsky's only novel after *Notes from the Underground* with a first-person narrator-protagonist), who is recalling a statement he made in the past. Widmann does not cite his motto's continuation: "And especially now, in our time, which you have so refashioned. Because it has never been worse than it is now. Things are not at all clear in our society, gentlemen. I mean, you deny God, and you deny great deeds, what sort of deaf, blind, dull torpor can make me act this way, if it's more profitable for me otherwise?" (p. 57).

64. *KGB* III 7/2:525; emphasis added.

65. See Carl Albrecht Bernoulli, *Franz Overbeck und Friedrich Nietzsche: Eine Freundschaft, nach ungedruckten Dokumenten und im Zusammenhang mit der bisherigen Forschung*, 2 vols. (Jena: Diederichs, 1908), esp. 2:104–6; also 450, 481–85.

66. Ibid., 105–6.

67. See primarily *KSA* 13:141–53, though, again, it is uncertain where Nietzsche's response to Dostoevsky stops, if it indeed does, in this notebook. He was reading both volumes of Fiodor Dostoïevski, *Les possédés*, trans. Victor Derély, 2 vols. (Paris: Plon, 1886). True, as noted by his friends (notably Franz Overbeck), Nietzsche had an uncanny way of knowing what was in a text, or rather what he *needed* in it, by merely hearing about it or by quickly perusing it. However, Dostoevsky's *Demons* is the most notable *exception*.

68. Note the centrality of *Nice* in this scenario—though that's a topic for another occasion.

69. *KSA* 5:47.

70. Style: "That all those Nietzschean charlatans in verbal revolt against all that exists . . . should have ended up by accepting it after all may well be the case . . . but this is a question of *style*, not 'theory.'" Antonio Gramsci, *Prison Notebooks*, cited in Waite, *Nietzsche's Corps/e*, 343; emphasis added. A question that could be asked many a Dostoevskian protagonist.

71. In one of his last wills, Lenin included a statue of Dostoevsky among the many to be erected in honor of the 1917 Revolution. It still stands today, in front of the Lenin Library in Moscow at the Arbatskaya entrance—silently

greeting "everyone and no one," as Nietzsche might have said, whether entering or exiting. Flowers are left at its base.

72. Walter Benjamin, "One-way Street" (1923–26), *Selected Writings, Vol. 1: 1913–1926*, ed. Marcus Bullock and Michael W. Jennings (Cambridge, Mass.: Belknap Press, 1996), 481.

73. "Silence *and* terror" is a millenarian mantra, as in more recently, e.g., the quasi-religion of Nikos Kazantzakis. Nietzsche *with* Dostoevsky shatter precisely this "and." In concert, they further shatter as premature the nihilism of Hamlet's "the rest is silence" or Wittgenstein's "whereof one cannot speak, thereof one must be silent."

74. See Geoff Waite, "Nietzsche's Baudelaire, or The Sublime Proleptic Spin of His Politico-Economic Thought," *Representations* 50 (Spring 1995): 14–52. Summarized, Carey read by Nietzsche provided a specifically politico-economic rationale and consequence for the Eternal Recurrence of the Same. Carey's "harmony of interests" eliminated class struggle. In dialectical terms, Difference was absorbed into Identity. See further Karl Marx, *Capital: A Critique of Political Economy*, 3 vols., trans. David Fernbach (London: Penguin, 1991), 3:759; also the several other references to Carey and other international "harmonizers" in the four volumes of *Das Kapital*.

75. Ernest Mandel, *Delightful Murder: A Social History of the Crime Story* (Minneapolis: University of Minnesota Press, 1984), 135; slightly amended.

76. *KSA* 13:150–51. This note ends with Nietzsche's apparently positive appraisal of Tsar Nicholas I (1796–1855), who had ordered the brutal massacre of the Decembrists in 1825, the year he ascended to power, and who was the Tsar who in 1849 drove Dostoevsky into exile. For Nietzsche, Nicholas was "cold, quiet, *raisonnable*—consequently he was more terrible than anyone else" (p. 151). When Dostoevsky was being transported to hard labor in Siberia in 1849, it was Decembrist wives who met Dostoevsky at the train to gift him the copy of the New Testament he cherished all his life.

77. Leon Trotsky, *History of the Russian Revolution* [1930], trans. Max Eastman (New York: Pathfinder, 1980), 35.

78. For this and Nietzsche's immediately following "sources," compare Dostoevsky, *Demons* (1871–72), ed. Ronald Meyer, trans. Robert A. Maguire (London: Penguin, 2008), 744–46.

79. *KSA* 13:142.

80. See, for example, Nietzsche's response to Savrogin and Kirilov at *KSA* 13:144.

81. *KSA* 5:399.

82. Shestov may be the first to remark both Nietzsche's united front with the Order of Assassins and also, in this context, the similar slogan in *The Brothers Karamazov*: "Everything is permitted, and that's that! And if you mean to swindle, what further need is there of the sanction of truth?" Shestov, *Dosto-*

evsky and Nietzsche, 253. Shestov is too cautious a writer to state that Nietzsche ever read the novel, thus correctly leaving unanswered the ongoing question of how this remarkable aspect of the collaboration came to be.

83. See Nietzsche's (Spinozan, anti-Cartesian) attack in *Beyond Good and Evil* on "grammatical habits": "A thought comes when 'it' wants, and not when 'I' want; so it is a *falsification* of the factual situation to say that the subject 'I' is the condition of the predicate 'think.' It thinks [*Es denkt*]" (*KSA* 5:31).

84. *KSA* 13:178–79; ellipses in original.

85. Compare Lukács: "'They say,' says a desperate character in Dostoevsky, 'that the well-fed cannot understand the hungry, but I would add that the hungry do not always understand the hungry.' There is apparently not a ray of light in this darkness. What Dostoevsky thought to be such a ray was only a will-o'-the wisp." Georg Lukács, "Dostoevsky" (1949), *Marxism and Human Liberation: Essays on History, Culture and Revolution*, ed. E. San Juan, Jr. (New York: Dell, 1973), 179–97; here 195. Lukács cites old Ichmenyev in *Humiliated and Insulted*, which Nietzsche wept reading. By contrast, the obvious Frankfurt School mantra has been: "Liberation from hunger and misery does not necessarily converge with liberation from servitude and degradation." Jürgen Habermas, *Theory and Practice* (1971), trans. John Viertel (Boston: Beacon, 1973), 169.

86. *KSB* 8:41.

87. Cited in Vladimir Bonch-Bruevich, "Lenin o knigakh i pisatelyah," *Literaturnaya gazeta* (April 21, 1955), as translated by Vladimir Seduro in "The Fate of Stavrogin's Confession," *Russian Review* 25:4 (October 1966): 397–404; here 398. As Seduro notes, the discovery of this remark by Lenin spurred the Soviet reception of Dostoevsky in new directions, including away from focus on "only the reactionary aspect of *The Possessed*."

88. Marx, *Theorien über den Mehrwert* (1862–63), Karl Marx and Friedrich Engels, *Werke*, 43 vols. (Berlin: Dietz, 1956–90), 26(1):363.

89. *KSA* 6:146–47. In Nietzsche's subtitle, the signifier "hammer" signifies not only a tool to drive nails (especially into The Cross of Dostoevsky's Christ) and to smash all other idols into their deserved twilight but also the "tuning fork" to test and retune musical instruments, including writing—not least Nietzsche's own.

90. Nietzsche was to make one more momentous discovery in this regard. He first recorded his reading of Spinoza at the end of April 1881 and a day or two later his revelation of the Eternal Recurrence of the Same, its impact on *Thus Spoke Zarathustra* being incalculable. See *KSB* 8:111 and *KSA* 9:494, respectively. But Nietzsche knew Spinoza far more indirectly (through Vischer's monumental history of philosophy) than he knew Stendhal and especially was to know Dostoevsky—their impact on him being far more direct.

91. *KSB* 8:27–28. Similarly enthusiastic, though sometimes slightly qualified remarks on his discovery of Dostoevsky occur in other letters to various correspondents from mid-February to July 1887.

92. See *KSB* 8:34.

93. *KSA* 5:57. Here Nietzsche, in admiration of Stendhal's style, cites him to the effect that to be a good philosopher one must be like a *banker*; that is, *pour faire des découvertes en philosophie, c'est-à-dire pour voir clair dans ce qui est* (to make discoveries in philosophy, that is to say to see clearly that which exists).

94. *KSA* 6:319. Nietzsche here recalls that it was following this maxim that he "first entered society," that is, with his challenge to David Friedrich Strauss in 1873. He takes his maxim from Prosper Mérimée's preface to Stendhal, *Correspondance inédite* (Paris: Michel Lévy, 1855), ix.

95. *KSA* 13:19. Nietzsche appears to have found this crucial remark in Stendhal's preface to his *Vie de Napoléon* (1817–18), 2nd ed. (Paris: Michel Lévy, 1877), xv.

96. Dostoevsky, *Notes from the Underground* (trans. Kentish), 7–8.

97. See Everett L. Wheeler's exceptional *Stratagem and the Vocabulary of Military Trickery* (Leiden: E. J. Brill, 1988). Equally crucial in the same regard is Marcel Detienne, *Maîtres de vérité dans la grèce archaïque* (Paris: Maspero, 1967).

98. Attributed to Nietzsche, the phrase "the prison house of language" has gained currency as being the sole epigraph of Fredric Jameson's *The Prison-House of Language: A Critical Account of Structuralism and Russian Formalism* (Princeton: Princeton University Press, 1972). Nietzsche never uttered this phrase. Emphatically, he wrote instead of "linguistic constraint." "*We stop thinking when we don't want to think within linguistic constraint* [*in dem sprachlichen Zwange*], we still barely touch even the doubt to see this limit qua limit" (*KSA* 12:193). Jameson has appropriated the dramatic mistranslation from Erich Heller, "Wittgenstein and Nietzsche" (1965), *The Importance of Nietzsche: Ten Essays* (Chicago: University of Chicago Press, 1988), 141–57; here 152. Anyone who has experienced both knows that constraint breakout is a piece of cake compared with prison breakout.

99. Here we hijack, for Nietzsche's relation to Dostoevsky, a line from socialist writer Dwight Macdonald's acerbic comment on Alexander Herzen's implication—in the "My Siberian Exile" section of *My Past and Thoughts* (1852–70)—that he was ever *actually* in prison: "Siberian exile, as Dostoevsky suffered in the same period (compare *The House of the Dead*), was to Herzen's as Leavenworth is to parole. Herzen was not a convict like Dostoevsky—or Bakunin, Lenin, or Trotsky later." *My Life and Thoughts: The Memoirs of Alexander Herzen*, trans. Constance Garnett, abridged with a preface and notes by Dwight Macdonald (Berkeley: University of California Press, 1973), 483–84, n. 19.

100. *KSA* 5:92.

101. *KSA* 5:251.

102. See again *KSA* 5:122.

103. The response to Lenin in chess notation is in deference to the passion for chess that he had to abandon for revolution. The "!?" after a move is the most

debated of symbols because it can signify: "perhaps not the best, but interesting"; "deserving further attention"; "enterprising"; "risky"; "involving speculative sacrifice"; "launching a dangerous attack"; "setting a cunning trap," sometimes in a hopeless position. Most commonly, however, "!?" indicates that the move is good if it initiates exhilarating or wild play. For a quite different but not wholly unrelated view, see Andrew Soltis, *Karl Marx Plays Chess: And Other Reports on the World's Oldest Game* (New York: Three Rivers Press, 1991).

Jeff Love

Violence and the Dissolution of Narrative

> . . . the basic fact of the human will, its *horror vacui*: *it needs a goal*—and it would rather will *nothingness* than not will.
> —Nietzsche, *On the Genealogy of Morality*

> It is necessary that every man have at least somewhere to go.
> —Dostoevsky, *Crime and Punishment*

HOW DOES ONE NARRATE VIOLENCE? This question may seem supernumerary, perhaps silly or obvious. We are surrounded by tales of violence, of war, theft, rape, beatings of all kinds. These acts of violence are the raw material of countless narratives, from the great books encountered in our universities and high schools to the crime dramas of prime-time television. Why would one possibly seek to question the patently obvious? Is that not a step into the "inverted world" (*die verkehrte Welt*), the upside-down realm of issues that neither demand nor offer an answer?

But that is precisely the point. Violence is essentially departure, a stepping away or over (*perestupit'*), a crossing of boundaries into a realm of uncertainty, of the indeterminate. One could say—and this is a preliminary definition of some moment, if not irony—that violence is the intrusion of the indeterminate into an otherwise determinate context: violence designates indeterminacy. This sounds like a slogan, impossibly precious and distant from the reality of violence. Nothing could be further from the truth.

Indeterminacy announces collapse, illness, the failure of definition, the failure of a way of getting about with things. The word *definition* is particularly appropriate here. To define is to take something in hand, to make it an "it" available for certain purposes, and those purposes have an architectonic role in our lives, in society, in everyday exchanges with others. To render these definitions questionable, to upset, overturn, or corrode them, is to do violence on an elemental level.

Thus, I pose the initial question again: how does one narrate violence? That is, how does one narrate that which in its resistance to definition would

37

appear also to resist narrative? And again the sheer obviousness of the re-sponse, the myriad narratives of violence, makes the question seem naive, foolhardy. But I may also frame the question differently now. For one might argue that narratives of violence are ways of eradicating violence, of trans-forming the fundamentally estranging force that is violence into what it is not, into a "regulated" violence, this being their seductive charm and power, whether these are expressed in the carefully wrought hexameters of Ho-meric epic or the simple patterns of resolution that characterize the sixty-minute crime drama.

Perhaps it would be hard to make a more banal claim. Narrative is expiation; it liberates us from violence by giving form to it, by putting it to work. Narrative finds a language, a way of definition, for that which has no definition: narrative tames violence as it depicts it. Narratives are means by which we protect ourselves. They are police gestures, normative, giving and enforcing patterns that ward away what is most uncanny about violence, that violence is unsettlement, deracination, eradication, a tearing away of all that allows us to orient ourselves in some manner or other.

Bluntly put, violence as typically understood, as a determinate act, though terrible and destructive, is but foreground disguising a far more threatening, potent, and elusive violence that is the violence of indetermi-nacy, complete collapse, dissolution. While there has been much focus on violence as exclusion, as taking a position, as asserting a judgment that favors some at the cost of others, there has been less focus on the arguably more fundamental violence which is the dissolution of the very frameworks in which exclusions, positions, and assertions are intelligible in the first place.[1]

Theodicy is at the core of the approach I take, and theodicy is by no means a transparent term. Precision would have us trace the term to its in-ventor, Gottfried Wilhelm Leibniz, who created it out of a combination of two Greek words with rich histories, *theos*, or "god," and *dikē*, or "justice."[2] The usual reading is, then, one that equates theodicy with God's justice, more or less along the lines of Milton's famous claim to attempt to explain the ways of God to men. That is the project of theodicy, and it is developed at formidable length in Leibniz's *Theodicy* published in 1710.

The conceptual framework provided by theodicy permits me to focus on the central issue of this essay, violence, because theodicy aims to offer not just an explanation of, but also a justification for, violence in the guise of evil. And, indeed, connecting evil with violence usefully broadens the context of my investigation. It does so because evil is primarily understood by Leibniz, drawing on a complex tradition, negatively; that is, as a being defined by its absence of being. This definition reaches back to the characterization of evil as *privatio boni* (absence of good) that gained exceptional authority in the Western Christian tradition with St. Augustine while also having important resonances in the East because of the pervasive influence of Neoplatonism and, in particular, figures like Pseudo-Dionysius, the Areopagite.[3]

Let me clarify here. The evident paradox, that evil's being is to have no being, or, in other terms that may be rather more precise, that evil is a sort of determinate indeterminacy, are of the utmost relevance. For the key notion, one which I mentioned above, is that violence is fundamentally a kind of indeterminacy; thus, the connection with evil serves to clarify this problematic aspect of violence. I say "problematic" because to assert that there is a kind of indeterminacy is surely peculiar, since "kind" offers a definition of something that should not lend itself to definition.

Why is this important? From the simplest standpoint, indeterminacy offers no orientation for action: indeterminacy, to borrow a metaphor whose power in our tradition remains undiminished, is a kind of darkness, and in our modern age it has been connected with nihilism, the utter inability to determine any sort of authoritative valuation or hierarchy of values. Violence of course possesses this inchoate power; it is the demolishing of determinate order, whether the collapse of an organism, the destruction of a person, or of an empire.

Theodicy plays an important role here because theodicy, like Aristotelian narrative, seeks to assign a positive teleological value to violence, to give it a place in a greater order—or, as we say now, economy—indicating that its apparent indeterminacy plays a crucial role both in reinforcing and establishing a firm determinacy, a holistic architecture. Hence, the venerable, and questionably credible, claim repeated countless times that a negative or destructive action took place for the "greater" good, meaning that it played a determinate role in a sort of master plan rather than pulling that plan asunder.

Nietzsche and Dostoevsky recognize the limitations of this view of violence; indeed, they are among the first to point out that the ameliorative interpretation of violence is a kind of palliative fiction.[4] More bluntly put, they both question the underlying assumption that violence can be tamed, or instrumentalized as the essential tool that fulfills the whole. This assumption, which Hegel develops so beautifully in his attempt at harnessing the *"ungeheure Macht des Negativen"* (monstrous power of the negative), is for Nietzsche and Dostoevsky a fiction at the brink of exhaustion.[5]

If Nietzsche and Dostoevsky both accept this view, their response to it differs considerably, and I would suggest that in this respect Dostoevsky may well be the more radical of the two. I say this because Dostoevsky explores in his grand narratives the possibility of creating a narrative that neither succumbs to the now bankrupt theodicean narrative impulse nor its simplistic antinarrative complement that finds its most pregnant expression in Dostoevsky's heroes of indeterminacy, characters of the underground like Ippolit

Jeff Love

Terentiev and Nikolai Stavrogin. Nietzsche, to the contrary, argues that such narratives are necessary illusions, though ones the truly superior man should mock as a sign of his courageous acceptance of their illusory quality, of the greater originary power of indeterminacy.

There is arguably a broader point here, and I might make it usefully by reference to Martin Heidegger's discussion of *Angst* in "What Is Metaphysics?"[6] In that essay Heidegger relates the attunement or *Stimmung* of *Angst* to an apprehension of nothingness, or to what Heidegger refers to as the "essential impossibility of determination" (*die wesenhafte Unmöglichkeit der Bestimmbarkeit*). Nietzsche and Dostoevsky both appreciate this attitude toward indeterminacy and seek in their own ways to overcome the terror before indeterminacy either by a kind of oblivious freedom from that terror or a delight in it that is truly the delight of the artist, the ostensibly fearless creator. In this respect, both Nietzsche and Dostoevsky are heralds of a new attitude to narrative and thus a new attitude to the assumptions that have hitherto informed narratives: they are explorers in a sort of post-narrative landscape.

Nietzsche offers what has now become familiar as post-modern irony, the narrative that upsets its own presuppositions but remains, for all that, a narrative nonetheless. I suggest that Dostoevsky tends to go further to question whether we need a narrative at all, whether we may live in a manner not beholden to narrative—the question that looms large here is whether a non-narrative life is even possible. Dostoevsky thus puts in question the value of narrative itself; in so doing, he also puts in question the value of action, and, as we shall see, Dostoevsky's concern about narrative is at the same time a concern about action. If Nietzsche retains the largely modern valorization of action, albeit in a complicated and indirect fashion, Dostoevsky is far more circumspect.

I should now like to examine these two positions, starting with Nietzsche, then moving on to Dostoevsky.

Nietzsche's famous preface to the second edition of *The Gay Science* deserves its reputation as a fascinating and beguiling document. Its initial focus is one that would be familiar to any reader of Dostoevsky: sickness. While we may be tempted to make much of the biographical element in Nietzsche's account of his own sickness, there is of course no doubt that Nietzsche employs with considerable frequency sickness as a guiding metaphor in his work.

The sickness Nietzsche discusses in the preface is remarkable for having been cured. The opening conceit of *The Gay Science* as viewed in retrospect is that it is a work of healing, of growing health and, thus, of hope as well. Nietzsche proceeds to identify the discoveries of *The Gay Science* with the Greeks, but the affinity of his account with Christian narratives ought

40

not to be overlooked. The narrative of sickness and healing accompanied by new hope recalls nothing so much as a Christian redemption narrative. Such narratives are quite foreign to those aspects of Greek thought which Nietzsche most fervently admires; and, hence, it is already somewhat curious that Nietzsche's central conceit in the preface holds a significance that his own focus on the Greeks would appear to belie.

But let us look a bit closer at this sickness. What kind is it? Nietzsche refers to his sickness in the following terms:

> [T]his stretch of desert, exhaustion, disbelief, icing up in the midst of youth, this interlude of old age at the wrong time, this tyranny of pain even excelled by the tyranny of pride that refused the *conclusions* of pain—and conclusions are consolations—this radical retreat into solitude as a self-defense against a contempt for men that had become pathologically clairvoyant—this determined self-limitation to what was bitter, harsh, and hurtful to know, prescribed by the *nausea* that had gradually developed out of an incautious and pampering spiritual diet, called romanticism—oh, who could reexperience all of this?[7]

The metaphors are striking: desert, exhaustion, icing up, old age in the midst of youth. They convey a sense of aridity and immobility, of lost vitality. When combined with disbelief, this assemblage of metaphors suggests that disbelief issues in a kind of stasis, a "conscious sitting with folded arms," in the words of Dostoevsky's Underground Man.[8] Moreover, stasis is a kind of sickness, a claim recalling one of Nietzsche's more famous aphorisms, his attack on Flaubert that ends with the memorable phrase: "Only thoughts won by walking have value" (*Nur die ergangenen Gedanken haben Werth*).[9] Why does disbelief issue into stasis? And what is so problematic about stasis? The answer to the first question should provide an answer to the second as well.

The connection between disbelief and stasis may be clarified by reference to the Underground Man once again. In chapter V of *Notes from Underground*, the Underground Man gives an account of his situation, of why inertia governs his existence and not action:

> For the direct, lawful, immediate fruit of consciousness is inertia—that is, a conscious sitting with folded arms. I've already mentioned this above. I repeat, I emphatically repeat: ingenuous people and active figures are all active simply because they are dull and narrow-minded. How to explain it? Here's how: as a consequence of their narrow-mindedness, they take the most immediate and secondary causes for the primary ones, and thus become convinced more quickly and easily than others that they have found an indis-

putable basis for their doings, and so they feel at ease; and that, after all, is the main thing. For in order to begin to act, one must first be completely at ease, so that no more doubts remain. Well, and how am I to set myself at ease? Where are the primary causes on which I can rest, where are my bases? Where am I going to get them? I exercise thinking, and, consequently, for me every primary cause immediately drags with it yet another still more primary one, and so on ad infinitum.[10]

The Underground Man employs an argument at the end of this passage that one can trace back to Aristotle's *Posterior Analytics*. Roughly speaking, the argument holds that knowledge of an unending causal chain is impossible since it is impossible to survey fully anything that is unending (*apeiron*).[11]

Stasis from this perspective is an inability to choose any course of action; that is, an inability to evaluate definitively the relative worth of one action vis-à-vis another, what Nietzsche otherwise seems to associate with nihilism. The ground for this inability is precisely the impossibility of finding a firm ground for acting, reasons and grounds having a similar meaning in this context. If we return to the issue of indeterminacy, we can readily admit that the impossibility of finding a ground is a kind of indeterminacy, since the actions which one must take as determinations or decisions whereby determinate ends might be realized simply cannot find justification—they must be arbitrary, choices made for no other reason than to make a choice, action for the sake of action alone.

Given the connections one might make between the putative author of *The Gay Science* and the Underground Man, Nietzsche's prescriptions for recovery from this sickness must be of abiding interest, for they seem to involve choice of a fundamental sort. That one may choose to recover from one's sickness shows the limits of the figuration. Physical illness may not be so pliant to choice; indeed, the real power and terror of illness are that one may not simply choose to recover. But Nietzsche does not linger on this difficulty; rather, he suggests by means of a curious analogy between a traveler and philosophers that the latter may indeed fall asleep, or fall into sickness, in the knowledge that they will once again awaken, whereupon they will see in a quite different light.

This different light is, above all, associated with malice, with making light of the suffering that drives philosophers into sickness. What awakens from sickness is an expansive lightness, a fleetness of spirit that mocks the seriousness imposed on us by suffering.[12] In this respect, it may be useful to recall the connection Nietzsche makes in *On the Genealogy of Morality* between pain and obedience—it is pain that makes memories in us, and these memories enforce a certain order that we must take seriously if we are to avoid further pain. In *On the Genealogy of Morality*, pain is a guarantor of authority; indeed, pain and the threat of death, as the most terrifying result of pain—complete dissolution of one's bodily existence, and for Nietzsche there is no other—are the wellsprings of authority.

Nietzsche's malicious spirit, his convalescent, turns against this authority. That is the significance of convalescence. For convalescence is precisely the liberation from the weight of authority, the authority of another, an authority behind which one finds the ultimate authority of suffering and death. Nietzsche's concern with authority is remarkable in so far as it makes the far-reaching assertion that authority arises from suffering or is a response to suffering. The corollary is that, without suffering, there would be no need for authority. This is a point that reflects Nietzsche's astute readings of tragedy where the connection between the fear of death and longing for authority emerges explicitly, as it does in *Oedipus Tyrannos*.[13]

Nietzsche's convalescent needs no authority, no expiating narrative, no theodicy—Nietzsche's convalescent is free of the concern with the horrors of indeterminacy and can in fact embrace indeterminacy as the most beautiful freedom, something the Underground Man is unable to do. While the Underground Man seems finally unable to delight in his ability to see things as they are, the Nietzschean convalescent accepts them—up to a certain point.

This "certain point" is the need for art that characterizes the convalescent: "No, if we convalescents still need art, it is another kind of art—a mocking, light, fleeting, divinely untroubled, divinely artificial art that like a pure flame, licks into unclouded skies."[14] Once again in *On the Genealogy of Morality*, Nietzsche accentuates this point with regard to the great artistic love of his life, Richard Wagner:

> . . . what? Was this Parsifal meant at all *seriously*? For one could be tempted to conjecture, even to wish the opposite—that the Wagnerian Parsifal was meant lightheartedly, a closing piece and satyr-play, as it were, with which the tragedian Wagner wanted to take leave of us, of himself, above all *of tragedy* in a manner fitting for and worthy of him, namely with an excess of highest and most mischievous parody of the tragic itself, of the entire gruesome earthly seriousness and wretchedness of earlier times, of the *coarsest form*— now finally overcome—found in the anti-nature of the ascetic ideal. This as noted, would have been worthy precisely of a great tragedian, who, like every artist, only arrives at the final pinnacle of his greatness when he is able to see himself and his art *beneath* him—when he is able to *laugh* at himself.[15]

The imagery in these two passages is telling. What kind of art is like a pure flame licking into unclouded skies? The image is extravagant but it also has a fairly traditional base: purification by fire, that is, purification by immolation—purification by destruction, a destruction so pure it ends up in emptiness, pure expanse, unclouded skies. And we might take the second passage to identify this purifying destruction with laughter that dissolves the "gruesome earthly seriousness" reflected in the tragic.

Here we have the basic elements of an interpretation of the tragic and the comic that may offer a helpful perspective on the convalescent. In a sense, tragic seriousness reveals a wound that can only be healed by comic laughter, by mockery. The tragic belongs to an age of futility where the impossibility of overcoming suffering forces us into bitter servitude, a kind of dampening humility whose outcome is a reticence to take action of any kind—one has only to recall the elder Oedipus, the blind and helpless wanderer.[16] The Underground Man finds himself in a somewhat similar situation, as does the sick philosopher. Action concludes with failure, and, as Nietzsche tells us, conclusions are consolations.

To mock this somber conclusion—any conclusion at all—seems to be the lasting value Nietzsche attaches to comedy, the satyr-play of the imagination that refuses to be humble but places itself above the merely human. But is this not in fact the other side of the Underground Man as well? By this I mean that we can interpret the Underground Man as displaying a fundamental or core ambivalence about his circumstances. On the one hand, he seems to bemoan his impotence, that he "never even managed to become anything: neither wicked, nor good, neither a scoundrel nor an honest man, neither a hero nor an insect."[17] On the other hand, he is boastful about his intellectual superiority to the simple actor, the one who can act because he or she stops thinking. This claim of superiority results in open disdain for those who act and, by inference, puts narrative as a shape of action in question. At least one of the more obvious aspects of part 2 of *Notes from Underground* is the parodic quality associated with the narratives, their evident (if pathetic) ridiculousness.[18]

Taking this ambivalence into account, we may argue that the Underground Man exemplifies the Nietzschean account. But this would be a substantial misstatement, because the Underground Man seems unable to decide between these alternatives—belief in a narrative, no matter how tragic, and comic mockery of that narrative—whereas the point of Nietzsche's account is that healing is itself a kind of decision. But what kind of decision exactly?

The decision is to become superficial, to become stupid, to forget:

No, this bad taste, this will to truth, to "truth at any price," this youthful madness in the love of truth, have lost their charm for us: for that we are too experienced, too serious, too merry, too burned, *too profound.* We no longer believe that truth remains when the veils are withdrawn; we have lived too much to believe this. Today we consider it a matter of decency not to wish to see everything naked, or to be present at everything, or to understand and "know" everything.[19]

Nietzsche then proceeds with a surprisingly obscene joke:

"Is it true that God is present everywhere?" a little girl asked her mother: "I think that is indecent"—a hint for philosophers! One should have more respect for the bashfulness with which nature has hidden behind riddles and iridescent uncertainties. Perhaps truth is a woman who has reasons for not letting us see her reasons? Perhaps her name is—to speak Greek—*Baubo*?[20]

Let me spend some time exploring these two statements, one acting almost as a parody of the other, as if in demonstration of Nietzsche's praise of mockery.

The first statement is an eloquent formulation of the notion that the truth is dangerous, and we have at least some inkling of why this may be so. What is striking, however, is the peculiar wager Nietzsche makes here. Having recognized the truth, that the truth is in some sense—and we will return to this "sense"—unattractive, Nietzsche beckons us to return to a new innocence, a new freedom, to be "reborn," as he says elsewhere in the preface. But this is an unusual innocence because it emerges from the most thoroughgoing lack of innocence, from a knowledge that has gone too far or penetrated too deeply, to use a metaphor that has some relation to Nietzsche's crude joke. Here is the wager: How can one forget what one knows? How can one become innocent again? While this might be possible for Goethe's Faust, it is not at all clear how Nietzsche can work this out. Nietzsche is of course not unaware of the difficulty himself. In a letter to Georg Brandes, dated January 4, 1889, little more than a year after the preface appeared in print, Nietzsche put the matter thus: "After you discovered me, it was no great trick (*Kunststück*) to find me: the difficulty now is to lose me."[21]

But Nietzsche wants his artists to lose their interest in truth, in seeing things as they really are, and he picks an appropriate image: nakedness. His subsequent joke teases out some of the implications of this metaphoric treatment of the truth, but first we might as well lay out the significance of his initial association of nakedness with the truth. Here Nietzsche makes a somewhat enigmatic comment: "We no longer believe that the truth remains when the veils are withdrawn." We might assume this image shows that truth and nakedness have no connection. But we might also say that there is no truth available at all when one withdraws all the veils, that like an object deprived of all qualities, one has only an indefinable X left over, not a truth of the object, but a nothing to explain. And this explanation must end up failing because to identify a nothing, as Heidegger famously indicated, is to transform it into a something, exactly what it cannot be if it is nothing. This is merely an awkward way of saying that one cannot talk about nothing successfully; therefore, the object in its "bare objecthood" is nothing at all, an emptiness, determinately indeterminate.[22]

Is this what Nietzsche means? The fact that he switches registers to a crude joke complicates the interpretation. Indeed, if God is everywhere, one would have to conclude that he finds himself *there* as well, and if that is the case God's intimacy with his creatures is far greater—and far more unsettling—than we are typically led to imagine. Moreover, the equation of truth with Baubo, normally represented as a face on the female genitalia, is a curious gloss, to say the least.[23]

We can perhaps be fairly sure of one thing: Nietzsche seems to connect the withdrawing of veils with something rather terrible, either because it reveals a "nothing" at the heart of things or an obscene image, perhaps an image of raw, protean fecundity itself, the reverse of elegance and simplicity compatible with both nakedness and nothingness.

What is the solution? One needs to return to the "clothed world," the world of appearances. It seems quite apparent that the philosopher still needs art for precisely this purpose, that is, for the purpose of forgetting what the philosopher may have glimpsed. In this sense, clothing is a fine metaphor because it hides the truth—or lack thereof. Yet, we may ask if this function is compatible with an art that is insouciant and ironic, an art of malice and laughter.

An art of malice and laughter cares nothing for truth—this is its peculiar refinement. As Nietzsche notes, one is "newborn" with "merrier senses, with a second dangerous innocence in joy, more childlike and yet a hundred times subtler than one has ever been before."[24] The new art is in this sense a mask, and everybody recalls that most notorious statement from *Beyond Good and Evil*: "everything that is deep loves the mask."[25] The depths reached in suffering clamor for superficiality, a sticking to the surface of things in order to heal oneself from the trauma of full disclosure.

In Dostoevsky there is also a crisis of full disclosure, a crisis of seeing. Robert Louis Jackson writes eloquently about Dostoevsky's insistence that we have an ethical duty to look at the way things are, that we may not hide from "reality."[26] But the fictional works seem to me to be far more equivocal. Let us take a further look at the Underground Man, for to this point I have attended to one aspect of his dilemma, which, though important, is only part of a far more complicated structure.

I have suggested that what the Underground Man sees is the impossibility of making choices, the impossibility of acting from an untroubled, firm basis. The infinite regress argument effectively eliminates the possibility of determining a final ground or a sequence of final reasons whereby one may safely make inferences that decide choices to act in one way and not another. The Underground Man faces a sort of abyss of freedom, as the later existentialists might claim with suitable pathos and gnashing of teeth.

But the Underground Man faces the opposite of this as well: he faces an abyss of necessity. If the Underground Man seems to feel burdened by an excess of freedom understood as the complete indifference toward choice, since no proper differential may be found to motivate choice, he is equally, if not more, burdened by the humiliating fetters that nature places upon him. As he says, "throughout my life, the laws of nature have offended me constantly and more than anything else."[27] Part 1 is riddled with comments on this aspect of his (and our) situation:

> "For pity's sake," they'll shout at you, "you can't rebel: it's two times two is four! Nature doesn't ask your permission; it doesn't care about your wishes, or whether you like its laws or not. You're obliged to accept it as it is, and consequently all its results as well . . . etc., etc." My God, but what do I care about the laws of nature and arithmetic if for some reason these laws and two times two is four are not to my liking? To be sure, I won't break through such a wall with my forehead if I've really not got strength enough to do it, but neither will I be reconciled with it simply because I have a stone wall here and have not got strength enough.[28]

How might we reconcile these two tendencies? Or what are we to make of them? I should like to entertain two different readings. The first makes the simple claim that there are two bold, mutually incompatible possibilities expressed by the narrator, two extremes: one is that the laws of nature govern all human activity, and those laws impose a dire necessity upon us because nature fates us to die. The other is that there is somehow an original freedom, a sort of initial indeterminacy that we are ultimately unable to overcome and to which we return again and again, as I have already suggested.

Put this way, the Underground Man seems to be caught in a Kantian dilemma, an attempt to reconcile a Newtonian view of nature with the possibility of freedom, which is an inheritance from faith.[29] It is not at all clear that such a dilemma admits of resolution. Yet, it seems fair to say that the kind of freedom expressed by the Underground Man is not consistent with natural necessity. After all, if there are indeed laws of nature, the Underground Man cannot exempt himself from them.

But this is exactly what he endeavors to do. The Underground Man moves to declare a peculiar freedom from arithmetical laws by declaring that two times two is five, "also a most charming little thing."[30] By declaring freedom from arithmetic, the Underground Man also declares freedom from the laws of nature whose basis is in an arithmetic or mathematical understanding of nature. Here is the problem: How can one possibly declare oneself free of these laws if they are truly necessary? This statement seems to be incoherent, and that is the point, for the Underground Man seems finally to seek out incoherence. One might associate this incoherence with paradox, but to do so confers a logic on the more radical claims of the Underground Man that those claims do not merit.

The Underground Man ends up asserting the primacy of irrational desire over reason, of desire unleashed from any reason to desire other than to desire. Indeed, the Underground Man links imagination to this desire as soon as he makes the claim that two times two equals five. This is an important link because one may well argue that the Underground Man (arguably like Kant) comes close to asserting that we imagine ourselves to be free or have to do so because no other freedom is available.[31] From this point of view, a stolidly finitist one, the Underground Man's infinite regress argument also becomes a creature of the imagination since no one can possibly know an infinite causal chain. If no one can know that chain, no one can make definitive claims about it, either that it is infinite or finite; to do so is to engage the imagination, to leap beyond the primary focus of science, observation and induction. The Underground Man asserts in effect that we prefer fiction over truth because truth enslaves us.

Coming from rather different conclusions, Dostoevsky's Underground Man valorizes fiction—artifice—just as Nietzsche does: illusion has more power than reality, art triumphs in this case over science. The difference is that Nietzsche seems to flee the tyranny of chance, of indeterminacy, where the Underground Man seeks to embrace them—his fictions are fictions of liberation, and finally liberation from death. For there is probably no more indeterminate state to pursue than that of immortality.

But what kind of immortality might this be? The consequences for narrative are rather complicated, and Dostoevsky explores them in the immense narratives that follow *Notes from Underground*. What I mean here is that Dostoevsky offers a series of fascinating "heroes of indifference," like Myshkin and Stavrogin, heroes, that is, of a strangely indeterminate sort who seem to represent attempts to create a narrative without laws, a narrative that is in some sense a nonnarrative. This is especially evident in one of Dostoevsky's neglected late narratives, *The Adolescent*, which deserves far more attention than it has garnered in the critical reception of Dostoevsky to this point.[32]

The critical reception has typically viewed *The Adolescent* as a novel of inferior quality, a failure in comparison with the four other major novels from the "great" period of Dostoevsky's artistic career. The critical complaints are that the novel meanders, is improbable and melodramatic, and is unconvincing as the portrait of a young man in the first person. There is also the more general complaint that the novel is simply clumsy and gauche. Some of these complaints have been leveled at *The Idiot* as well, and even at *Demons*, although one might say that the latter is saved by the strong plot that takes over as the novel progresses. Indeed, the underlying concern in all these cases seems to turn on a failure of plotting, of structural felicity, that haunts these novels.

Now, one argument that has been advanced is that this lack of structural felicity reflects Dostoevsky's concern to depict a reality in dissolution, a reality in flux, a centrifugal reality; and this line of argument is a more or less transparent assertion of the death of God thesis with Dostoevsky taking the place of the madman.[33] But one wonders if this is really so or the exclusively appropriate reading. Dissolution might also be evaluated differently, as the prelude to a freedom from narrative, from the chains of action. Both views seem to be at large in Dostoevsky's novels, as the strange twins, Myshkin and Stavrogin, seem to show. For Myshkin is not a hero of the will, but rather of the lack of will; Myshkin's beauty is in his "presentness," in his sovereign freedom from the will. If he is a figuration of Christ, he is so to the extent that he has liberated himself from the chains of narrative. The acidic irony of the novel emerges in large degree from the contrast between Myshkin's freedom and the fetters the other characters wear, fetters of ambition and desire, fetters arising from the predominance of nature in us. The obverse portrait of freedom is that of Stavrogin in *Demons*. Stavrogin also seems to be a hero lacking in will; he is the "absent center" of the immense novel. He is enigma and mystery, giving directions to the others more by withdrawal than active advising. The other characters place their designs on him, reading him in ways that justify their own actions, but Stavrogin himself does not seem inclined to give any direction. Yet, this freedom, a freedom of apparent indifference, forms a marked contrast with Myshkin because it leads to a radically different conclusion: suicide. This conclusion suggests that behind the appearance of indifference is will, that Stavrogin's indifference is a product of will, not freedom from willing as should be the case with Myshkin. Like many other characters in *Demons*, Stavrogin is an imposter, a suggestion hinted at broadly at several points in the novel.[34]

As an imposter, however, Stavrogin provides an interesting gloss on the Underground Man. While I have suggested that the Underground Man valorizes fiction, Stavrogin's fate qualifies that valorization. Fiction for the Underground Man is also a product of will. As a product of will, this fiction is bound to fail; it cannot achieve the results it might claim to achieve. In place of the Underground Man, we have a hero like Myshkin, who is a hero of letting go, of dispensing with the will.

49

We end up with a deft interpretation of the Underground Man as a creature of will, and of frustrated will at that. The polemic in *Notes from Underground* from this viewpoint centers on a consideration of will. The result, it seems to me, is that will is just as much a disease as consciousness, which, incidentally, gives birth to the possibility of will understood as the manner in which one becomes not only free of the laws of nature but of all laws. This radical mode of emancipation, an emancipation that assumes as its condition of possibility the triumph over death, seems to meet with little success in *Notes from Underground*, and the same could be said for the ostensibly Napoleonic striving of Raskolnikov in *Crime and Punishment*. At least it is clear in the latter novel that emancipation even from the laws of men is not possible, much less emancipation from the laws of nature.

Failure of will reflects the complicated problem that becomes the centerpiece of one of Dostoevsky's principal and most famous passages, the "Grand Inquisitor" chapter from *The Brothers Karamazov*. Put simply, failure of will reveals sharp ambivalence toward willing, an ambivalence that the Underground Man describes as well with perfect clarity in a crucial passage reprised in "The Grand Inquisitor":

> Allow me an observation. I agree: man is predominantly a creating animal, doomed to strive consciously towards a goal and to occupy himself with the art of engineering—that is, to eternally and ceaselessly make a road for himself that at least goes *somewhere or other*. But sometimes he may wish to swerve aside, precisely because he is *doomed* to open this road, and also perhaps because, stupid though the ingenuous figure generally is, it still sometimes occurs to him that this road almost always turns out to go *somewhere or other*, and the main thing is not where it goes, but that it should simply be going, and that the well-behaved child, by neglecting the art of engineering, not give himself up to pernicious idleness, which, as is known, is the mother of all vice. Man loves creating and the making of roads, that is indisputable. But why does he so passionately love destruction and chaos as well? Tell me that! Can it be that he has such a love of destruction and chaos (it's indisputable that he sometimes loves them very much, that is a fact) because he is instinctively afraid of achieving the goal and completing the edifice he is creating?[35]

Here are two essentially different narrative attitudes. On the one hand, we have narrative understood as a creation and articulation of struggle without end—the resulting pattern must be circular and recalls the kind of narrative one might associate with *The Iliad* except that the noble tragic desire to overcome the sanctions of the gods, or to be oneself a god, turns out to be leavened by a desire not to be a god. On the other hand, we have narrative understood as a cessation of struggle, a path toward equilibrium or, indeed, the relinquishment of desire, if not narrative itself. The differences between these two narratives are fundamental. The circular narrative of struggle as the Underground Man frames it, is somewhat deceptive because it retains in fact the primacy of desire—we will even our own failures, and as that astute student of Schopenhauer, Jorge Luis Borges, notes, there "is no more cunning consolation than the thought that we have chosen our own misfortunes; that individual theology reveals a secret order, and in a marvelous way confuses ourselves with the deity."[36] The narrative of overturning struggle has two variants, the first being the creation of the patriarchal government of the Grand Inquisitor, the second being the overturning of any government—perhaps more radically, of any narrative—by the Grand Inquisitor's curious guest, the ostensive "prisoner."

The first variant is deceptive because the Grand Inquisitor is an avatar of the Underground Man. He claims the same arguments about human beings, that they are free and necessarily unhappily so because they both love and hate their freedom. The difference is, perhaps, that the Grand Inquisitor emphasizes the latter aspect of the attitude toward freedom. But this, too, is consistent with the Underground Man, who refers to consciousness as a "disease" that causes one to collapse into indecision or constant struggle in regard to what action one might take. It would be reductive and an exaggeration to suggest that the Underground Man demands to be freed from his freedom and, in so doing, exemplifies the dilemma that the Grand Inquisitor describes.

The second variant is radically different: the prisoner does not speak. The prisoner acts only once, at the end of the Grand Inquisitor's monologue when he kisses the latter, an enigmatic gesture to be sure. The reticence and passivity of the prisoner are perhaps appropriate to his role as a Christ figure, and the Grand Inquisitor ends up letting the prisoner go because he knows that the prisoner will not encourage resistance, direct action in the world against the Grand Inquisitor. The prisoner is not a revolutionary in this respect, not a model for action, but a model for reluctance to act. The prisoner is in this sense a distillation of tendencies one might associate with Myshkin and, finally, with Alyosha in *The Brothers Karamazov*: he moves with his interlocutors but is essentially static from the point of view of narrative. More radically, he may even be too enigmatic for narrative, hanging on its edges, moving through it like a cipher.

What I want to argue here is that the Grand Inquisitor's apparently patriarchal attitude to his rebellious children, his claim that they wish to give up their freedom, is mere foreground. The Grand Inquisitor's argument is a noble lie he deploys out of his own *Menschenverachtung* (contempt for humanity), a contempt that recalls nothing so much as the contempt Nietzsche bids us have in *The Antichrist* when he asserts that "one must be superior to mankind in force, in *loftiness* of soul—in contempt . . ."[37] The Grand Inquisitor is thoroughly Nietzschean (and Machiavellian) in his promotion of a noble lie that has the effect of raising and preserving his own advantage at the expense of others.[38] This is the real issue: the Grand Inquisitor arrogates to himself authority to judge and dispose of other human beings in order to protect and preserve his own freedom; he is aristocratic both in his anti-egalitarian views and in the broadness of the generalizations he makes to justify his own authority. Foremost among these is the claim that human beings cannot dispose of their own freedom adequately; born rebels—and to quote the "poem," "Can rebels be happy?"—they seek to relinquish as much freedom as possible. The Grand Inquisitor merely assists them in this task, and this constitutes his supreme benevolence.

The homology, however ironic, between the Nietzschean philosopher and the Grand Inquisitor seems undeniable and has been noted by critics of Nietzsche's progeny. But what of the other position? Are we to align the Dostoevskian view with the prisoner? Of course this is a perilous task. One of Dostoevsky's most important readers in the Russian tradition argues strongly against such an alignment.[39] Putting this question aside for the moment, let me tease out some of the implications of the prisoner's attitude to the Grand Inquisitor's monologue. Silence—this is the main element of the prisoner's response. The Grand Inquisitor gives us a ready-made interpretation of this silence by suggesting that the prisoner has no need to add to what he has already said. This comment has special significance if one considers the end of history thesis yet again, albeit from another perspective. There is indeed nothing to add for the prisoner; the Grand Inquisitor needs to add, not only, as he says, to correct, but indeed to do anything at all. The Grand Inquisitor cannot accept the terminal state he associates with the prisoner: he is a creature of action, a Quixote having become cynical, repulsed by the cycle of defeat to which Quixote is subject. Like those characters who impose interpretations on Myshkin and Stavrogin, the Grand Inquisitor demonstrates his anxiety before that which cannot be determined; he is in this sense an avatar of the one who feels *Angst* before the possible indeterminacy of things.

The prisoner is this indeterminacy, but he differs markedly from an enigmatic character like Stavrogin. This difference lies in his only act, his kissing the Grand Inquisitor at the end of the monologue, at once a peculiar twist on another famous kiss of betrayal, and a clue to the prisoner's power. Not only does the prisoner betray the Grand Inquisitor in that the prisoner cannot be brought to accept his authority or, indeed, any authority at all, he emphasizes his complete equanimity through the kiss. This power is of a person at the end of time, freed from the delusions of action, from the need to exercise will. The prisoner's sovereign gesture is his freedom from the temptation to participate in the cycle of action and response; indeed, the prisoner is no longer a prisoner of any kind because he is free of the struggle between action and inaction, activity and passivity, announced by the Underground Man. With the prisoner, Dostoevsky offers a new kind of character that is no longer a character of will or even relinquishment of will; rather, the novelty of the prisoner is that he represents an overcoming of this opposition, thus an overcoming of opposition. The prisoner is thus the end of history, liberation from history and the deadlock that comes with it.

If the prisoner is really a Christ-figure to rival other Christ-figures strewn throughout Dostoevsky's major works, then the significance of the *imitatio Christi* is to advocate pursuit of freedom as freedom from the struggles that constitute narrative. The Christ-figure lives beyond narrative, a seeming contradiction in terms because the Christ-figure does not thereby succumb to circular or linear narrative trajectories, given that both are bound to struggle, either as a perpetuation or final resolution. Perpetuation and finality are not determinative in the post-narrative world of the Christlike figure.

Is this a utopian "end of time"? Can one live an indeterminate narrative, one without direction, without a specific structure that implies limitation, the assertion of authority? These questions, which accompany Myshkin and Stavrogin in differing ways, also accompany Alyosha in *The Brothers Karamazov*. The fundamental question that arises, then, is whether Alyosha embodies the post-narrative world of the Christlike figure. The handy response points to the end of the novel, which, as ending, is entirely appropriate as an ending to the novel *tout court*. One may certainly snicker about this ending. Harold Bloom referred to it as the most embarrassing pages written by a major author, and his reaction is entirely appropriate if one interprets this ending as a coda to literature, an absurd and wild one, to be sure (at least for the Grand Inquisitor).

But it may be better to suggest that this post-narrative world is not simply without narratives but rather is without narratives that seek to eradicate indeterminacy; indeed, Alyosha does not renounce narrative per se but the narrative impulse that expresses the terror of indeterminacy. The question here—one that is not finally answered in *The Brothers Karamazov*—is what this ostensibly new narrativity might possibly be, a narrativity of "active love."

What remains is a radical counterpoint to the Nietzschean narrative of impossible conquest and to narrative itself. The horror of the indeterminate that shapes Nietzsche is let go in Dostoevsky, at least in this respect. Perhaps this bold narrative move is what Lukács sensed when he famously claimed that Dostoevsky had gone beyond the novel.[40]

We have initially identified a significant apparent confluence between Nietzsche and Dostoevsky, and it is centered in their common valorization of fiction over reality, of imagination over the given experience of a time period. Tracing the course of my argument back to its origins, we might say that Nietzsche shows a complicated, arguably Platonic attitude to fiction, an attitude that entails a sort of split identity for the philosopher. After all, it is the philosopher who emerges out of the most profound sense of the shapelessness and impermanence of the world to take up the artist's prerogative to create the diverting fictions that are supposed to protect and foster a new innocence, a rebirth. The philosopher awakens from the elemental violence of indeterminacy to give order while retaining that violence within, as it were, on some level. That is, the philosopher would seem to retain an awareness of the openness or excess of possibility that his role as an artist must eliminate or suggest is not there. Nietzsche would not claim that the laws of nature somehow transcend that openness.

For Dostoevsky this seems to be the great problem. The laws of nature turn us into little more than animals or robots, as the Underground Man says, a "piano key or sprig in an organ."[41] The Underground Man seeks to create an openness, to celebrate the elemental violence of indeterminacy through the agency of the unfettered imagination. The powerful equation between imagination and violence is a crucial aspect of Dostoevsky's fictions, which attempt to deal with the pursuit of freedom the Underground Man praises so highly. The point here is that freedom is inherently dangerous and destructive: as an astute reader of Dostoevsky noted, freedom is evil.[42] And thus Dostoevsky presents another course, that of renunciation, a freedom not based in the contradictory process of action but in liberating oneself from action, from the contrasting pair of inaction-action, the dilemma that the Underground Man is unable to resolve in any fashion whatsoever.

The difference between Nietzsche and Dostoevsky that I wish to emphasize is not, however, simply reducible to an advocacy of war against peace, the philosophical creator against the ruminative hero who lets beings be. Rather, the cutting edge in this distinction seems to reveal profoundly opposed attitudes to indeterminacy. The rejection of indeterminacy results in struggle; the violence of creation emerges from a primordial violence, the chaos of indeterminacy; and the cycle of violence replicates itself. The acceptance of indeterminacy leads to a certain quiescence that is no longer quiescence, however, since the conceptual duality of struggle and relinquishment of struggle, whereby the one defines the other, implicates the other, depends on the other, is finally overcome. Whether this overcoming may ever take place or what it might look like are haunting questions, the mere posing of which reveals our entrapment within the very pattern from which we mean to escape.[43] The final irony is, I suppose, that the achievement of overcoming must be a silent one outside of philosophy, literature, or parasitic essays like the one you have just read.

NOTES

1. I have no wish to downplay the horrible acts of violence that take place within a normative framework or to suggest that they are not violent or terrible in their way. But I think there is a difference between the violence that takes place within and with reference to a specific normative framework—a regulated violence, as I have noted, and the ostensibly more fundamental (and total) violence which threatens to dissolve that framework entirely or suggests that no such framework is possible in the first place. For a discussion of the latter pertinent to Nietzsche, see Martin Heidegger, *Introduction to Metaphysics*, trans. Gregory Fried and Richard Polt, 2nd ed. (New Haven: Yale University Press, 2014), 163–200.

2. G. W. Leibniz, *Theodicy*, trans. E. M. Huggard (La Salle: Open Court, 1985).

3. A useful starting point might be: Mark Larrimore, ed. *The Problem of Evil* (Oxford: Blackwell Publishers, 2001).

4. For an interesting discussion of this thinking, see Susan Neiman, *Evil in Modern Thought: An Alternative History of Philosophy* (Princeton: Princeton University Press, 2002), 113–202.

5. G. W. F. Hegel, *Phenomenology of Spirit*, trans. A. V. Miller (Oxford: Oxford University Press, 1977), 19.

6. Martin Heidegger, "What Is Metaphysics?," in *Basic Writings*, ed. David Ferrell Krell (London: Harper Perennial, 2008), 93–110.

7. Friedrich Nietzsche, *The Gay Science*, trans. Walter Kaufmann (New York: Vintage Books, 1974), 33.

8. Fyodor Dostoevsky, *Notes from Underground*, trans. Richard Pevear and Larissa Volokhonsky (New York: Vintage Books, 1993), 17.

9. Friedrich Nietzsche, *Twilight of The Idols*, trans. R. J. Hollingdale (London: Penguin Books, 1968), 36 (translation modified). Geoff Waite offers a rather pithy rendering of this line.

10. Dostoevsky, *Notes from Underground*, 17.

11. Aristotle, *Posterior Analytics*, trans. Hugh Trendennick and E. S. Forster (Cambridge, Mass.: Harvard University Press, 1960), 37.

12. This cliché of Nietzsche reception has of course been made famous by Milan Kundera and finds ample (if covert) expression in the ostensibly "antiphilosophical" works of Vladimir Nabokov.

13. I am referring to the fact that it is the threat of death, the awful plague, that moves the citizens of Thebes to appeal to Oedipus at the very beginning of the great drama. See the sensitive translation of Frederick Ahl, *Two Faces of Oedipus* (Ithaca: Cornell University Press, 2008), 136–37.

14. Nietzsche, *Gay Science*, 37.

15. Nietzsche, *On the Genealogy of Morality*, trans. Maudemarie Clark and Alan J. Swenson (Indianapolis: Hackett Publishing, 1998), 69.

16. Sophocles, *Oedipus at Colonus*, trans. Hugh Lloyd-Jones (Cambridge, Mass.: Harvard University Press, 1994).

17. Dostoevsky, *Notes from Underground*, 5.

18. At least in regard to the "contest" with the officer and the notorious dinner party: the scene in the brothel is a rather more complicated one, a model of pathos and mockery that would have enormous influence (one has only to think of the novels of Samuel Beckett or Juan Carlos Onetti) in the twentieth century.

19. Nietzsche, *Gay Science*, 38.

20. Ibid.

21. See Friedrich Nietzsche, *Sämtliche Briefe*, ed. Giorgio Colli and Mazzino Montinari (Berlin: Deutscher Taschenbuch Verlag, 1986), 8:573. My translation.

22. Heidegger, "What Is Metaphysics?," 97.

23. See, for example, Francis Nesbitt Oppel, *Nietzsche on Gender* (Charlottesville: University of Virginia Press, 2005), 150 *et passim*.

24. Nietzsche, *Gay Science*, 37.

25. Friedrich Nietzsche, *Beyond Good and Evil*, trans. R. J. Hollingdale (London: Penguin Books, 1973), 69.

26. Robert Louis Jackson, "The Ethics of Vision I: Turgenev's 'Execution of Tropmann' and Dostoevsky's View of the Matter," in *Dialogues with Dostoevsky* (Stanford: Stanford University Press, 1993), 29–54.

27. Dostoevsky, *Notes from Underground*, 16.

28. Ibid., 13.

29. See Evgenia Cherkasova, *Dostoevsky and Kant* (Amsterdam–New York: Rodopi, 2009), 29–51.

30. Dostoevsky, *Notes from Underground*, 34.

31. See Stanley Rosen, *Hermeneutics as Politics* (Oxford: Oxford University Press, 1987), 4.

32. The negative consensus regarding this work is overwhelming. For a soberly balanced account, see Victor Terras, *Reading Dostoevsky* (Madison: University of Wisconsin Press, 1998), 101–12.

33. See James Scanlon, *Dostoevsky the Thinker* (Ithaca: Cornell University Press, 2002), 15.

34. See Nancy Anderson's interesting and neglected book on imposture in *Demons*: Nancy Anderson, *The Perverted Ideal in Dostoevsky's "The Devils"* (New York: Peter Lang, 1997).

35. Dostoevsky, *Notes from Underground*, 33.

36. Jorge Luis Borges, "Deutsches Requiem," in *Collected Fictions*, trans. Andrew Hurley (New York: Penguin Books, 1999), 231.

37. Friedrich Nietzsche, *The Antichrist*, trans. R. J. Hollingdale (London: Penguin Books, 1968), 125.

38. Many commentators have noted this similarity, perhaps too easily.

39. Vasilii Rozanov makes the claim that Dostoevsky sides with the Grand Inquisitor. He thus participates in a tiresome debate as to which position seems to prevail in the novel. See Vasilii Rozanov, *Dostoevsky and the Legend of the Grand Inquisitor*, trans. Spencer E. Roberts (Ithaca: Cornell University Press, 1972).

40. See Georg Lukács, *The Theory of the Novel*, trans. Anna Bostock (Cambridge, Mass.: MIT Press, 1971), 152.

41. Dostoevsky, *Notes from Underground*, 24.

42. See Yevgeny Zamyatin, *We*, trans. Natasha Randall (New York: Modern Library, 2006). This is of course hardly a new connection: it is deeply embedded within the texture of Christian discourse, emerging quite explicitly in St. Augustine's important treatise on the will, *On Free Will* (*De libero arbitrio*) and F. W. J. Schelling's influential *Philosophical Investigations into the Essence of Human Freedom* (1809).

43. This is a way of describing an aspect of Derridean *différance*, the "x-à-venir" (democracy for example) that haunts his later works. The question is: How does one escape the dialectic of struggle, what I refer to as the struggle between the active and the passive here? Is there a middle voice that overcomes the opposition?

Jeffrey Metzger

Truth, Will, and Reactivity in Nietzsche and Dostoevsky

> And outside, the silent wilderness surrounding
> this cleared speck on the earth struck me as
> something great and invincible, like evil or
> truth, waiting patiently for the passing away of
> this fantastic invasion.
> —Conrad, *Heart of Darkness*

FOR BOTH NIETZSCHE AND DOSTOEVSKY, truth is connected with violence. Does this mean that truth somehow springs from or relies on physical violence, so that truth is simply an effect of power or domination? Or, on the contrary, is truth itself violent, both spawn and progenitor of suffering, violence in its most comprehensive and fundamental sense, of which physical violence is just one instance among many, perhaps not even the most painful or disturbing? Does truth, in other words, effect a violent displacement of one's basic sense of self? If so, how does the individual, or the order or arrangement that constitutes the individual, adapt and restructure to assimilate or simply repulse the truth?[1] Or is this phrase in fact misleading, does violence, particularly violence suffered at the hands of another, impede one's ability to perceive the truth? If these questions are too specific, we can ask this more fundamental question about the status of truth: is it perceived or produced? Which is primary in human beings, the will or the intellect, desire or knowledge?

For both Nietzsche and Dostoevsky these questions are bound up with the question of reactivity or *ressentiment*.[2] For Nietzsche, *ressentiment* is the rancorous negation of reality that acts as perhaps the strongest and most poisonous skin protecting the individual from truth. For Dostoevsky, or at least his Underground Man, the relation between truth and reactivity is much more ambiguous. We can very briefly sum up the basic positions of both by saying that for Nietzsche, the will is prior to the truth (if indeed the will itself is anything other than a fiction),[3] and it is only due to the violent incursion of a particular, contingent truth that *ressentiment* leaps up to shield the

58

individual from that truth, though in doing so it permeates and warps the individual. For the Underground Man, the will is prior to the truth in the sense that one can choose to believe a lie, but the truth cannot be simply silenced or ignored, and the necessary result of this contingent state of affairs is a kind of reactive inhibition, an inability to act and, ultimately, to will or choose at all. For Nietzsche, the intellect is subordinate to the will (again, an imperfect formulation, with both "intellect" and "will" being highly questionable entities for Nietzsche): a healthy nature "interprets" the world to suit itself, which is largely a matter of creating fictions, but the violent intrusion of truth, or the intrusion of a truth too violent to be digested or interpreted, forces one to abandon instinctive or unconscious fictions and to actually lie to oneself. For the Underground Man, on the other hand, the will is subordinate to the intellect in the sense that one's beliefs about reality can inhibit and even enervate the will, but at the same time the choice of beliefs is a moral as well as a theoretical act, and thus relies on the will as well as the intellect. As this sketch makes clear, I see both Nietzsche and Dostoevsky as writing in the tradition that sees distinctly human action as possible only if the will is informed by reason or intellect, and so ultimately by the truth. In rejecting this vision of the will and its relation to the intellect, Nietzsche thus rejects the traditional notion of the human being (and of course calls for the creation of an *Übermensch* defined largely by a new conception of will and its relation to the intellect, the body, and truth). Dostoevsky, or his Underground Man, suggests a picture of human action in which the truth is primary but its apprehension is not chiefly the work of reason or rationality.[4]

In pursuing this argument I attempt to do justice to the complex and difficult texts in which these questions are explored, and thus concentrate on close readings of the First Essay of *On the Genealogy of Morals* and the first five sections of "Underground," part 1 of *Notes from Underground*. This chapter thus aspires to belong to the genus of interpretations that Geoff Waite has described as "excruciatingly meticulous close readings of many Great Books,"[5] though given its length it can be only so meticulous (and, one hopes, only so excruciating). I have chosen these two texts because both center on questions of vengefulness, truth, will, morality, and the often unsteady and obscure interplay between these things, and also because in comparing the two we begin to see the fundamental and characteristic differences between Dostoevsky and Nietzsche. While both writers examine reactivity, ultimately Nietzsche speaks of *ressentiment*, a psychological phenomenon, while Dostoevsky speaks of wickedness, a moral phenomenon. The entry point for this comparison is the question of whether truth is produced (and thus ultimately simply a fiction) or perceived (and thus in a sense imposed on an often unwilling human mind by an independent reality). The rest of this section is devoted to a general discussion of reactivity in these two texts; subsequent sections deal with the First Essay of the *Genealogy* and with the first five sections of "Underground."

Nietzsche first encountered Dostoevsky in the form of a book titled *L'esprit souterrain*, which consisted of "The Landlady" and a modified version of *Notes from Underground*, presented together as a sort of unified composition (though Nietzsche was able to tell that they were in fact two distinct works).[6] Nietzsche appears to have read *L'esprit souterrain* in the interval between completing *Beyond Good and Evil* and beginning *On the Genealogy of Morals*. One of the major theoretical innovations of the *Genealogy* is its introduction of the concept of *ressentiment*.[7] Although Nietzsche, as is his wont, never pauses to give a definition of the term, it can be described as a kind of poisonous, obsessive hatred born of suffering harm at the hands of another and being unable to avenge oneself; this harm may include the psychological or emotional harm of being forced to acknowledge another's superiority—indeed, this experience of someone else's superiority is the crucial wellspring of *ressentiment*. Nietzsche first presents *ressentiment* in the course of explaining slave morality and how it differs from noble morality. The introduction of this concept marks not only the emergence of a new idea or term in Nietzsche's thought but a significant revision of the account of the two basic types of morality that he provides in *Beyond Good and Evil*, attention to which helps clarify what is distinctive about both *ressentiment* and Nietzsche's broader preoccupations and attitudes in the First Essay of the *Genealogy*.[8]

In the final part of *Beyond Good and Evil* ("What Is Noble?"), Nietzsche devotes a long aphorism to contrasting what he there calls "master morality" (*Herren-Moral*) and "slave morality" (*Sklaven-Moral*) (*BGE* 260). The First Essay of the *Genealogy* deals with the same basic subject, though Nietzsche titles the essay "'Good and Evil,' 'Good and Bad,'" choosing to highlight the conceptual opposition that defines each type of morality, rather than the political class in which it originates. Unsurprisingly, the two treatments are largely similar, with many of the major points made in the First Essay of the *Genealogy* already present in embryonic form in the passage from *Beyond Good and Evil*.[9] There are, however, subtle and interesting differences; especially pertinent here is Nietzsche's decision to drop any mention of "masters" (*Herren*) in the *Genealogy*. In the First Essay, Nietzsche refers to the ruling classes only as "nobles," and never uses the term "master" to categorize their distinctive morality. Nietzsche does not explain his reasons for doing this, but one of the major effects of this change is to move away from a notion of "master morality" in which a conscious awareness of the differences between masters and slaves, and an accompanying negative view of the slaves, is a necessary and perhaps even sufficient condition for the creation of master morality. In other words, "master morality" as it is described in *Beyond Good and Evil* seems to rely on or instantiate a mild but still unmistakable reactive disvaluing of the slaves, the sort of moral-affective activity that Nietzsche identifies in the *Genealogy* as the essential feature of slave morality (compare *GM* I, 10): "The moral discrimination of values has originated either among a ruling group whose consciousness of its difference from the ruled group was accompanied by delight [*welche sich ihres Unterschieds gegen die beherrschte mit Wohlgefühl bewusst wurde*]—or among the ruled, the slaves and dependents of every degree" (*BGE* 260). This does not mean that master morality as Nietzsche describes it in *Beyond Good and Evil* is motivated by *ressentiment*, but it does make it hard to see it as born solely of an overflowing sense of power, vitality, and self-affirmation, as Nietzsche presents noble valuation in the *Genealogy*.

In the *Genealogy* Nietzsche not only drops the references to masters and master morality, but stresses that noble morality is born of an act of pure self-affirmation that owes nothing to the slave or the noble's awareness of his difference from the slave (*GM* I, 2), and that in fact contrasts nobility with slavishness only as an afterthought (*GM* I, 10).[10] Nietzsche also accents the predominance of *ressentiment* in slave morality, which he maintains is simply an obsessive attempt to negate the powerful in the purely imaginary or mendacious terms of a morality that thoroughly falsifies both the strong-noble and the weak-slave, by pretending that it is good to be weak and, before anything else, evil to be strong (*GM* I, 10, 13–14). This negation takes the form of imagined physical revenge (*GM* I, 15), but above all it is expressed through valuation, which for Nietzsche is the essential human activity and the one through which revenge must be accomplished. And because it is revenge, the real thrust of the valuation is concentrated on condemnation or negation of the powerful and noble, only secondarily on affirmation of the weak and humble; that is, of the ones actually producing this valuation.

This is what is largely new in the *Genealogy*—the notion that a form of morality could be simply an attempt to negate another, more powerful or vital form of life (though Nietzsche had adumbrated the idea previously: *BGE* 195). In *Beyond Good and Evil* (260), the argument was that dependent classes create moralities that honor the virtues that make their lives easier and possibly more pleasant. At the very beginning of the *Genealogy* Nietzsche rejects the notion that moral values would ever originate with weak or dependent classes (*GM* I, 2)—and although he then has to explain how "slave morality" came into existence at all (through the agency of a sickly type of noble, the priest [*GM* I, 6 and following]), his account in the First Essay focuses solely on revenge as the motive, not the attempt to make the lives of the weak or poor more bearable.[11]

Morality as negation, as an imaginary moral-affective revenge—this is the major innovation of the *Genealogy*, or at least of the First Essay, and it is also the essence of the morality produced when *ressentiment* becomes creative (compare *GM* I, 10). The Underground Man exemplifies this mode of thinking and feeling at least as well as Nietzsche's slaves or priests. The Underground Man radiates reactive energy from the first page of *Notes from Underground*; his manner of writing, especially in the first part of the *Notes* ("Underground"), seems to embody Nietzsche's description of *ressentiment*: "in order to exist, slave morality always first needs a hostile external world; it needs, physiologically speaking, external stimuli in order to act at all—its action is fundamentally reaction" (*GM* I, 10). The Underground Man's reactive passion shapes and drives his reflections in "Underground," manifesting itself in the jagged form and disruptive energy of his speech. He is constantly and suddenly zig-zagging from one subject to the next, usually without any clear order or logical purpose to his discourse; sometimes there is not even a tangential conceptual relation between two or more subjects that succeed one another in his writing (which is not to say that he does not succeed in making a coherent argument in "Underground," or that he can be taken simply as an exemplum of reactivity). Any passing thought or memory that momentarily touches upon his mind irritates him and provokes a negative and aggressive reaction, an abrupt striking out at and striking off toward a new topic or theme.[12] Nietzsche would describe this in terms of *ressentiment* and its defensive reaction to what it experiences as a hostile external world; the Underground Man himself speaks later of his "permanent, morbid irritability" (48).[13]

The particular episode that seems best to embody or illustrate *ressentiment* is the Underground Man's rancorous (and eventually pathetic) fixation on a nameless officer who casually moves him out of his way in a tavern one night. As the Underground Man says of the event, "I could even have forgiven a beating, but I simply could not forgive his moving me and in the end just not noticing me" (49). The relation between the officer and the Underground Man mirrors almost exactly that between noble and slave in Nietzsche's account of *ressentiment* and the creation of values in the First Essay of the *Genealogy* (*GM* I, especially 10). The officer has strength and power and thus barely notices the Underground Man; if he did, his reaction would no doubt be one of contempt or dismissal, but he would hardly consider such contempt central to his way of thinking or valuing (much like Zherkov's treatment of the Underground Man later in the book). The Underground Man's inferiority in physical strength is as nothing compared to the officer's complete lack of attention to him. Although the Underground Man does not, like Nietzsche's slaves, construct an entire system of values based on the negation of the officer (that system already exists in the nineteenth century, but does nothing to help the Underground Man respect or affirm himself, either in this encounter or elsewhere), the officer does dominate his consciousness while not even recognizing or remembering him. The Underground Man's emotional, psychological, and even physical reactions embody much of what Nietzsche means by *ressentiment*, while the relation between the officer and the Underground Man illustrates the crucial revision the *Genealogy* makes to the moral typology that Nietzsche had presented in *Beyond Good and Evil*.

There are of course significant, even fundamental, differences between Nietzsche's depiction of his slaves and priests and Dostoevsky's depiction of the Underground Man. Perhaps the cardinal difference concerns the power and status of truth. I noted above that the Underground Man, for all his unruly reactivity, makes a coherent argument and cannot be taken as simply an embodiment of *ressentiment*. But his treatment of these questions is best approached after examining Nietzsche's more direct and clearly defined approach to the question of truth, particularly the question of whether truth (philosophic, historical, moral, practical) is produced or perceived.

Nietzsche's argument in the First Essay of the *Genealogy* relies on specific archetypes, which are not mere illustrations of his argument but its actual subject. Despite the often dramatic differences between these diverse types, they all ultimately demonstrate Nietzsche's contention that truth is produced, and this because of Nietzsche's deeper contention that valuation, and particularly the need to value and respect or affirm oneself, is the most fundamental human activity or need. Nietzsche first sets forth this contention that truth is produced in the Preface to the *Genealogy*, where the type he is discussing is himself, the philosopher. As noted above, I will try to stay as close as possible to Nietzsche's text and his presentation of these questions, then sum up the basic or broader points at the end of this section.[14]

Each major part of the *Genealogy* (the Preface and each essay) begins with a brief sketch of what truth or knowledge is and how it relates to the psychology of the individual (or more precisely of different kinds of individuals, including different kinds of seekers after knowledge). These short sketches, however, do not set the stage for the rest of the essay. In other words, they do not identify the problems that must be answered (at least not in any straightforward way), or the framework in which the problems the essay does address must be understood or answered. The Preface, for instance, begins with a discussion of the "men of knowledge" (*Erkennenden*) and of their inability to know themselves or to comprehend—or experience—their own experience, but the rest of the Preface deals with that question only obliquely. The First Essay begins with a discussion of the "English psychologists," their motivations in pursuing knowledge of the history of morality, and the relationship between truth and desirability, but the rest of the essay addresses these questions only very indirectly or by implication. The Preface begins with confusion and proceeds to a sense of certainty, or at least hope, in the example of Nietzsche. The other three begin with the hope or prospect of greater knowledge and autonomy, but by the end have shown that prospect to be largely illusory. In the case of the First Essay, Nietzsche suggests that it is possible to educate oneself to sacrifice desirability to truth (*GM*, I, 1), in contrast to the picture of truth, of one's truths, being simply the necessary and mostly nonrational product of one's basic needs or constitution. Throughout the rest of the essay, however, it is this latter picture of knowing that prevails—it is exemplified in the nobles, priests, and slaves—and at the end of the essay it is unclear how or why the first type of knowledge would be either possible or desirable.[15]

Truth is presented in the Preface to the *Genealogy* in images that carry over throughout the book.[16] While the opening passage suggests a very mild form of truth as violence (being woken from reverie by a tolling bell [representative of "experience" generally]), the Preface as a whole uses organic metaphors to represent the act of thinking and knowing. Knowledge appears either as the outcome of natural growth (trees, soil, sun [Preface, 2]), or as something incorporated through the natural process of digestion (Preface, 8). The Nietzschean sun, one of the metaphors he uses to illustrate his own philosophic growth and activity, is like the Platonic sun in being a necessary condition for philosophy, but while Plato's sun simply illuminates the world for the philosopher to see (*Republic*, 515c–516c), the light of Nietzsche's sun is absorbed by the philosopher and, along with the nutrients he absorbs from a particular soil, incorporated into an organic whole that yields a partially idiosyncratic or particular truth; even the light of the sun, universal and the same for all, produces particular truths rather than universal truth. Those who cannot bring forth their own fruit can ingest Nietzsche's, inevitably incorporating only part of what they ingest but still being changed in the process (though if we take the cow metaphor seriously, it seems they could only eat the grass produced by the sun and soil, which indeed may not be Nietzsche's at all—though this is perhaps pursuing the metaphor too far).

The basic picture of truth as the inevitable outcome of one's nonrational constitution continues into the First Essay with Nietzsche's discussion of his predecessors, the "English psychologists" (*GM*, I, 1–3). Whether because their irrational (and perhaps subconscious) needs always drive them to the same conclusions, or simply because they are "old, cold, tedious frogs" (though Nietzsche refuses to believe this explanation), previous genealogists of morals were reverse alchemists who took the gold of our richly ambiguous and complicated moral experience and turned it into the lead of reductive superficialities through exposure to their own inner needs, drives, and experiences. As in the images from the Preface, truth, or at least thought, is the product of an organic process that is both necessary and particular.

In answer to the basic question of whether truth is perceived or produced, Nietzsche seems so far to be clearly saying that it is produced.

As we read on, however, we see that Nietzsche offers three criticisms of his predecessors; the first is psychological or even moral (*GM* I, 1), the second historical (*GM* I, 2), and the third logical (*GM* I, 3). The logical refutation is obviously meant to convince his readers through reason, and he goes on to offer evidence for his historical argument about the origin of the value judgment "good" (beginning at *GM* I, 4). There is thus also a suggestion that Nietzsche thinks that at least some truths or some aspects of truth can be discovered and absorbed by a reason acting independently of one's particularity. Similarly, at the end of Nietzsche's psychological critique of the "English psychologists," he writes that he hopes that they are "fundamentally brave, magnanimous, and proud animals, who know how to maintain control of their heart and their suffering, and who have educated [*erzogen*] themselves to sacrifice all desirability to the truth, *every* truth, even plain [*schlichten*], bitter, ugly, repellent, unchristian, immoral truth . . . for there are such truths [*Denn es geibt solche Wahrheiten*]" (*GM* I, 1). The clear implication is that these truths exist independently of whether a given individual can see them (i.e., truth is not simply the product of an individual's needs or turn of mind). Nietzsche continues his use of organic images by referring to these researchers as "animals" (*Thiere*), but complicates the picture by saying that animals can be educated (by themselves) to recognize difficult truths that require sacrifice to apprehend. Thus while Nietzsche gives indications that truth is both produced and perceived, overall his statements and especially his practice in these opening sections seem to lean toward a view of truth as perceived.

Yet this picture is almost immediately complicated or even erased in the second section of the essay, in which Nietzsche begins to consider the relation of violence to truth. The "English psychologists" had held that the value judgment "good" originally meant "useful," and was first pronounced by those for whom something useful was done. Nietzsche insists that the contrary was the case: "The viewpoint of utility is as remote and inappropriate as it possibly could be in face of such a burning eruption of the highest rank-ordering, rank-defining value judgments . . . The pathos of nobility and distance, as aforesaid, the constant and dominating total and fundamental feeling of a higher ruling type in relation to a lower type, to a 'beneath'—*that* is the origin of the opposition 'good' and 'bad'" (*GM* I, 2); the emphasis on value judgments "erupting" from within the nobles, as well as on the hierarchical social relations required for such experiences, suggests both emotional and physical violence.

Already we have three different basic types of approach to or experience of the truth: truth as the product of an organic, somewhat particular or idiosyncratic process; truth as something discovered by those brave and proud enough to sacrifice desirability to it; and truth as something created by an eruption of elevated feeling, specifically the pathos of distance. The first and third cases clearly resemble each other. In the first case the mediation of rational thought is necessary to manipulate the canons or principles of historical inquiry (even if not wholly successfully), but ultimately truth is still the product of nonrational drives and experiences. In the third case, the experience is pure and unmediated: the nobles feel themselves to be superior and this feeling instantly issues in the creation of value judgments.[17] Each case is also, at best, ambiguously true in the ordinary sense of the word—while these judgments or beliefs may be supported by or correspond to some reality, they may well just be fictions believed according to the requirements of a certain human type.

Even so, the nobles' value judgments are believed or felt to be true by them, and they form the basis of the political and social reality Nietzsche finds encoded in the etymologies he traces in the fourth and fifth sections of the First Essay. Moreover, Nietzsche himself seems to agree with the nobles' view of themselves as "the truthful" and of the lower orders as mendacious (*GM* I, 5; for Nietzsche's view of the slaves as liars, see especially I, 13–14). The nobles' beliefs are true according to a kind of psychological correspondence theory of truth—their beliefs about what they feel or experience correspond to what they actually feel, experience, desire, etc. This is true of the priests as well, even though their case is more complicated. Though Nietzsche seems not to believe the priests' own explanation or interpretation of their experiences (i.e., their beliefs about their experiences do not correspond to reality), they are not dishonest about their experience; their beliefs about themselves are true according to the psychological correspondence theory of truth: they really do value and aspire to what they say they do (e.g., "purity"), and they really do despise and abhor what they say they do (blood, dirt, brute physical violence, etc.). The slaves lyingly pretend to abjure physical violence and cruelty, but secretly lust after these things and fantasize about the day when they will be able to exult in the torture of the nobles (*GM* I, 15). In their own way the priests are just as incapable as the slaves of participating in the life of the warrior, but that is due to internal, psychological inhibitions, not physical or political weakness.

The priests are therefore more interesting than the slaves, and more important than either the nobles or the slaves for human development. It is, according to Nietzsche, "on the soil of this *essentially dangerous* form of human existence, the priestly form, that man first became *an interesting animal* . . . only here did the human soul in a higher sense acquire *depth* and become *evil*—and these are the two basic respects in which man has hitherto been superior to other beasts!" (*GM* I, 6). Here we see the return of the soil metaphor (as we see the return of the tree metaphor in I, 8, when Nietzsche discusses Jewish and therefore priestly love-hatred), which Nietzsche had used to describe (his own) philosophy in the Preface, and Nietzsche again refers to human beings as animals; both of these biological metaphors apparently suggest either that this is a natural development for human beings, or that it becomes a kind of second nature. This is an odd suggestion: the priests are the first to reflect on and change themselves, but they do it out of a dire necessity, because they are sick and are desperately (and, fatefully for all of humanity, unsuccessfully) seeking a cure—there is no natural impulse to self-reflection or self-creation, at least not if the natural is the healthy (though perhaps it is not for Nietzsche: see *GM* II, 1). Even so, Nietzsche's discussion of the priests in section six clearly rises to something like admiration at the end, and he deploys several richly organic metaphors to describe their achievement.

As with previous individuals or archetypes described with organic metaphors, the priests also exemplify the creation of truth from within, not the discovery of or surrender to an external truth. This is perhaps not surprising, since one can still see the basic noble mechanism or process of valuation at work in them: if they despise or turn against part of themselves, they still honor and indeed revere their own highest or purest spiritual states and experiences. Their values are still born of the pathos of distance; they have simply internalized it, and feel both the high and the low, the noble and the base, the pure and the dirty, to be states within themselves.

A less positive example of the picture of truth as irrational product of organic necessity is the "free spirit" who interrupts Nietzsche in *GM* I, 9. Nietzsche describes him as "an honest animal" (*ehrlichen Thiers*); the implication seems to be that his honesty is simple or simplistic and naive, not the honesty (*Redlichkeit*) or truthfulness that Nietzsche praises elsewhere. A further implication seems to be that Nietzsche cannot rouse him from his way of seeing the world, from his "truth"—the "free spirit's" wholeness or animality successfully resists much of Nietzsche's argument and narrative. Here we have an "honesty" so complete it is invincible to the violence of truth.

It is in the tenth section of the First Essay that the theme of violence and truth comes to the fore. Here Nietzsche introduces *ressentiment*. The case that particularly concerns him is that of *ressentiment* stymied and become creative: "The slave revolt in morality begins when *ressentiment* itself becomes creative and gives birth to values: the *ressentiment* of natures (*Wesen*) that are denied the true reaction, that of deeds, and compensate themselves with an imaginary revenge." This notion of slave morality, the morality of *ressentiment*, as an escape from reality into an imaginary revenge is one of the major themes of the rest of the essay. While Nietzsche acknowledges that the nobles sometimes "blunder and sin against reality," he maintains that "even supposing that the affect of contempt, of looking down from a superior height, *falsifies* the image of that which it despises . . . [it is] a much less serious falsification than that perpetrated on its opponent—*in effigie* of course—by the submerged hatred, the vengefulness of the impotent." Later in the section Nietzsche describes "strong, full natures in whom there is an excess of the power to form, to mold, to recuperate and to forget." It is the "strong, full natures" of the nobles that enable them to produce the truths that help them to thrive, and to ignore those that might be harmful to them.

We have now canvassed the three major human types presented in the First Essay, the noble, the priest, and the slave. We can return to the questions asked at the beginning of the essay and attempt to answer them. Is truth simply an effect of power or domination? Though there may be passages in the First Essay that suggest this, it is clear that the slaves do not simply accept the nobles' beliefs; their own perspective produces its own beliefs, as they interpret the actions of the nobles in a very different light than the nobles interpret their own (Nietzsche discusses this especially in *GM* I, 11). This underground truth is preserved among the slaves, among the priests (who have their own set of values and truths), and even embedded in myth and poetry (*GM* I, 11).

The view that emerges from the First Essay is not that truth is simply an effect of power or violence but that truth is primarily an effect of the physical and psychological needs of a particular type of animal; truth or knowing is an organic process, very similar to digestion, in which certain material is taken into the organism and what is necessary or nourishing is absorbed while what is harmful or unnecessary is refused. This, at least, is the picture of a healthy animal nature that Nietzsche presents in the Preface and in the First Essay. As he indicates at times in the First Essay and especially later in the *Genealogy*, it is indeed possible for this process of psychic incorporation and nourishment to go awry, and when it does the animal takes in and retains the wrong kinds of truths, truths that can be harmful or even poisonous (see especially *GM* II, 1 and III, 16; compare *BGE* 230). Thus the further question of how suffering at the hands of another affects one's ability to see the truth. Nietzsche repeatedly and emphatically suggests that such an experience, if profound or frequent enough, "poisons" those who suffer it; it forces them to lie to themselves about the person or group at whose hands they are suffering. The strong or nobles, as Nietzsche says, are themselves not perfectly "objective"; they too falsify reality, but much less than the weak or slaves do. To use the distinction made at the beginning of the chapter, the strong unconsciously create and believe fictions, while the weak must take the further step of lying (though they must also believe this lie).[18] The priests, as in so many other cases, do not really fit into this simple schema, for although their beliefs about themselves are not true, this is less because they have created either fictions or lies than because they have, for the first time in human history, ventured to explain something they could not understand. While they are still moved by the need to affirm themselves, they cannot satisfy this need without hazarding a solution to a wholly new human problem.[19]

The reason for this points to the primacy of the will, or more precisely the need to value and affirm oneself, that is at the heart of Nietzsche's argument and concerns in the First Essay. The reason that the weak need to lie is ultimately not the need to deal with trauma but the need to affirm or value oneself; put differently, the real trauma is not suffering physical violence but suffering the awareness of another's greater power or standing; even more fundamentally, this experience of another's superiority is only the cause or condition of the true crisis, the inability to affirm or honor oneself. This becomes especially clear in *GM* I, 13, in many ways both the theoretical and rhetorical high point of the essay, when Nietzsche denounces the mendacities of the weak: "'we weak ones are, after all, weak; it would be good if we did nothing *for which we are not strong enough*'; but this dry matter of fact, this prudence of the lowest order which even insects possess . . . has, thanks to the counterfeit and self-deception of impotence, clad itself in the ostentatious garb of the virtue of quiet, calm resignation, just as if the weakness of the weak—that is to say, their *essence*, their effects, their sole ineluctable, irremovable reality—were a voluntary achievement, willed, chosen, a *deed*, a meritorious act." Somehow the weak cannot accept that they are being prudent; they have a need for self-affirmation that is at least as deep and urgent as their need for self-preservation, and it apparently requires them to believe that they are acting for more than mere self-preservation (compare *GM* III, 7). Especially striking is that Nietzsche again uses natural or animal imagery here, but in this case the animal (the insect) creates neither truth nor lies. The insect represents simply the instinct for self-preservation; it is distinctively human to lie, but also to need to affirm oneself morally. In this way, the desperate belief in free will appears less as the means to blame the strong and more as the means for the weak to affirm themselves; indeed, by the end of the thirteenth section, Nietzsche's focus has shifted to this as the actual motive of the weak in clinging to the belief in free will.

Though Nietzsche is elusive even in the most schematic essay comprising his "polemic," we have seen that he advances a relatively clear and consistent argument that truth is produced and that the intellect is therefore subordinate to the will (and is indeed perhaps just an ancillary instrument of the will). We have seen that this argument is somewhat paradoxical, for the same reason that any attempt to deny the existence of a perceived truth is paradoxical, but it is lucid and direct enough not only to indicate Nietzsche's position but to act as a foil to help clarify the Underground Man's even more ambiguous, paradoxical treatment of these questions.

The first part of *Notes from Underground*, "Underground," presents many of the same interpretive challenges as the *Genealogy*, probably in an even more severe form: the polemical purpose and tone that blurs the line between incisive argument and combative overstatement, the digressions that at times seem to signal a loss of emotional as well as discursive control, the interpolations by an uncomprehending and vaguely dismissive imagined reader. The text of "Underground" as a whole is of course rich, nuanced, and complicated, and too much focus on the most dramatic or well-known passages produces a distorted picture of the work (another similarity with Nietzsche). Despite the fame of the opening sentence, for instance, by his own account the Underground Man is sick and wicked only in very qualified and uncertain ways.

Issues like this are of course common to all texts, but the exceptional and arguably the greatest interpretive difficulty posed by "Underground" is the reactive energy pervading the Underground Man's notes, especially in the first part of the work. The reactive tone and attitude is of course hardly unique to the *Notes*; Dostoevsky uses a very similar voice in *Winter Notes on Summer Impressions*, but the contrast with that work highlights the obstacles presented by "Underground." The narrator of *Winter Notes* shares with the Underground Man a tendency to be carried away by his own bitterness to the point where he knows he begins to sound ridiculous, and yet to continue in the same vein, his self-awareness doing nothing to stop him or temper his acrimony. Much of the ethical and cultural critique of both works is delivered from a vantage point that eschews a conventional stance of moral superiority, though this does nothing to weaken the force of the critique for either the author or the reader. The narrator of *Winter Notes*, however, with his mordant portrait of the French bourgeoisie (*"Mon arbre, mon mur,"* "My tree, my wall") and his crushing account of the human sacrifice required for English wealth, could presume a certain common ground with his readers. Some might have found his depiction of Europe too acerbic and partial, but in a sense he was choosing easy targets, and few would rise to the defense of the profiteering French bourgeois or of the scenes he encountered in London's poorer quarters, or indeed of the rank hypocrisy he found everywhere, especially among the English clergy. The Underground Man makes no such concessions to his readers, or rather he starts from (and continues in) a very different place than the narrator of *Winter Notes*. He indicates this almost immediately with his mocking and dismissive mention of medicine. He starts by suggesting an opposition between respect for medicine and superstition, but then reduces respect for medicine to mere superstition, saying that he is superstitious enough to respect medicine. He begins, in other words, by setting up the appearance of sharing his readers' beliefs, only to quickly dissolve or explode that appearance and state his hostility to medicine by collapsing it into the superstition it was meant to overcome and supplant. He thus also expresses his hostility to his modern readers who would agree with such an understanding of both the purpose and success of modern medicine; this hostility is, of course, one of the hallmarks of "Underground." Unlike the narrator of *Winter Notes*, the Underground Man is attacking the core beliefs that constitute his readers' moral and cultural sense of self, rather than attacking cultural realities on the basis of more radical or intransigent versions of those beliefs.

But from where then does the Underground Man attack these beliefs? Does he believe anything himself, or is he rather pure reactivity or hostility, a kind of negating chimera with no real center or content, so that trying to assign a position to him is pointless and even wrong-headed? That is the specter that haunts any interpretation of "Underground," but readers have generally agreed that the Underground Man makes a recognizable, coherent, and indeed compelling argument in this part of the *Notes*. Here I will focus specifically on his discussions of wickedness, truth, consciousness, and will (though the will is largely dealt with only implicitly in the first half of "Underground"). Despite the overwhelming reactive energy of the Underground Man, and his striking similarity to Nietzsche's portrait of *ressentiment*, he himself speaks not of reactivity but of wickedness, and attention to this shows us how he differs from Nietzsche by showing us the fundamental concern and argument that runs even deeper than the mass of reactivity that emanates from his text. As with the previous section, I will follow the text closely (though selectively), then make more general points at the end of the section.[20]

The Underground Man says he is sick, but he refuses to see a doctor or be treated for his illness. "I refuse to be treated out of wickedness," he explains. His ascription of wickedness to himself here is somewhat strange; he refuses to do what is in his best material or physical interest, but is such a refusal really wicked? This notion of interest or good seems to be the same as that against which the Underground Man inveighs in the second half of "Underground"; his description of his refusal to seek treatment for his sickness as wicked thus seems questionable, if not ironic.

Wickedness, as the Underground Man understands it here, seems rather to consist in causing suffering, or at least in wanting to cause suffering: "I will not be able to explain to you who is going to suffer from my wickedness." The idea seems to be that causing pain is the whole point of wickedness, its final cause. It is clear that the Underground Man himself will suffer from refusing to be treated, as he will from refusing to cross out his bad witticism, and his ability (and desire) to take pleasure in his own suffering is of course one of the major themes of these first five sections. But his formulation here suggests that wickedness is more than anything a matter of making others suffer. The notion of wickedness as defined by causing suffering to others also seems implicit in his suggestion that he was a wicked official as compensation for not taking bribes: wickedness does not consist in profiting oneself dishonestly or illegally. Wickedness has nothing to do with profit, it is about causing harm and taking pleasure in it. To the extent that there is any profit or advantage in his wickedness, it seems to consist in gaining mastery or at least some power or control over others by causing them harm or, failing that, by "upsetting" them. The similarity to Nietzsche, and specifically the will to power, is obvious.

This seems to be the sense in which the Underground Man says that he was a wicked official (he upset and intimidated those who sought his help), though he soon adds that he was in fact not a wicked official, and was indeed never able to become wicked at all. This does not seem to mean that he was not able to upset people (e.g., the timid petitioners), but rather that he was never able to become wicked in some deeper sense; he was "simply frightening sparrows in vain, and pleasing myself with it." True wickedness would seem to require more than simply gnashing one's teeth at petitioners in a government office. The Underground Man is even prone to waxing tenderhearted; his false wickedness is perhaps akin to the "literariness" he criticizes at the end of the book. "The greatest nastiness," he says, consisted in being aware of this falseness, of knowing that he was in fact not wicked and not even embittered. He cannot escape or obscure the truth, nor can he reject it as a standard.[21]

In the course of explaining that he was not wicked and was never able to become wicked, the Underground Man says, "And I lied about myself just now when I said I was a wicked official. I lied out of wickedness." Given that this statement comes in the course of explaining that he was not wicked and was never able to become wicked, what are we to make of it? Is the Underground Man simply playing around with paradox? Or is he rather suggesting an essential connection between lying and wickedness? And perhaps further, that lying is the one kind of wickedness of which he is capable?

Of course, the Underground Man does not seem to be interested in resolving questions like this for the reader. In any case, he here presents himself as not wicked but (at least potentially) tenderhearted, but perhaps more than anything emotionally volatile, swinging from anger and pretended wickedness to tenderheartedness, then on to shame and insomnia at his tenderheartedness. In some sense his most irrepressible self appears to have been tenderhearted or at least anti-wicked, as he says that all his life he was "conscious every moment of so very many elements in myself most opposite to that [wickedness]. I felt them simply swarming in me, those opposite elements. I knew they had been swarming in me all my life, asking to be let go out of me, but I would not let them, I would not, I purposely would not let them out. They tormented me to the point of shame." This is of course the reverse of the usual picture one would expect, of wicked elements swarming within one, struggling to get out but being repressed, and of people lying about their success in overcoming their wicked impulses, rather than lying about their success in realizing them. It is not clear why the Underground Man would want to fight so hard to be wicked, and further be ashamed of the instincts within him that run counter to that, but based on the picture of him that emerges from the second part of the *Notes* it seems likely that it is because he has a strong desire to dominate others but is unable to do so through conventional forms of success and power (best embodied in Zherkov), and so must attempt to do so through wickedness. In any case, the mere thought of his failure to become wicked seems to inflame his sense of shame anew, as he becomes concerned with his readers' opinion of him, and in particular becomes concerned that they think he is trying to repent or ask forgiveness, and thus again failing to be wicked (and indeed ceding power to them).

Here we see a picture of identity and moral agency, if not truth, arising from within and moving outward: here moral character is produced by the individual's nonrational constitution, not formed in relation or response to the external world. This character, however, is repressed and overlaid, perhaps even deformed, by a lie, or at least an attempted lie, the Underground Man's efforts to be wicked.

The recollection of how he was unable to become wicked leads into the larger discussion of how he was unable to become anything, and how it is further impossible to become anything, at least for "an intelligent man of the nineteenth century." The Underground Man refers to this thought as a "spiteful and utterly futile consolation" (only the Underground Man could "taunt [him]self" with a consolation). The consolation may be spiteful simply because it is futile, but the word used here, *zlobnym*, is related to *zloi*, the word the Underground Man uses to describe himself as wicked in the opening sentence. The consolation that it is impossible to become anything thus could be merely spiteful, or it could be positively wicked or evil; if the latter, it must be wicked in large part (perhaps solely) because it is not true.[22] That this idea is untrue is further suggested by the fact that unintelligent people ("fools") apparently can become something; it is not impossible simply, but only impossible for a certain type of person who believes certain things.[23] Even so, this belief appears true to the intelligent; this is perhaps why they "should be morally obliged to be primarily a characterless being," because they should be morally obliged to accept the truth.

The Underground Man concludes the first section by responding to his readers' imagined irritation with him by giving a brief account of himself (characteristically stressing his refusal to leave Saint Petersburg for prudential reasons). He begins the second section with the intention of explaining why he was never able to become even an insect, though the closest he comes to answering this directly (at least here) is commenting on how too much consciousness is a sickness. His sickness thus appears to reside primarily in his consciousness rather than in his liver. The theme of consciousness as sickness leads into the question of why being conscious of inspiring ideals did nothing to prevent him from acting basely.

> Tell me this: why was it that, as if by design, in those same, yes, in those very same moments when I was most capable of being conscious of all the refinements of "everything beautiful and lofty," as we once used to say, it happened that instead of being conscious I did such unseemly deeds, such deeds as . . . well, in short, as everyone does, perhaps, but which with me occurred, as if by design, precisely when I was most conscious that I ought not to be doing them at all? The more conscious I was of the good and of all this "beautiful and lofty," the deeper I kept sinking into my mire, and the more capable I was of getting completely stuck in it. But the main feature was that this was all in me not as if by chance, but as if it had to be so. As if it were my most normal condition and in no way a sickness or a blight, so that finally I lost any wish to struggle against this blight. (7)

The simplest answer would be that this was due to some personal depravity or failing of the Underground Man, but this would go against both his and Dostoevsky's view that he is somehow exemplary and revealing. Another possibility is that it was due to the falseness, and perhaps the foreignness, of these ideas of the "beautiful and lofty" of which he was so acutely conscious: had the Underground Man tried to steer his life by a true moral code rather than sentimental and grandiose fantasies (which is how he presents them in "Apropos," 2) he would have been spared this "blight." This makes some sense, and obviously accords with the image of Dostoevsky as anti-Western polemicist. It is perhaps also supported by the parallel with the Underground Man's later insistence, contra the rationalist utopians, that human beings will act against their best interest to know they are free. There are obvious differences, chiefly that the "beautiful and lofty" is about moral uplift, not hard-eyed calculations of personal advantage, but the basic idea seems to be the same—in both cases one acts contrary to how one "should," because in both cases this "should" is false.

Yet the Underground Man says that "everyone does" the things he did, so it seems the blight is universal, if not always as complete or corrosive, or as perverse in its timing, as it was in his case. This interpretation also relies on the assumption that the problem is not consciousness itself but merely its contents, which seems obviously at odds with the Underground Man's position, especially in this second section. Moreover, the rebellion against utopianism is conscious and intentional, if not rational; the Underground Man's actions here are presented as somehow involuntary and inscrutable. Finally, and perhaps most importantly, the Underground Man's strictures against the rationalist utopians tend toward the view that one must be self-destructive at times in order to know that one is free. In this case the falseness of both the "beautiful and lofty" and the utopians' rationalist morality resides primarily not in their foreignness or modernity but in their lack of an element of self-destructiveness (what Nietzsche might call *Untergehen*), or the lack of an ability or outlet to act against one's own interests. In this case the goal would perhaps become not so much finding a set of ideals from which one will not deviate but finding the right way to deviate, the way to be self-destructive in a manner that expresses and preserves one's moral agency rather than destroying or debasing it. Here the traditional notion of the will as a faculty or appetite directed toward the rational apprehension of the good becomes very hard to maintain, but this does not mean that one abandons a notion of truth as perceived and sovereign, for the need to be self-destructively free is real and cannot be satisfied by a fiction of freedom.

The Underground Man closes the second section by introducing the villain of these early sections of "Underground," the laws of nature, and along with them the theme of blame and vengeance. On the subject of vengeance, he notes that if he wanted to take revenge he "surely wouldn't dare to do anything even if I could." This question of his inability to take revenge requires special attention and is explicated in a new section; he begins that section by discussing "those who know how to take revenge and generally how to stand up for themselves" (I, 3). This ability, however, at first seems to have nothing to do with knowledge but rather with the ability to shut off thought altogether: "Once they are overcome, say, by vengeful feeling, then for the time there is simply nothing left in their whole being but this feeling." He compares them to a bull; in this animal imagery we see something like a picture of truth as product, as the product of the bull's rage. Quickly, however, the Underground Man undercuts that conclusion: the active figures fold quite sincerely before a wall, the truth of which they accept as given. Ultimately, then, the active figures seem to perceive or submit to the truth rather than create it. Their vengeful rage produces truth until it confronts the wall, at which point truth becomes something apprehended or imposed; in both cases, they are honest, genuinely believing in the truth—and justice—of both their own vengeful anger and of the wall.

On the other hand, the "man of heightened consciousness, who came, of course, not from the bosom of nature but from a retort . . . this retort man sometimes folds before his antithesis so far that he honestly regards himself, with all his heightened consciousness, as a mouse and not a man." This mouse is unable to take revenge because it does not believe in the justice of its vengeance; *l'homme de nature et de la vérité* (the natural and truthful man) is able to take revenge because, "with his innate stupidity, [he] regards his revenge quite simply as justice." It is thus not a matter of simply being overcome by an irrational rage and a demand for vengeance, but of believing in the justice of that demand. In obvious contrast to Nietzsche, justice limits vengeance; it is not simply an instrument or pretense deployed by vengeance.[24] More generally, neither the active men nor the mouse escape into the realm of imaginary revenge that Nietzsche describes as the work of *ressentiment*. Both remain bound to the world of reality or truth, though truth appears differently to each based on their different levels of intelligence, and bound to what that reality tells them justice is. Here, probably more than anywhere else in these first five sections of "Underground," we have a picture of the will as subordinate to the intellect.[25]

The Underground Man's position is further clarified by his imagined exchanges with his readers. A particularly sharp and revealing contrast comes in the fourth section, which begins with his listeners laughing derisively. They appear, however, to be laughing at his comments about taking pleasure in his own feelings of inertia and helplessness, not at the comments with which he had ended section three, about the pain caused by that same inertia. It is as if they have somehow not heard or read what immediately precedes their laughter. It is a common situation in Nietzsche's writings, including in the First Essay of the *Genealogy*: his contemporaries have read but not understood, nor even been able to fully see or grasp what he is discussing.[26] It is also, and more to the point for Dostoevsky, a recurring theme in the Bible. Especially relevant here are the following lines from Psalms:

> The idols of the heathen are silver and gold, the work of men's hands.
> They have mouths, but they speak not; eyes have they, but they see not;
> They have ears, but they hear not; neither is there any breath in their mouths.
> They that make them are like unto them: so is every one that trusteth in them.
> (Psalm 135:15–18, AV)

The idols of the modern understanding of nature and the political and social hopes built upon it cannot see or account for the longings and the pain the Underground Man describes, and neither can those who have made them or believe in them.[27] All that they can perceive is an image of the Underground Man absurdly delighting in a sense of uncertainty and paralysis that is itself risible and pointless. Here there is a limit or blockage that prevents one from perceiving the truth—specifically, the simple truth of what another person believes—but it is the result of adopting certain beliefs or idols, not of the natural or intrinsically human constitution of the Underground Man's readers. Not comprehending this reality, his listeners both mock it, thinking the Underground Man's pleasure in inertia trivial and ridiculous (like pleasure in a toothache), and fail to understand the consequences of the pain he describes.

The Underground Man's speech largely comes full circle in section five, where he returns to his inability to take revenge (and the related, largely prior inability to become wicked). He explains how he would "hoodwink" himself into feeling things he wouldn't otherwise: repentance, offense, love. He hoodwinked himself out of mere boredom—not, as in Nietzsche's account of the bad conscience, out of a desire to create or even to will and so experience some kind of mastery and freedom, but simply because he was "crushed by inertia." Again, the fruit of consciousness is inertia, while active figures are able to act only because they are "dull and narrow-minded." To explain this he returns to the example of vengeance: active types are able to take revenge because they believe they have found a "primary cause" and so an "indisputable basis" for acting, which he later clarifies is justice (i.e., a subjective sense of one's own justice, or the justice of one's own sense of grievance, that ignores all the factors that may have led one's enemy to harm one and that may have been completely beyond the enemy's control). The Underground Man, by contrast, sees no justice in his own desire for revenge, and so could take vengeance only out of wickedness, but of course he is not actually able to be or become wicked. Without wickedness (*zlost'*), his spite (*zloba*) "undergoes a chemical breakdown," the offence he wanted to avenge loses human meaning and becomes a *fatum* (fate), like a toothache, and vengeance (or any other action) becomes impossible.[28] He concludes the fifth section by assuring his readers that they will despise themselves for hoodwinking themselves; again, the truth is primary, and provides both an external check on one's own subjective experience and feelings and a basis for valuation, a criterion by which one can judge one's actions and beliefs as good or bad, admirable or despicable.

We have seen how the Underground Man consistently suggests that an independent, perceived truth limits the human intellect and especially the will. Here we see in more detail how his moral psychology differs from Nietzsche's, specifically on the question of vengeance and reactivity. For Nietzsche the belief in the justice of one's vengefulness, however false and venomous that belief, is the product of *ressentiment*, while for the Underground Man belief in the justice of one's revenge is independent of and largely immune to any pressure exerted by the desire for vengeance, as we see especially in the case of "people who think and consequently do nothing," and is thus the necessary condition of actually seeking vengeance. For Nietzsche, the desire for vengeance creates the belief in justice; for the Underground Man, the belief in justice creates the ability to act on the desire for vengeance, and the lack of belief in one's own justice stifles it. In section five we see a similar contrast concerning the nature and efficacy of spite. For Nietzsche, spite or *ressentiment* is damned up or blocked by weakness, not the absence of wickedness (which, to the extent that it exists for Nietzsche, is largely synonymous with *ressentiment*). For the Underground Man, however, wickedness is something real, and its absence prevents one's spite from being an effective spur to action. For Nietzsche spite that cannot be discharged does not "break down" but insinuates and articulates itself in other ways, and even takes control of the mind or soul, warping it to serve its demands. What would enable the spite to express itself is simply the power or opportunity to do so, not wickedness or belief in one's own justice (which, again, the spite or *ressentiment* itself produces in Nietzsche's view); for Nietzsche, the check on spite is purely external; for the Underground Man, purely internal. The Underground Man needs something to fill his mind or to set himself at ease, so he can act and give expression to his spite or vengefulness. Without that basis for action, the spite simply dissolves, or perhaps is directed back at oneself. It neither forces nor enables one to deceive oneself, and it does not become creative and give birth to new values and self-understandings.

We can now return to the questions about truth and violence asked at the beginning of the chapter. Is truth simply an effect of power or domination? Nothing the Underground Man says suggests that this is his view, and a great deal points in the opposite direction. Likewise, the Underground Man does not seem to think that suffering harm at the hands of another affects one's ability to see the truth. For the highly conscious like the Underground Man, the truth restrains even the most ardent desire for revenge, as well as the desire for deceptive self-affirmation (though it is always possible that for Dostoevsky and the Underground Man this restraint is the work of some deeper, unacknowledged need or desire). The active men or bulls are able to believe in the justice of their revenge, but this is only because of their natural stupidity, not because of the power their desire for vengeance wields over their minds. The point can be made more generally by saying that, for the Underground Man, the will is subordinate to the intellect, at least in the case of vengeance; this formulation leaves aside the question of whether or not the intellect must lay hold of the truth to have this power (both thinking and unthinking people seem to be the same in this respect, despite having mutually exclusive beliefs about justice and revenge).

To say that the truth is primary in this sense is not to say that human beings never believe falsehoods; the embrace of falsehoods or idols may indeed be the most common situation, though exactly why or how this comes about is not explained. A likely explanation, one that coheres or harmonizes with other points in the Underground Man's speech (as well as others of Dostoevsky's writings), is that they embrace the falsehoods or idols for an illusory feeling of mastery, for an experience of autonomy and complete exercise of the will, in the form of remaking the world along rational lines; paradoxically, this ends up destroying any meaningful understanding or even basic experience of the will. This embrace of a falsehood, however, is presented not as the natural or normal condition but as somehow an aberration (even if a common or attractive one), and one which necessarily distorts or disfigures the human beings engaged in this embrace.

All of this is in clear contrast to Nietzsche, at least the Nietzsche of the First Essay of the *Genealogy*. For Nietzsche, the truth is violent enough to make the slaves recognize it, and thus to lie to repulse it. The nobles simply believe a fiction (though even they must "guard themselves" against certain aspects of reality). The priests are the most introspective and self-aware of these three primeval types, but even they are truthful only in an extremely qualified and ambiguous sense. For all of them, truth is produced according to the requirements of their own particular needs and drives, and the fact that the truth appears differently to each type is a result of these inherent constitutional differences, not of different levels of intelligence or probity (these qualities themselves being simply the product of different necessities and conditions of life). All of this clearly goes against the picture presented by the Underground Man of truth as primary for human beings, something necessarily grounding and so limiting their thoughts, emotions, and actions. Nietzsche sees the (healthy) self as enveloped by fictions of its own making, its own, necessary organic covering or protection. The Underground Man sees such fictions as do envelop the self as false beliefs more or less consciously adopted by the individual. These beliefs or idols keep it from seeing the truth, or rather keep the self inwardly sealed off from its own true experiences, those the Underground Man himself explores and reveals.

We can conclude and sum up by asking three overarching, related questions, about reactivity, the will, and the picture of the willing subject that emerges from each text.

What is reactivity? Is it real? Is it productive? For Nietzsche, reactivity is *ressentiment*. It is real but not fundamental or universal; as I said at the beginning of the chapter, it is the necessary reaction to a contingent situation. Although it replaces many traditional moral concepts, both as an explanation for particular acts and as the cause or origin of many of these traditional concepts, it is itself a psychological rather than a moral term, and names a phenomenon wholly explicable in psychological or organic terms. It is of course very productive, but what it produces is poisoned, warped, and mendacious. Although the Underground Man exhibits many reactive characteristics, perhaps as much in "Underground" as in "Apropos of the Wet Snow," in his view wickedness is the more fundamental reality. If both wickedness and reactivity are real, reactivity appears in "Underground" as something closely linked to inhibition, though inhibition caused by consciousness, not, as for Nietzsche, physical or political weakness; it is not productive of anything other than impotent spite and perhaps pleasure in one's own inability to choose or act. Wickedness, on the other hand, is both real and productive. Though the Underground Man himself lacks wickedness, and thus can do nothing in the face of personal insult (or any other *fatum*), wickedness would pull him out of the world of empty and mute *fata* and make it possible for him to exist and act in a world of recognizably human experiences and motives. If reactivity belongs with inaction and paralysis, wickedness belongs with action (and, in a sense, power—a further difference from *ressentiment*).

What is the will? What is the deepest, most fundamental will or desire of human beings? Of course everyone knows that the Nietzschean answer is the will to power. As we saw above, however, ultimately this does not mean the will to simple physical or political power, but at the deepest level the will to affirm or respect oneself. In other words, the will to power expresses itself in human beings through the act of valuation, not simply through mindless physical domination. For the Underground Man the deepest or most essential will is the wanting or will he discusses in the second half of "Underground," "[o]ne's own free and voluntary wanting" (25), according to which one may even "purposely, consciously wish for himself even the harmful, the stupid, even what is stupidest of all . . . *to have the right* to wish for himself even what is stupidest of all and not be bound by an obligation to wish for himself only what is intelligent" (28). This "preserves for us the chiefest and dearest thing, that is, our personality and our individuality" (28–29). As this description makes clear, "wanting is very often, and even for the most part, completely and stubbornly at odds with reason" (29).

What then is the relation between will and intellect? More generally, what is the new picture of the willing subject? The traditional view, the view that largely constituted the Western sense of self, held that for an action to be distinctly human, it must be conscious, voluntary, and rational; the will was regarded as a rational faculty or appetite inherently directed toward the good or the natural or moral law. Reason apprehends the good (or, for Kant, the moral law), then the will wills or chooses it. As we have seen above, Nietzsche rejects or displaces most of that account. The will is neither conscious nor rational (see especially *GM* I, 13), and thus cannot be voluntary in the traditional or classical sense.[29] The intellect is therefore clearly subordinate to the will for Nietzsche, but the will to power takes the form of consciousness among human beings, and consciousness takes specific historical forms, and in particular takes distinct historical forms as conscience; thus, under certain historical conditions, the demand for truth becomes a cultural imperative (as Nietzsche explains at the end of the Third Essay of the *Genealogy*), and the true must or at least should be chosen over the desirable. Even so, however, Nietzsche's vision of the will excludes the classical view, for here as always, according to Nietzsche, the will is not rational, and not directed to the good (compare, for example, *GM* III, 7; *BGE* 188).

For the Underground Man the situation is somewhat more complex. He also largely rejects the notion of a willing subject defined by a rational will, arguing instead for a picture of will or wanting as essentially nonrational, unpredictable, disruptive, and, like Nietzsche, not concerned with the good (indeed, even purposely choosing the bad or harmful in order to know it is free to do so). His position on the will is thus much more radical than is often supposed: he rejects not only the rationalist egotism of his day but the picture of the rational will at the center of Western thought. Yet we have also seen that, for the Underground Man, consciousness or intellect can inhibit the will. This can be suffocating or enervating, as when the consciousness of the laws of nature makes any human action, and ultimately any action at all, impossible, but the Underground Man also suggests that the will is restrained by a belief in justice that is independent of the will or desires of the subject. This is not to say that unjust vengeance is impossible, simply that it requires wickedness, a conscious decision to harm another knowing that this harm is not justified.

NOTES

1. Though the use of the term "individual" is certainly questionable in Nietzsche's case, I use it here both because I think this use, especially in the question above, is in line with Nietzsche's critique of the notion of individuality, and because in *On the Genealogy of Morals* (which, as I explain below, will be the focus of my discussion of Nietzsche) Nietzsche presents us with clear individual archetypes, especially in the First Essay (noble, priest, slave).

2. In this essay I abstain from questions about whether Nietzsche and Dostoevsky are implicated in this phenomenon themselves, and how that implication may manifest itself in their writings. For a highly intelligent and perceptive argument that Nietzsche's texts are themselves moved at times by *ressentiment*, see Henry Staten, *Nietzsche's Voice* (Ithaca: Cornell University Press, 1990), especially 8–39. Dostoevsky's occasionally prickly personality is well known, and one may see a certain reactivity mar his fiction in his portrait of the Polish characters in *The Gambler* (among other places). The richest and most powerful exploration of reactivity in the person and work of Dostoevsky I have seen is Leonid Tsypkin, *Summer in Baden-Baden*, trans. Roger and Angela Keys (New York: New Directions, 2001).

3. See Friedrich Nietzsche, *Beyond Good and Evil*, trans. Walter Kaufmann (New York: Vintage Books, 1966), section 19 and part 1 generally. *Beyond Good and Evil* is hereafter abbreviated as *BGE*.

4. Of course with writers as canny and elusive as Nietzsche and Dostoevsky the matter is never quite as clear as the above summary suggests, and no less a commentator than Robert Louis Jackson takes the opposite tack and argues that Dostoevsky ultimately embraced illusion while Nietzsche rejected it (Robert Louis Jackson, "Counterpoint: Nietzsche and Dostoevsky," in *Dialogues with Dostoevsky: The Overwhelming Questions* [Stanford: Stanford University Press, 1993], 246–47). While I agree that Nietzsche rejected illusion, I believe that this was because of his particular historical situation, not because he thought this was the fundamental or natural imperative for human beings (I come back to this point briefly at the end of the chapter). As for Dostoevsky, Jackson himself writes that "reality for Dostoevsky always is pregnant with an inner truth, a poetry that can at any moment suddenly make itself felt (and *suddenly* is one of his favorite words); a poetry that in spiritual-religious terms is revelation but in purely aesthetic terms for Dostoevsky means a triumph over naturalistic surface reality, a disclosure of the rich but usually masked interiority of man and human reality" (240). This statement is more in line with what I argue below, and indeed is almost the unstated basis or presupposition of it.

5. Geoff Waite, *Nietzsche's Corps/e: Aesthetics, Politics, Prophecy, or, The Spectacular Technoculture of Everyday Life* (Durham, N.C.: Duke University Press, 1996), 160.

6. On Nietzsche's discovery of Dostoevsky and questions of possible influence see C. A. Miller, "Nietzsche's 'Discovery' of Dostoevsky," *Nietzsche-Studien* 2 (1973): 202–57, and Eric v. d. Luft and Douglas G. Stenberg, "Dostoevskii's Specific Influence on Nietzsche's Preface to *Daybreak*," *Journal of the History of Ideas* 52 (1991): 441–61 (for details on Nietzsche's immediate reaction to Dostoevsky, see Miller, 206 and following). Miller makes an argument deprecating the importance of *Notes from Underground* for Nietzsche's enthusiasm for Dostoevsky; although I find this unconvincing, her extended comparison of "The Landlady" with Nietzsche's thought, and her reconstruction of Nietzsche's reading of it, are very interesting. Luft and Stenberg, 442–43, n. 4, includes a useful overview of the changes that *L'esprit souterrain* made to *Notes from Underground*, including mistranslating "the name of the dentist Wagenheim as *la grande Inconnue*."

7. Given the importance of *ressentiment* to Nietzsche's arguments about morality in the *Genealogy* (especially in the First and Third Essays), one may expect that it would form an essential, even foundational or organizing component of his moral philosophy in subsequent works. In fact, however, Nietzsche barely uses the term at all again after the *Genealogy* (though it does appear in a few passages in *Der Antichrist*). Though this may seem surprising or even odd,

the same fate is suffered by other striking and seemingly fundamental new concepts Nietzsche introduces in previous works—the superman, the last man, and even the Eternal Recurrence of the Same, which is barely mentioned in most of Nietzsche's published work after *Zarathustra*.

8. Although questions of influence are necessarily speculative here (Nietzsche's copies of Dostoevsky's works are not among the books included in his library at the Nietzsche Archive in Weimar), it is not unreasonable to think that Nietzsche's encounter with the Underground Man may have inspired him to think more fully about this phenomenon and to see it more clearly.

9. Compare also *Human, All Too Human*, I, 45, Nietzsche's earliest, and somewhat different, formulation of the idea that different social classes will produce radically different moralities (compare *GM* Pr., 4).

10. Though I—or perhaps Nietzsche—may be overstating this, since Nietzsche still speaks of noble values in terms of the pathos of distance; that is, "the protracted and domineering fundamental feeling on the part of a higher ruling order in relation to a lower order, to a 'below'" (I, 2). Friedrich Nietzsche, *On the Genealogy of Morals: A Polemic*, trans. Walter Kaufmann and R. J. Hollingdale (New York: Vintage Books, 1969), abbreviated as *GM*.

11. Nietzsche does discuss this as a motive for morality in the Third Essay, but morality as a system of actions to help the weak is more the invention of the priest (*GM* III, 15), and both the priest and the sickly use it to increase their feeling of power (*GM* III, 18), not, as in *Beyond Good and Evil*, to increase the convenience or comfort of the weak.

12. Perhaps the effectiveness of this constant, disorderly, but obviously intense and often penetrating motion of his speech is part of why Dostoevsky chose never to restore the material expurgated by the censor from section ten of "Underground"—because he realized that the Underground Man's crucial truth was best expressed by brilliant and caustic incoherence rather than by didactic exposition. For a brief account of the cuts made by the censor and Dostoevsky's reaction to them, see Richard Pevear's foreword to Fyodor Dostoevsky, *Notes from Underground*, trans. Richard Pevear and Larissa Volokhonsky (New York: Vintage, 1993), xviii–xix.

13. Parenthetical references to page numbers of *Notes from Underground* refer to the Pevear and Volokhonsky translation cited in the previous note.

14. The *Genealogy* has been the subject of several very good, book-length commentaries, especially in recent years. They include Aaron Ridley, *Nietzsche's Conscience: Six Character Studies from the "Genealogy"* (Ithaca: Cornell University Press, 1998); Daniel Conway, *Nietzsche's "On the Genealogy of Morals": A Reader's Guide* (New York: Continuum, 2007); Christopher Janaway, *Beyond Selflessness: Reading Nietzsche's Genealogy* (New York: Oxford University Press, 2007); David Owen, *Nietzsche's "Genealogy of Morality"* (Montreal and Kingston: McGill-Queen's University Press, 2007); and Lawrence J. Hatab,

Nietzsche's "On the Genealogy of Morality": An Introduction (New York: Cambridge University Press, 2008).

15. Nietzsche's procedure here is somewhat paradoxical. Though the psychology of knowledge or truth that Nietzsche presents throughout the First Essay seems to imply a view of truth as something produced rather than perceived, his presentation is part of an argument that seems clearly intended to convince the reader of its truth; that is, to convince the reader that Nietzsche has discovered or perceived the truth, both about the character of truth and about the history of morality.

16. Here and throughout the rest of the chapter I am leaving aside the question of Nietzsche's attitude or relationship to (traditional) philosophic notions of truth, and simply following Nietzsche's own usage in some of the many and varied statements he makes about "truth" in the early parts of the *Genealogy*. Tamsin Shaw, *Nietzsche's Political Skepticism* (Princeton: Princeton University Press, 2007), 62–69, provides a summary of some recent work on the question of Nietzsche and truth, which shows that there is still no real consensus. Major works on the subject include Maudemarie Clark, *Nietzsche on Truth and Philosophy* (New York: Cambridge University Press, 1990); Peter Poellner, *Nietzsche and Metaphysics* (New York: Clarendon Press, 1995); and Christoph Cox, *Nietzsche: Naturalism and Interpretation* (Berkeley: University of California Press, 1999), especially 69–168.

17. Nietzsche frequently writes about the nobles in very evocative and romantic terms, and here I am mostly taking those statements at face value. A fuller reckoning with the First Essay and the *Genealogy* as a whole would obviously have to address the question of whether these various romantic (and often Romantic) tropes, tonal registers, etc., are genuine or ironic, and the further question (if they are ironic) of whether their purpose is sinister or educative (or somehow both).

18. The difference between fictions and lies here largely reduces to the presence or absence of *ressentiment*, especially as the source of the lie.

19. Though their solution ultimately relies on *ressentiment*, not against the nobles but against existence itself. See *GM* III, 11.

20. Like the *Genealogy*, *Notes from Underground* has generated a great deal of commentary. Especially good and relevant for our purposes here are the close readings by Joseph Frank, *Dostoevsky: The Stir of Liberation, 1860–1865* (Princeton: Princeton University Press, 1988), 310–47 (316–23 on the portion I discuss here), and James Scanlan, *Dostoevsky the Thinker* (Ithaca: Cornell University Press, 2002), 57–80.

21. Here I am suggesting that Dostoevsky gives the Underground Man a certain set of experiences in order to make his own points about the primacy of truth, not that the Underground Man is here advancing his own theoretical argument or is fully aware of the significance of his experiences. For the most

part I think that this is what Dostoevsky is doing when the Underground Man describes his own experiences, especially in the first three sections of "Underground," while in the Underground Man's discussion of vengeance and active men in sections four and five I tend to ascribe his views to Dostoevsky himself, since I think they accord with the larger philosophical picture that emerges from Dostoevsky's sketch of the Underground Man. On Dostoevsky's distance from the Underground Man, see Frank, *Stir of Liberation*, 310–16, and Scanlan, *Dostoevsky the Thinker*, 73–76.

22. Though it is perhaps unwise to try to hang too much on this peg, as *zloi* and related words are much more common, and have a broader and more prosaic range of meanings, than the English "wicked."

23. This is not to say that the foolish, natural type is simply bad or contemptible for the Underground Man: "I envy such a man to the point of extreme bile. He is stupid, I won't argue with you about that, but perhaps a normal man ought to be stupid, how do you know? Perhaps it's even very beautiful." In this passage he takes a somewhat Nietzschean swipe at Rousseau (natural man is stupid and vengeful, not stupid and compassionate), but the conflicted attitude here and throughout this discussion is clear. The natural or stupid man obviously shares much in common with Nietzsche's nobles, and the Underground Man's posture toward them, while less positive than Nietzsche's toward the nobles, shares some of his ambivalence because he shares Nietzsche's ambivalence to human development and civilization. For a somewhat different reading of both the Underground Man and Nietzsche on these points, see Edith W. Clowes, "Self-Laceration and Resentment: The Terms of Moral Psychology in Dostoevsky and Nietzsche," in *Freedom and Responsibility in Russian Literature: Essays in Honor of Robert Louis Jackson*, ed. Elizabeth Cheresh Allen and Gary Saul Morson (Evanston: Northwestern University Press, 1995), 122–24.

24. Though Nietzsche is emphatic that genuine justice, as opposed to the mendacious and vindictive use of that word, does not originate in *ressentiment* (*GM* II, 11).

25. But why can consciousness restrain and even dissolve the impulse to vengeance but not the impulse to debauchery? Is it because consciousness somehow has a power over the irascible that it does not over the concupiscent, or over *thumos* that it does not over *eros*? Or is it not a question of the power of consciousness but of the substance of the Underground Man and other thinking people? Are they lacking in some inner spark or wrath (perhaps akin to wickedness) that would overpower consciousness?

26. See, for instance, the story of the madman in section 125 of *The Gay Science*.

27. Does the Underground Man (and, more interestingly, Dostoevsky) reject the modern understanding of nature as governed by wholly impersonal and de-

terministic laws? If not, then the Underground Man's refusal to accept the laws of nature—"My God, but what do I care about the laws of nature and arithmetic if for some reason these laws and two times two is four are not to my liking?"—would seem to be pure willfulness—which may indeed be Dostoevsky's point, and the Underground Man's rejection of these laws, or at least the manner of that rejection, may ultimately be another symptom of the condition he is meant to illustrate (on this see Scanlan, *Dostoevsky the Thinker*, 74–76). The other possibility is that the Underground Man (and behind him Dostoevsky), like Nietzsche (but probably more radically), sees nature as something very different from what is represented by modern science (for Nietzsche, compare, for example, *BGE* 22; *GM* III, 7).

28. So then are we left with the only alternative being between paralysis in the face of an inhuman *fatum* on the one hand and a relatively mindless but efficacious vengefulness on the other? Is the problem inherent in the Underground Man's worldview, or in the nature of vengefulness itself? Nietzsche's answer, of course, is to overcome the spirit of revenge through *amor fati*. It seems reasonable to suppose that Dostoevsky's answer also relies on love, though not of a null *fatum*.

29. Indeed, it may be the case that for Nietzsche, who sees humans as so often blind to the true ends or motives of their acts of will (both beliefs and actions), the human will is less voluntary than the will of animals was for Aquinas, who thought that animals acted for an end but with only an imperfect understanding of the end (*Summa Theologica* IaIIae Q 6, Art. 2).

Michael Allen Gillespie

Dostoevsky's Impact on Nietzsche's Understanding of Nihilism

NIETZSCHE'S INTELLECTUAL DEVELOPMENT was decisively shaped by his accidental discovery of three books: Schopenhauer's *World as Will and Representation* when he was twenty-one, Stendhal's *The Red and the Black* at thirty-five, and Dostoevsky's *Notes from the Underground* at forty-three.[1] The impact of Schopenhauer has long been recognized and the importance of Stendhal is similarly clear to most Nietzsche scholars. The role that Dostoevsky played, however, is less obvious, in large part because Nietzsche discovered his work only a little more than a year before the collapse that ended his productive life. Yet in that short time he read as many of Dostoevsky's works as he could find, including "The Landlady," *Notes from the Underground*, *The House of the Dead*, *Crime and Punishment*, *The Demons*, and perhaps *The Idiot*.[2] There thus can be little doubt that in Nietzsche's last feverish year of philosophical activity, Dostoevsky was a nearly constant presence in his thoughts. In what follows I will try to describe the way in which this encounter shaped Nietzsche's thinking, and particularly Dostoevsky's impact on Nietzsche's exploration of the death of God, nihilism, and the possibility of the superhuman.

NIETZSCHE'S FINAL TEACHING

Nietzsche's thought, by his own account, falls into three periods. Under the influence of Wagner and Schopenhauer, his early work aimed at cultural renewal. During his middle period, which began with *Human, All Too Human*, he became pessimistic about the possibility of such renewal and turned his efforts toward the analysis and praise of the decisive role of distinctive individuals who as firstlings he believed were invariably opposed to prevailing cultural norms, criminals in thought if not in deed. This project gave way after 1881 to a new (and ultimately final) project which aimed at producing what Nietzsche called "the Great Noon," an apocalyptic transformation that he believed would overcome nihilism and set humanity on a path to the superhuman.

In Nietzsche's view, the advent of this Great Noon was coterminus with the proclamation of the idea of the Eternal Recurrence of the Same. This idea apparently first came to Nietzsche along with the idea for *Thus Spoke Zarathustra* during a walk around Lake Silvaplana in the vicinity of Sils Maria in the Swiss Alps in late September of 1881.[3] From the very beginning he considered it his deepest thought and made it the cornerstone of all his thinking. Indeed, he came to believe that everything he had previously written or done had been merely a preparation for this thought.[4]

At the core of this idea is the notion that everything that has been and everything that will be is inextricably connected in a chain of causes that forms a great circle, so that every moment depends upon all of the preceding moments and is also responsible for all of the moments that come after it. Consequently, one cannot affirm or condemn any one moment without affirming or condemning all of the others. So conceived, the world must be accepted or rejected as a whole. Schopenhauer in Nietzsche's view had followed the path of absolute negation and renunciation, treating the world as the delusive appearance of a demonic will that made us all both perpetrators and victims. By contrast, Nietzsche sought to affirm the whole by affirming the idea of the Eternal Recurrence. Such an affirmation, in his view, meant willing everything that had ever been or would be.[5]

Nietzsche initially presented this idea as the teaching of the Persian wise man Zarathustra in an effort to give the doctrine a mythic significance it would otherwise have lacked.[6] This decision was in part the result of his rejection of the worldview and methodology of positivism and utilitarianism. His intended audience was not the scientific or scholarly community of his time but the moral and cultural elite. *Thus Spoke Zarathustra* in this sense was a counter-Gospel which Nietzsche hoped would appeal not only to reason but to the hearts and wills of his contemporaries.[7] Nietzsche's Zarathustra in this context plays the role of an Antichrist, not a God who becomes a man but a man who becomes godlike, not a Christlike figure who evokes great pathos but a playful and benevolent character, even if at times he appears to be inhuman and pitiless. And perhaps most importantly, Zarathustra does not preach a doctrine of sin and the need for repentance or redemption but a doctrine of innocence and self-overcoming.

Nietzsche believed that this doctrine would ultimately produce a new order, but he recognized that in the short term its effect would be cataclysmic: "To build a new temple," Nietzsche asserted, "an old temple must be destroyed."[8] Thus, while the doctrine might open up extraordinary possibilities in the more distant future, Nietzsche knew that "uncountably many will die" on its account in "wars the like of which the world has never seen."[9] To affirm and proclaim this doctrine, it is thus necessary to accept the inevitability of its cataclysmic consequences.

Nietzsche himself hesitated in the face of such an apocalyptic vision, but not for the reasons one might imagine. The fact that many ordinary human beings would be swallowed up in this transformation did not much concern him. These are the ones Zarathustra refers to as the superfluous, the human-all-too-human, and the many-all-too-many. Nietzsche is much more concerned about the suffering and fate of those Zarathustra calls "higher men," the intellectuals and artists of his time who have recognized that God is dead but who are unable to find a way out of the abyss opened up by this event. The final barrier to proclaiming this teaching was thus what Zarathustra calls his final sin, "pity for the higher man." It is the suffering of these "higher men" and not the rest of humanity that worries Nietzsche. They are the only ones who matter. They are high but not high enough, not truly above man. They thus must perish in order for the superman to come into being.

THE IMPACT OF DOSTOEVSKY ON NIETZSCHE

It was in the context of his struggle to overcome nihilism that Dostoevsky came to play an important role for Nietzsche. Nietzsche considered Dostoevsky to be a preeminent example of slave morality, as he admitted in a letter to Brandes, but he was attracted to Dostoevsky because of his psychological insight into the intellectual nihilists.[10] Dostoevsky's portrayals of such characters as the Underground Man, Raskolnikov, and Kirillov confirmed and deepened Nietzsche's understanding of such higher men. Like Nietzsche Dostoevsky recognized that these men were daring enough to try to become something more than their human-all-too-human contemporaries, but he also recognized that they were not strong enough to achieve this goal. Dostoevsky thought that their failures marked out the limits of human striving, thus demonstrating the futility of pursuing a superhuman god-manhood, and consequently the need to return to God. Nietzsche, by contrast, concluded that their failures were due to the residue of Christianity that informed their moral sensibilities, leaving them paralyzed with feelings of pity and guilt. Like the tightrope walker in *Zarathustra*, they were stuck at the midpoint of the line between beast and superman, on the verge of the Great Noon, but unable to take the step from believer to destroyer because they could not bear the suffering it would bring to their fellow human beings. They thus had to perish. As Nietzsche portrays this event in *Zarathustra*, they fall from the tightrope when they are leaped over by those who are stronger and harder than they are, by sardonic jesters who have no pity or patience for their moral scruples.

While Nietzsche first laid out this project in *Zarathustra*, the book did not have the impact he anticipated. He had expected it to produce an event of European importance, but it disappeared beneath the surface of the intellectual sea of the 1880s with scarcely a ripple. The Biblical and mythic imagery, the epigrammatic and parablistic style simply made it too strange and alien not merely for the average reader, but also for Nietzsche's friends and admirers. Although profoundly disappointed, Nietzsche did not lose faith in the teaching that lay at its heart. Instead, he concluded that the work was "untimely"—that the public was so mired in positivism, utilitarianism, and Christianity that they simply could not see the truth. He realized he needed to further prepare them for the task he had set before them. The period after *Zarathustra* was thus what Nietzsche later characterized as the no-saying part of his task, the effort to demolish not merely the idea of the Christian God but everything that was built upon it, including all of European morality, in order to prepare the public for the reception of the idea of the Eternal Recurrence and the advent of the Great Noon.[11]

From the beginning this demanded that Nietzsche change the way he was perceived by the public. His previous work had led his readers to assume he was a disciple of Schopenhauer and Wagner or like Carlyle and Stendhal a worshiper of heroic men rather than the teacher of the Eternal Recurrence. To change this misperception, he realized that he would have to re-present himself to the public. This required him to reflect on his own intellectual development. In doing so he came to see that each of the "false" steps he had taken had been a "necessary error," a stage in his passage through and recovery from nihilism. By affirming the idea of the Eternal Recurrence Nietzsche felt that he had finally bitten off the head of the snake that had been poisoning him and thereby set himself on the road to recovery. Everything that he had thought and written before 1881 thus had to be reconceived as a preparation for this great realization. He had to show his readers that his works charted a course that they not only could but had to follow, a path that led beyond the higher man to the superman, and a new health and innocence beyond good and evil. As part of the effort to make this path clear to his contemporaries, he thus republished all of his earlier works with new prefaces that placed them in the context of his intellectual journey from sickness to health. By reissuing the works in this way, however, he also re-presented them to his readers as a propaedeutic for his new teaching.[12]

It was in the midst of writing these prefaces that he discovered Dostoevsky. Dostoevsky's impact was immediate and strong, as is evident in the new preface for *The Dawn*, in which he identifies the author of the work as a subversive mole, drawing on Dostoevsky's portrayal of the Underground Man.[13] This allusion is a clue to the nature of his reception and use of Dostoevsky. The purpose of the new prefaces was to describe the stages of Nietzsche's passage through decadence and nihilism to a new health. In tying the author of *The Dawn* to Dostoevsky's Underground Man, Nietzsche portrays not his current but his former self as mired in the same sickness that characterized Dostoevsky's protagonist. This was a form of life that Nietzsche believed he had overcome. Dostoevsky's mole thus represents one of the stages in the development of nihilism, one form of the "higher man."

Nietzsche thought that Dostoevsky had given a masterful account of this kind of man in *Notes from the Underground*. He particularly admired Dostoevsky's analysis of what he calls "the psychology of the psychologist."[14] With this phrase Nietzsche refers to what we might call the psychology of modern self-consciousness or subjectivity. Modernity rests upon the belief that self-consciousness reveals the truth of what we are, providing us with the solid foundation (an "Archimedean point," to use Descartes's famous phrase) for science and the mastery of nature. Even in his earliest works Nietzsche rejected this view. What Dostoevsky investigates and portrays more fully than anyone else, according to Nietzsche, is the psychology of this form of self-consciousness, the unconscious or subconscious foundation of such self-consciousness and the notion of truth that is founded upon it.[15] He thereby also reveals the emptiness of modern philosophy and the culture upon which it is built.

The problem with this form of thinking for Dostoevsky lies in the fact that while the Cartesian notion of self-consciousness liberates man from divine deception and gives him the capacity to set his own course through life, this godless self-consciousness is an empty shell or solipsistic universe without moral direction. Dostoevsky's literary examples thus reinforced Nietzsche's notion that the spiritual problems facing Europe were insoluble within the parameters of the modern notion of consciousness. Without God, self-consciousness reveals only a looming abyss, the absolute aloneness of the self without any goals or purposes other than those revealed by one's momentary desires. Within self-consciousness, the atheist thus cannot understand himself or find his way in life.[16] All of the efforts to better the human condition through science and the hopes of progress are thus in vain because at its foundation this scientific enterprise is the source of aimlessness. The unreflective masses (Nietzsche's last men) may find solace in the notion of progress preached by the utilitarians and displayed in monuments such as the Crystal Palace, but the higher men cannot. For them the material pleasures of such a life cannot make up for the lack of spiritual direction. Such a life is profoundly dissatisfying and leads nihilist intellectuals not merely to boredom and despair but to murder, madness, and suicide.[17] In such characters as Raskolnikov, Kirillov, and Stavrogin, Nietzsche believed that Dostoevsky had revealed the psychopathology of this hypersensitive self-consciousness. Dostoevsky for him thus provided the clearest and most compelling account of the inner life and ultimate fate of the nihilist.[18]

While Nietzsche accepted Dostoevsky's portrayal of the nihilist, he rejected his conclusions about what should be done. Dostoevsky believed that self-reflection and modern science were rooted in the systematic doubt of Cartesian skepticism that undermined faith, which alone could give direction and meaning to life. He hoped for a revival of this faith by pointing Russians to their Slavic tradition and away from Western rationalism.[19] In this way he believed that it would be possible to escape from the mirrored box of self-consciousness.

Although Nietzsche shared many of Dostoevsky's concerns about the debilitating character of Cartesian egoism, he drew different conclusions about the ultimate source of the problem. For him the return to any form of Christian faith would fail, because the inwardness of such hyper-self-conscious individuals was not the consequence of a turn away from Christianity, but the product of Christianity itself. Nietzsche was thus convinced that all of Europe would eventually be engulfed by the same nihilism he had passed through and that afflicted Dostoevsky's nihilistic protagonists. For Nietzsche the solution to nihilism lay in going where Dostoevsky was unwilling to go, where Dostoevsky believed no human could go. Dostoevsky's nihilists can find no way out of the aporia of self-consciousness. They are defeated by guilt, by pity, and by despair. Nietzsche concluded that these "higher men" were not strong or hard enough. Overcoming nihilism thus depended upon the formation of a harder people, tempered by years of brutal conflict, who in contrast to Dostoevsky's nihilists would be able to move beyond this impasse and forge a stronger European civilization.[20]

Here too the encounter with Dostoevsky aided Nietzsche in formulating his solution, although contrary to Dostoevsky's intentions. What particularly struck Nietzsche in this regard were not Dostoevsky's peasants and holy men, but the sturdy, fatalistic criminals he had encountered during his exile in Siberia and that he described in *The House of the Dead*. The fact that the strong often found themselves at odds with prevailing mores was certainly not surprising to Nietzsche. Byron's *Manfred*, the favorite work of his youth, presented just such a character. Stendhal's Julian Sorel was another. Dostoevsky's Siberian criminals, however, added a final element, because they exemplified a fatalism that was often missing in their Western European counterparts. This fatalism apparently played a role in the development of what Nietzsche came to call *amor fati* (love of fate), which he closely associated with the doctrine of the Eternal Recurrence. It was from such men and not out of the hyper-self-conscious, nihilist intellectuals that the superman in Nietzsche's view would be born.[21]

DOSTOEVSKY'S VISION OF THE NIHILIST

Dostoevsky, of course, was not the first to portray the nihilist. Turgenev's Basarov (1862) and Chernyshevsky's Rakhmetov (1863) antedate all of Dostoevsky's nihilists. However, in all previous literary examples the nihilist hero is described from the outside looking in, more as a rare and incomprehensible phenomenon than as a living, thinking, and above all self-reflective human being.[22] The greatness of Basarov, for example, is only visible in his effects on others. We never see the inner workings of his mind. Rakhmetov is a strange and mysterious being who stands apart and is held in awe by those around him. Dostoevsky's portrayal of the nihilists' internal struggles is a new and more psychologically enlightening account.

Although Nietzsche is often thought of as the preeminent philosopher of nihilism, the term does not appear in his notes until 1880 or in his published work until 1886.[23] The concept thus plays an explicit role only in his later thought. That said, the issues behind nihilism had occupied Nietzsche since the beginning of his thinking. As he began to reflect more carefully on nihilism in the 1880s, however, he came to distinguish different forms of the phenomenon.[24] The most fundamental distinction, as he saw it, was between incomplete and complete nihilism. Incomplete nihilism stretches back to Plato and includes all of Christian thought and modern philosophy up to Hegel. Complete nihilism begins in the middle third of the nineteenth century and recognizes the death of God and the essential aimlessness of human life. This form of nihilism is either passive or active. Passive nihilism includes Schopenhauer and his followers. It is characterized by pessimism, spiritual negation, and a renunciation of life. Within this category Nietzsche includes most Russian nihilists, whom he believed were fundamentally influenced by Schopenhauer.[25] Active nihilism, according to Nietzsche, does not merely renounce the world but seeks to destroy it, to assert its freedom through negation. In this category he includes revolutionary nihilists such as Bakunin and Nechayev who use violence to disrupt and destroy the existing order. Dostoevsky's nihilists, such as Stavrogin and Kirillov, stand on the border between active and passive nihilism. Stavrogin rejects the moral order of his time but cannot bring himself to destroy it. He violates its norms, but is unwilling to participate in the revolutionary movement. In the end for him there is nothing to do except hang himself.

Kirillov was the most extreme nihilist that Nietzsche encountered in Dostoevsky's works. He is a positivistic atheist akin to Turgenev's Basarov.[26]

He is horrified by the "stupid, blind, insane and problematical" reality of a world deprived of God. His nihilism is total and all-engrossing. It is also not a merely passive despair that leads to ascetic renunciation but a form of active nihilism. However, he does not direct the negative energy of his will against the prevailing order. Indeed, he is unwilling to inflict pain and suffering on others. This contradiction leads him to suicide.[27] Everything in his view depends upon humanity rising above the fear of death because the idea of God is given force and reality by this fear. To kill oneself simply in order to demonstrate that one does not fear death will, he believes, enable him (and through him the rest of humanity) to become god-men.[28] By killing himself he thus hopes to redeem humanity.[29] However, he does not and cannot attain the liberation he longs for, and remains trapped by his ideas and his fellow nihilist conspirators. While he kills himself, he is thus not able to affirm life and remains rooted in negation.

None of Dostoevsky's characters ever moves beyond such active nihilism to what Nietzsche calls radical or Dionysian nihilism. This form of nihilism in his view accepts and affirms the idea of the Eternal Recurrence. It thus requires a harder, more fatalistic type of human being who can not only endure the burden of nihilism but also turn it into a new form of cheerfulness. Taken to its end, Nietzsche thus believes that nihilism need not end in murder, madness, or suicide but opens up the possibility of an exuberant, joyful, and potentially superhuman existence.

IVAN KARAMAZOV

Dostoevsky's most comprehensive exploration of the nihilist mentality was his portrayal of Ivan Karamazov in the *Brothers Karamazov*. While Nietzsche never read this work, Dostoevsky's Ivan poses the greatest challenge to Nietzsche's reading of nihilism and reveals in a particularly vivid fashion the gulf that separates the two thinkers. Moreover, the demands of the radical nihilism that Nietzsche describes in his final teaching become more concrete in the light of Ivan's response to the death of God, his recognition of human mortality and the meaninglessness of human striving.

Like many students of his generation, Ivan fell under the spell of modern Western ideas while at the university. Positivism, utilitarianism, and natural science led him to question the existence of God and the possibility of life after death. Like Turgenev's Bazarov (and unlike Chernyshevsky's Rakhmetov, and Dostoevsky's own Kirillov) Ivan is not obviously involved in revolutionary political activity. Nihilism for him is principally a moral-theological problem only tangentially related to politics. His studies have led him to believe there is no natural impulse or law of nature that men should love one another and thus no natural ground for communal life. All such love, he concludes, must therefore be due to a belief in immortality. Hence, if belief in Christianity with its promise of a final judgment dries up, there will no longer be any restraint on egoism, for if nothing is immoral, everything including cannibalism will be lawful.

Ivan expresses such opinions brashly and without regard to their consequences. Despite the apparent daring with which he proclaims these ideas, however, they impose real psychological costs on him. In this respect he is a much more serious character than Pyotr Verkhovensky, the leader of the nihilist group in *The Demons* who plays at being a nihilist revolutionary but never suffers the spiritual torments that beset Dostoevsky's other nihilistic protagonists. Dostoevsky gives us a graphic indication of the burdens such thinking imposes on Ivan in three chapters of *Brothers*, "On Rebellion," "The Grand Inquisitor," and "The Devil. Ivan's Nightmare." The first two are part of a lengthy discussion between Ivan and his pious younger brother Alyosha. The third is a dialogue between Ivan and the devil when Ivan is suffering from a brain fever. The three chapters taken as a whole spell out with great force the nihilist position that Dostoevsky rejects.

In "On Rebellion" Ivan suggests that either there is no God and then nothing is evil or there is a God and he is utterly complicit in evil. The example he uses to prove this thesis is the torture and murder of innocent children, those who have not "eaten of the apple," and are thus without sin. The fact that such crimes occur indicates to Ivan that God does not exist or that he is not just or merciful. In either case existence is meaningless.

Ivan is aware that there is a traditional Christian answer to this charge, that such evil is only apparent and not real because finite beings cannot understand God's infinite purpose. Humans thus cannot understand how the justice and goodness of the whole may require the apparent injustice of specific parts. Moreover, scripture indicates that at the end of time God's justice will be made evident and everyone will be reconciled with one another in him. Ivan, however, asserts that even if there is a final revelation of the necessity of the suffering of the innocent, it cannot justify that suffering, nor the God that allowed it. No future knowledge or event can undo the suffering of innocent children or reconcile them with their tormentors. Such actions are simply unjustifiable. There is no theodicy. Thus Ivan declares that he "gives back his ticket." Either there is no God and the world is simply a set of random events in which everything is permitted, including the torture and murder of innocent children, or there is a God who created and rules the world, and he is evil. In either case, Ivan wants no part of it. He renounces existence.

Ivan is convinced that if God exists he is guilty of allowing such abominations. Like Kirillov he rejects the notion that there could be a utilitarian justification for such suffering, pointing out that the happiness of all cannot be purchased by the sacrifice of even one innocent. In contrast to Kirillov, however, he loves life more than the meaning of it. As he puts it, "I have a longing for life, and I go on living in spite of logic. Though I may not believe in the order of the universe, yet I love the sticky little leaves as they open in spring. I love the blue sky, I love some people, whom one loves sometimes without knowing why. I love some great deeds done by men, though I've long since ceased perhaps to have faith in them, yet from old habit one's heart prizes them."[30] As a result and in contrast to Kirillov, Ivan is not defeated by his nihilistic ideas.[31] He is sustained by his sensuality (what he calls the Karamazov baseness). In this respect he is closer to Nietzsche than to the hyper-rational Kirillov. Reason and a desire for justice and an end to evil are important for him but there is a deep wellspring of love that sustains him.

Ivan's second argument is developed in "The Grand Inquisitor," which extends the argument in "On Rebellion" by showing that not only God the creator but God the redeemer is complicit in human suffering. It is thus directed not against the idea of an omnipotent and omnibenevolent Father but against the gnostic notion of a divine Son who can redeem the evil Father's errors. The argument is presented through a story set during the Spanish Inquisition in Seville. The city is dominated by a Grand Inquisitor, a hardened old man who rules through a mixture of religious awe and terrifying violence. Just a day after an auto-da-fé in which almost one hundred heretics were burned alive, Christ appears in the midst of a crowd. Although he is there only for a short visit, he is immediately recognized and adored by the people. The Grand Inquisitor has him taken into custody and imprisoned in a cell, where the Inquisitor visits him in the middle of the night. The rest of the story is a monologue in which the Inquisitor explains and attempts to justify his life to Christ. It is a defense of his own actions and a condemnation of Christ for failing to alleviate human suffering.

The Inquisitor's basic accusation against Christ is that God granted all human beings free will but granted only a tiny number of them the ability to make good use of it. Freedom thus causes suffering for most human beings. Only a few benefit from it by entering into paradise, while all of the rest are condemned to eternal damnation. The Inquisitor suggests that Christ could have saved all of humanity from such suffering but chose not to do so. Drawing on the account of Satan's temptation of Christ in the wilderness, he argues that Christ rejected the three keys to human happiness and well-being, all of which were revealed to him in Satan's three temptations. He argues that miracle, mystery, and authority are crucial to human happiness: the miracle (of converting stones to bread) because it satisfies the basic human instinct for survival, mystery because it provides human beings with something to live for, and authority because it removes the burden of freedom and choice that most men cannot bear. Christ, according to the Inquisitor, knew how necessary all three of these were to human well-being, but rejected them, leaving human beings with an absolute freedom so that a small number could prove themselves worthy of salvation.

The Inquisitor asserts that he and those like him took a more humane path, entering into league with Satan against Christ in the interest of the vast majority of humanity, taking the burden of freedom upon themselves and providing the masses with bread and a comforting belief in salvation, thus relieving them of the terrible necessity of a choice that they could not make or endure. It is wrong, the Inquisitor tells Christ, to blame the weak for what they can never do, and it would be wrong to blame him and his fellows for deceiving and ruling over them for their own good. They, he claims, love men more than Christ does, and thus should not be blamed for what they have done because it was done not for personal gain but for the love of mankind. To put the argument in theological terms, the Inquisitor argues that it is not possible to love both God and one's neighbor, and that his choice of the latter was more "Christian" than Christ's choice of the former. Christ does not answer but simply kisses the Inquisitor on the lips, and the Inquisitor then lets him depart.[32]

When Ivan finishes, Alyosha realizes that the entire story was only a reflection of the struggle going on in Ivan's soul. This terrifies him. He argues that no one can live with such notions in one's heart. This also seems to be Dostoevsky's opinion since in the end Ivan is driven mad when confronted with the realization of his ideas. The precipitating cause of Ivan's collapse is his discovery that his arguments have persuaded his half-brother Smerdyakov that all things are lawful and, as a result, he has killed their father and let the blame fall on their fourth brother, Dmitry. Ivan comes to believe that he is responsible for his father's murder and cannot bear his guilt. He berates Smerdyakov for misunderstanding him and leaves. This pulls the moral rug out from under Smerdyakov's feet, and with no further way to justify his action to himself, he hangs himself. Back in his room, Ivan falls into a fever and in his delirium has a discussion with the devil.

Throughout this feverish dialogue, Ivan is never sure whether the devil is an independent being or his alter-ego, some darker part of himself.[33] Ultimately, however, this does not matter, since the devil has all of the limitations of human beings, and thus has no knowledge that transcends human experience. Like Ivan he exists in doubt, certain only of the "I think, therefore I am" of Descartes, but uncertain whether anything outside of himself, including God, exists. The devil is thus as trapped in the prison of self-consciousness as Ivan himself.

In his dialogue with the devil, Ivan is brought face-to-face with the consequences of his earlier arguments against faith. If there is no God, then man is god, as Kirillov recognized, but, if so, then this god or man-god is indistinguishable from the devil, and thus incapable of doing good, whatever his intentions. Without God, man or the man-god is lost without hope on the empty sea of self-consciousness.

At the core of modern self-consciousness is a will to know and to command that seeks certainty and security. The path to such knowledge and power, however, depends upon the negative force of methodological doubt. To know for modernity is not to rely on authority, however sacred or august, but to grasp the truth oneself. This truth, as Descartes put it, must be confirmed by the mind as indubitable. The test of knowledge for modernity is thus methodological doubt that calls everything into question and seeks to ground knowledge on a *fundamentum inconcussum absolutum veritatis*, on an "absolutely immoveable foundational truth." It is for this reason that the critical spirit that calls everything into question is the basis of Western rationalism. As Hegel and his successors recognized, self-consciousness is thus negativity. Goethe personified this element in Mephistopheles, who describes himself as "the spirit that always negates."[34] Ivan's devil is only another in a long line of these demonic, critical spirits. His negativity, however, is ultimately greater than that of Mephistopheles. Mephistopheles tried to do evil but always ended up doing good because God had ordered the world so that all actions have a happy ending. Kant shared this teleological assumption. Ivan's devil, by contrast, wants to do good but always ends up doing evil. The world, as the Grand Inquisitor correctly made clear, is out of joint and everything as a result inevitably ends in tragedy.[35] Thus, even the most powerful god-man-devil lives in unhappiness and dreams like Ivan himself of being a simple merchant's wife who is able to believe and live happily in ignorance. The fate of the devil in this sense is no different from the fate of any man who lives without faith.

Ivan's devil understands that this negativity also has a political dimension, but he discounts its importance. He knows that the "new men," the nihilist revolutionaries, are bent on destroying everything. He argues, however, that such revolutionary measures are unnecessary. When men deny God, he asserts, the old conception of the universe and the prevailing moral order will come to an end without the need for the cannibalism these revolutionaries want to practice. The universal rule of God, according to Ivan's devil, will then be replaced by the reign of the man-god who will infinitely extend humanity's power over nature.[36]

Dostoevsky does not deny that this process will eventually make life better here on earth. In this respect the utilitarian dream of progress is not vacuous. What he suggests is that in the absence of God and immortality no one will have any reason to love one another or act in concert with one another. Indeed, each person who realizes the truth and thus becomes a man-god will have every reason to act on purely egoistic principles as Smerdyakov did.

Such a life, however, is not worth living even if one can live in a crystal palace. The path that rests on doubt and negation rather than love thus leads only to madness, murder, and suicide. With nothing to give man direction he will wander over the earth without a home, without a destination, and without anyone to accompany him on his journey.

DOSTOEVSKY AND NIETZSCHE'S FINAL TEACHING

Nietzsche learned a great deal from Dostoevsky's account of the nihilist psyche but was not convinced that Dostoevsky had finally understood nihilism or that he had adequately grasped the possibility of finding a way through nihilism to a higher form of existence. He knew from his reading of *The Demons* that Dostoevsky had considered such a possibility but had rejected it as an impossible attempt to transcend the limits of human nature. Viewed against the backdrop of this daunting account of nihilism, we can begin to glimpse the daring character of Nietzsche's final teaching, which charts a path into and through the abyss that swallows up Dostoevsky's heroes. Nietzsche realizes that following this path is extraordinarily dangerous, but he believes it is the only alternative to the pessimism and despair of passive nihilism and the desire for revenge that characterizes revolutionary nihilism.

Both Kirillov and Ivan exemplify the moral and psychological burden of nihilism. Both seek to live without God, but the effort to do so drives them to madness and suicide. Affirming the doctrine of the Eternal Recurrence, however, demands that one live an even more demanding atheistic life. It does not mean just saying that one does not believe in God, as Kirillov and Ivan do, but willingly living without God, as they are unable to do. Moreover, this willing is not simply the willing of what one finds pleasing or entertaining or even "most beautiful," but willing *everything*, that is, everything that is beautiful, everything that is ugly, and everything that is horrible. Ivan argued that one could not believe in or affirm a God who allowed the innocent to be tortured. Such a world was either ruled by blind chance or an evil demon. Kirillov more or less agreed but thought that the world could be redeemed by his suicide. Nietzsche's teaching of the Eternal Recurrence is an effort to force men to confront just such a purposeless universe. In Nietzsche's view his teaching is a hammer that will shatter most men—even such higher men as Ivan and Kirillov—because it demands that they affirm the torture of the innocent, not as the act of a malicious deity or the product of blind chance but as what they want, as what they will, and as what they do. Ivan is shattered by the discovery that Smerdyakov murdered their father because he followed Ivan's ideas to their logical conclusion. When faced with this fact, Ivan (like Raskolnikov) is plunged into guilt and wants to be punished.[37]

Nietzsche argues that the Ivans and Kirillovs of the world who want to overcome nihilism must not merely affirm such deeds done in their name or in the name of their ideas but want to do such things themselves. This extreme affirmation is crucial for escaping from the spirit of revenge and living joyfully in the face of suffering. The guilt that Dostoevsky's nihilists feel, in Nietzsche's view, is a reflection of their weakness, a consequence of their pity and thus a reflection of the continued dominance of Christian values. This weakness is not shared by Dostoevsky's Siberian criminals whom Nietzsche so admires, and in this sense these criminals are better models for the type of human beings who can deal with nihilism than the intellectuals Dostoevsky portrays. What is needed is not a guilty conscience but a hard fatalism, *amor fati*. Such men not only do not flinch from affirming such deeds, they actually draw strength and joy from such an affirmation. For Nietzsche such men as Kirillov and Ivan are decadents, sick and weak, and thus unable to pass through nihilism, unable to move beyond the midpoint between beast and superman at which the believer must become a destroyer. They therefore must perish in order to make room for a stronger, healthier human being, the true man-god who is beyond good and evil but still the foremost proponent of life itself.

Such an affirmation carries Nietzsche beyond Kirillov, Ivan, and even the Grand Inquisitor. Like Kirillov, the Grand Inquisitor seeks to take the burden of guilt upon himself, to rule human beings, to provide them with their daily bread, give some purpose to their lives, and subordinate their rebellious instincts to authority. Despite his obvious strength and power he is driven not by a desire for self-overcoming or a desire to create something greater than himself but by pity. He had the strength to be one of the elect but apparently concluded (as Ivan did) that a God who allows suffering when he can alleviate it is not worthy of his worship. The Inquisitor is thus the image of a paternalistic authoritarian ruling humanity for its own good, perhaps modeled on Hegel's notion of a universal class of philosophically educated bureaucrats or Plato's philosopher kings. Nietzsche believes that such rule would only perpetuate the weakness at the heart of contemporary human beings who seek solace in the dream of a better world.

The construction of such an imaginary world may seem to be an act of charity, but for Nietzsche it is an act of weakness, an attempt by the slaves to realize an imaginary revenge on their masters by creating a place that is everything that this world is not, an eternal realm of being in place of the actual world of becoming, a place where the strong cannot do what they want and where the meek do in fact inherit the earth. The preeminent source of the desire for revenge in Nietzsche's view is the inexorable character of becoming. Individuals may believe that they are free in some sense, but even the strongest are always governed by the dead hand of the past, by antecedent causes that not only limit the scope of human willing but form it into the sort of will it is. As Zarathustra puts it, the "It was" is the great rock against which the will itself shatters. Because we find ourselves always subject to this power, we attempt to exact revenge in the present by punishing ourselves and others for what occurs as if we were the actual cause of the event. The lust for revenge, however, is an entirely reactive passion, and as long as we are driven by it we are incapable of acting freely or actually willing or creating anything at all.

In order to overcome the spirit of revenge, according to Zarathustra, it would be necessary to will backward, which on the surface seems impossible. However, Zarathustra suggests that it is possible if in willing forward one also willed "backward." This could only be the case, however, if the order of all events forms a circle. This is, of course, nothing other than the idea of the Eternal Recurrence of all things, which consequently opens up the possibility for overcoming the desire for revenge.[38] But the idea of the Eternal Recurrence is just an idea, a possibility that may or may not be true. Why then does Nietzsche take it so seriously?

Many scholars have pointed out that while the Eternal Recurrence Nietzsche describes is possible, it is not necessary and is indemonstrable. It thus seems a slender thread upon which to hang his teaching. Nietzsche was not unaware of this fact. In his notes after 1881 he occasionally tries to piece together something like an empirical or scientific explanation for the idea, but he never put any of this into print and it seems unlikely that he ever considered these speculations actual demonstrations.

A scientific proof of the idea would in any case undermine the psychological effect Nietzsche imagines the idea will have. The idea is a test, an experiment in which one attempts to live one's life as if the idea were true. To affirm the idea of the Eternal Recurrence in this sense is not just to accept the possibility of the worst but its actuality, to will it, to believe in it. For Nietzsche in contrast to Dostoevsky it is thus important to imagine a world in which innocent children are tortured and killed in order to be able to say not "I give back my ticket," but "Once more," to want to be the author of such deeds, to want to be eternally both the pain and the joy of becoming.

For Nietzsche, only someone who can will in this way can overcome the pessimism and despair that destroy Kirillov and Ivan. The Grand Inquisitor is a step in this direction but he too is driven not by his desire for a higher humanity but by pity and a longing to ease man's earthly burden.[39] The superman that Nietzsche imagines is the Grand Inquisitor freed from pity and his desire for revenge, the Grand Inquisitor (or as Nietzsche put it, Caesar) with the soul of Christ, an active rather than a reactive being who guides and shapes humanity not as a result of pity or out of charity but according to his own aesthetic sensibilities and desires. He is supremely alive and does not seek to ease his own burden or that of his fellow human beings but to increase both. He is an artist and a tyrant. This superman, in Nietzsche's view, however, does not yet exist and can only come into being as the result of a long process of breeding tougher, more pitiless human beings. Such beings, however, can only come to be through a centuries-long process of tempering under the harshest conditions of war and struggle.[40] Only then, when the last vestiges of Christianity have been eliminated, will the superman be possible.

Nietzsche did not complete the task of spelling out this final teaching. What form it would have taken remains unknowable. That he imagined it would provoke the Great Noon, an apocalyptic day of decision for European civilization, however, seems incontestable. Here too the parallel to Dostoevsky is enlightening. Dostoevsky imagined that it was the Russian national destiny to bring about the advent of the Kingdom of God as the consummation of human history.[41] Moreover, he was convinced that the critical turning point in human history was near at hand. The appearance of the man-god in his view was an indication that the Antichrist had arrived. He was convinced that the reappearance of the God-man could not be far behind, and that his return would redeem not merely man but nature itself. Nietzsche adopted a position that was radically opposed to that of Dostoevsky. The new world would be brought into being in his view not by the appearance of the God-man but by the coming to power of the true man-god, Nietzsche's superman. For Nietzsche, however, this event lies on the far side of two centuries of war and destruction. The true enemies for him in the present are Christianity and Christian values. This fact is spelled out clearly and unequivocally in the phrase Nietzsche places at the end of his final work, *Ecce Homo*: "Dionysus versus the Crucified." Ironically, these words might have been penned by Dostoevsky as well, although he certainly would have been pulling for the other side.

FINAL REFLECTIONS

Despite their shared analysis of the origins of nihilism, Dostoevsky and Nietzsche diverge in a profound way when it comes to the appropriate response to this problem. For both the central question turns on man's relationship to God within the broader context of Christianity. They both recognized that Cartesian skepticism and modern science had undermined faith in Christianity. They also recognized the looming disaster that the loss of faith entails. This disaster in their view was evident above all in the careers and fates of the nihilist intellectuals. Both Nietzsche and Dostoevsky felt a profound kinship with such men. Both, however, found a way out of the nihilistic abyss they encountered. Their paths out of nihilism and their prescriptions for dealing with it, however, were quite different.

Dostoevsky believed that the path that humanity has to follow is the path of faith, a path rooted in the love of God and his creation. This relationship in his view is made possible through the mediation of Christ, the God-man, whose incarnation is the demonstration of the divinity of all created things. Dostoevsky identifies such a religious stance with the traditional faith of the Russian peasant, exemplified in Father Zosima in *The Brothers Karamazov*. Zosima's faith fills him with a love for all things that gives meaning and purpose to his life.[42] By contrast, Nietzsche believes what is needed is not a return to Christian faith, but a hardening and culling of humanity by war and a struggle for preeminence. In his view the ultimate source of nihilism lies in Christianity and hence a return to it would be pointless. War and conflict are also inevitable given the irreversible decline in faith. The consequent hardening of humanity will then produce not Dostoevsky's imaginary God-man but an elite out of which the superman will arise. This superman will be able to overcome the spirit of revenge by affirming the doctrine of the Eternal Recurrence of the Same, which will allow him to become truly active and creative and thus able to give human beings new values and purposes for their lives. This superman is clearly related to the man-god whom Dostoevsky sees as the epitome of all that is wrong with modern life. Dostoevsky rejects the path of willfulness in favor of faith and Nietzsche rejects the path of faith in favor of will.[43]

All this said, it would be a mistake to conclude that their differences can simply be described as a disagreement between a believer and a nonbeliever. Both Dostoevsky and Nietzsche stand within the larger penumbra of Christianity. Christianity has always been a syncretistic religion that combines many different streams of thought.[44] From the very beginning Christians have debated the very nature of their God, and this question was resolved in favor of Trinitarianism (as opposed to Arianism) only by imperial power. Even after the settlement of this fundamental question, however, the relationship between the three persons of the godhead remained a continuing point of dispute that erupted time and time again. Moreover, even when Christians agreed about the nature of God, they often disagreed about the nature and weight of God's attributes. On this question Nietzsche and Dostoevsky clearly part company.

Both Nietzsche and Dostoevsky reject the scholastic view of a preeminently rational God, just as they both reject the Enlightenment notion of a rational humanity and a rational cosmos.[45] Their differences seem to turn more around their view of the other two principal attributes of the divine: omnibenevolence and omnipotence, that is, love and power. For Dostoevsky the principal attribute of God and his creation is love, while for Nietzsche the central principle that governs the cosmos is the will to power. Dostoevsky sees such willfulness as the key element in nihilism that leads to the man-god. Nietzsche sees a reliance upon transcendent love in face of the manifestly tragic circumstances of life a debilitating self-deception. For Dostoevsky the only way to escape nihilism is faith in the coming God-man. For Nietzsche it is only by means of an affirmation of the doctrine of the Eternal Recurrence of all things that the superman can come to be.[46]

Both Dostoevsky and Nietzsche see human beings playing a decisive role in overcoming nihilism. For Dostoevsky the people are the fount of all salvation. The particular people Dostoevsky has in mind are the Russian peasantry, who in his view are the true repository of Orthodox faith, which alone has sustained an authentic Christianity in the face of modern Western rationalism. Salvation is only possible if the intellectuals and rulers bow down to the people and follow their pious lead. Poets and other artists like Pushkin who hearken to the people's sensibility give this spirituality form. Indeed, Dostoevsky sees himself playing a similar role in demonstrating concretely the possibility of a truly Christian life of love.

Nietzsche discounts the importance of the existing people but recognizes the need for the formation of a new people in order to bring about the transformation he longs for. This people will be formed, however, not by love or a reliance on existing traditions but by war and struggle that will obliterate the old faith and create a new people capable of instituting a new one. Nietzsche's vision of the future is thus much more aristocratic and less communitarian than Dostoevsky's. It is also much less nationalistic. For Dostoevsky it is the Russians and particularly those who have clung to Slavic traditions who are the way into the future. Nietzsche rests his hopes not on Frenchmen or Germans but on "good Europeans." It is from among this cosmopolitan group tempered by war and by the affirmation of the Eternal Recurrence that a superhuman artist-tyrant-poet-legislator will arise. This "genius of the heart" as Nietzsche refers to him in *Beyond Good and Evil* will give men new values and new goals.

While on the surface Nietzsche's prescription may seem atheistic and the epitome of secular humanism, there are many reasons to see it as deeply connected to a vision of God that focuses almost exclusively on divine will to the exclusion of all other characteristics and attributes. Nietzsche points us in this direction with his references to Dionysus and to "the golden wonder" "for whom only future songs will find names," as he puts it in *Zarathustra*.[47] For him the artist plays a crucial role in unveiling this new god and founding this new faith. It is, however, finally a faith for the valiant and the powerful rather than the meek and pious. While Nietzsche learned a great deal from Dostoevsky, he parts company with him on basic moral questions. While Dostoevsky believed that the death of God leads to madness, murder, and suicide, Nietzsche was convinced that at least for the few it opened up the possibility of a new cheerfulness and a tragic nobility.

NOTES

1. Nietzsche wrote to Overbeck on Feb. 23 and Mar. 7, 1887, describing his discovery of Dostoevsky and comparing it to his discovery of Schopenhauer. C. A. Miller, "Nietzsche's Discovery of Dostoevsky," *Nietzsche-Studien* 2 (1973): 202. Nietzsche's references to Dostoevsky in his letters can be found in Friedrich Nietzsche, *Nietzsche Briefwechsel: Kritische Gesamtausgabe*, ed. Giorgi Colli and Mazzino Montinari (New York and Berlin: de Gruyter, 1975–84), III, 5: 21, 24, 27, 41, 50, 75, 106, 451, 457, 483.

2. Nietzsche knew Dostoevsky only through French translations. On the texts Nietzsche read see Janko Lavrin, "A Note on Nietzsche and Dostoevsky," *Russian Review* 28:2 (Apr. 1969): 160. "The Landlady" and *Notes from the Underground* were presented in the French translation as two chapters of a single story. For evidence on *The Idiot* see the suggestive passage in the *Nachlass*: Friedrich Nietzsche, *Werke: Kritische Gesamtausgabe*, ed. Giorgio Colli and Mazzino Montinari (Berlin: Walter de Gruyter, 1967), VIII, 3: 59. The *Werke* is hereafter abbreviated as *KGW*.

3. See *Ecce Homo*, *KGW* VI, 3: 333.

4. According to Janz he imparted it only to his closest friends, and then in hushed tones, apparently hoping to gather them together into a secret society to help spread this teaching. Curt Paul Janz, *Nietzsche: Biographie*, 3 vols. (Munich: Hanser, 1978–79), 2: 149, 267, 280.

5. The idea of the Eternal Recurrence in this way solves the problem Kant poses in the Third Antinomy of the contradiction between freedom and natural necessity. If in fact all things do recur eternally, then the possible coincidence of a causality through nature and a causality through freedom that Kant hypothesizes would be realized, and absolute freedom would be identical with absolute necessity.

6. Zarathustra was thus not merely a literary creation but the supreme deed of a world-governing spirit and creator of truth. Janz, *Nietzsche*, 2: 164.

7. C. A. Miller, "The Nihilist as Tempter-Redeemer: Dostoevsky's 'Man-God' in Nietzsche's Notebooks," *Nietzsche-Studien* 4 (1975): 166.

8. *Genealogy of Morals*. *KGW* VI, 2: 351.

9. Cited in Janz, *Nietzsche*, 2: 289.

10. Nietzsche to Georg Brandes, Nov. 20, 1888.

11. This was the task of his next two works, *Beyond Good and Evil* and *The Genealogy of Morals*. Nietzsche conceived the *Genealogy* as a continuation of *Beyond*, and even considered republishing them as a single work. The connection of these works to *Zarathustra* and his final teaching is evident in his reference to *Beyond* in one of his notes as a "Preface to a Philosophy of the Eternal Recurrence." *KGW* VII, 2: 233–35. See also VII, 3: 209–11.

12. In the three related works of 1888, *Twilight of the Idols*, *The Case of Wagner*, and *Ecce Homo*, Nietzsche lays out this path in much greater detail.

Michael Allen Gillespie

13. On this point see Erik von der Luft and Douglas Stenburg, "Dostoevskii's Specific Influence on Nietzsche's Preface to *Daybreak*," *Journal of the
History of Ideas* 52:3 (July–Sept. 1991): 442. He could not have seen the work
before November 20, 1886, when it was published, and must have read it before
he sent the preface to the publisher on December 22, 1886. Ibid., 443. Miller
suggests that the imagery is not dispositive as an allusion to Dostoevsky and may
have come from *Beyond Good and Evil*. Miller, "Nietzsche's Discovery," 210–12.
See also Richard Avremenko, "Bedeviled by Boredom: A Voegelinian Reading of
Dostoevsky's *Possessed*," *Humanitas* 17:1–2 (2004): 108–38.

14. *Friedrich Nietzsches Gesammelte Briefe*, 5 vols. (Leipzig: Insel, 1902–9),
4: 285.

15. Miller, "Nietzsches 'Soteriopsychologie' im Spiegel von Dostoevskys
Auseinandersetzung mit dem europäischen Nihilismus," *Nietzsche-Studien* 7
(1978): 130–31.

16. Miller, "Nietzsches 'Soteriopsychologie,'" 132–33.

17. Luft and Stenburg, "Dostoevskii's Influence," 446–47. See also Lavrin,
"A Note," 165, and Ekaterina Poljakova, "Die 'Bosheit' der Russen: Nietzsches
Deutung Russlands in der Perspektive russischer Moralphilosophie," *Nietzsche-
Studien* 35 (2006): 213.

18. Miller, "Nietzsches 'Soteriopsychologie,'" 142–44.

19. On this matter he was deeply influenced by the nineteenth-century revival of Russian monasticism led by monks at the Optina Monastery, and by the
philosophical-theological work of his young friend Vladimir Soloviev. On Soloviev see L. M. Lopatin, "The Philosophy of Vladimir Soloviev," *Mind* 25:100 (Oct.
1916): 425–60.

20. In his late notes Nietzsche spoke of two hundred years of war and destruction necessary for the hardening of humanity and establishing the foundation of a thousand-year Dionysian empire. On this point see *KGW* VIII, 2: 41,
313, 431.

21. On this matter Nietzsche, intentionally or due to misrepresentations by
the translators, transforms Dostoevsky's praise of the decency of these men into
a praise of their criminal and militaristic backgrounds. See Hartwig Frank, "Die
Metapher Russland im Denken Nietzsches," *Nietzsche-Studien* 36 (2007): 351–53.
In other words he assimilates them to Stendhal's (anti)heroes rather than por-
traying them in their true light. This misunderstanding or misconstruction makes
it difficult to draw any more comprehensive conclusions about the impact of this
work on Nietzsche.

22. For a fuller account of the depiction of nihilists in Russian literature see
my *Nihilism before Nietzsche* (Chicago: University of Chicago Press, 1995), 135–73.

23. The source of the term is almost certainly Russian. On this point see
Elisabeth Kuhn, "Nietzsches Quelle des Nihilismus-Begriffs," *Nietzsche-Studien*
13 (1984): 262–63.

24. On this point see Elisabeth Kuhn, *Friedrich Nietzsches Philosophie des europäischen Nihilismus* (Berlin: de Gruyter, 1992), and my "Nietzsche and the Anthropology of Nihilism," *Nietzsche-Studien* 28 (1999): 141–55.

25. He was misled on this point by Mérimée and Bourget. On this point see Elisabeth Kuhn, "Nietzsches Quelle," 262–63. Feuerbach was almost certainly more important for their thinking than Schopenhauer.

26. Miller, "The Nihilist," 212.

27. Ibid., 193.

28. On Kirillov's man-god see Miller, "The Nihilist," 168, 188, and Lavrin, "A Note," 166.

29. Miller, "The Nihilist," 209.

30. Dostoevsky, *The Brothers Karamazov*, trans. Constance Garnett (New York: Modern Library, 1996), 242.

31. Kirillov is ultimately dominated by logic rather than life, and is defeated by his idea. He is a decadent who over-intellectualizes everything. Miller, "The Nihilist," 205–8.

32. A great deal of this story reflects Dostoevsky's hatred of Catholicism and the Jesuits in particular, who he believed sought such dominion over men, but Ivan discounts this element, suggesting that this Inquisitor is motivated not by self-interest or a longing for power but by a love of humanity. For a thoughtful discussion of the chapter see Ellis Sandoz, "Philosophical Anthropology and Dostoevsky's 'Legend of the Grand Inquisitor,'" *Review of Politics* 26:3 (July 1964): 353–77.

33. Michael Stroeber argues that the devil is Ivan's hallucination. Michael Stroeber, "Dostoevsky's Devil: The Will to Power," *Journal of Religion* 74:1 (Jan. 1994): 38.

34. Goethe, *Faust*, line 1338.

35. As Lavrin points out, if God is dead then the universe is the vaudeville of the devil. "A Note," 162.

36. The argument for the man-god that the devil develops here and that Kirillov articulates in *The Demons* has its origins in the thought of the Left Hegelian Ludwig Feuerbach, who claims that the necessary turning point of history will be the moment when man becomes aware and admits that his consciousness of God is nothing but the consciousness of man as a species. Ludwig Feuerbach, *The Essence of Christianity*, trans. Marian Evans (London: Chapman, 1854), 267. This notion played a powerful role among Russian nihilists.

37. Stroeber, "Dostoevsky's Devil," 36.

38. Dostoevsky's devil mentions this possibility in his discussion with Ivan but considers it only in passing, and draws no conclusions about its significance.

39. On the similarity of the Grand Inquisitor and Zarathustra, see Lavrin, "A Note," 167.

40. In this respect he perhaps most closely resembles Shigalov, who was also willing to sacrifice 90 percent of the population so that the other 10 percent

could be truly free and creative. This element of Nietzsche's thought is already clear in his early essay *The Greek State*. See also *KGW* VII, 2: 81.

41. Miller, "The Nihilist," 185.

42. On this point see Geoff Uyleman, "Nietzsche and Dostoevsky's Creative and Resolving Existential Despair," *Aporia* 15:1 (2005): 32; Lavrin, "A Note," 170; Stroeber, "Dostoevsky's Devil," 42.

43. Miller, "Nietzsche's Discovery," 254. Miller suggests that Dostoevsky's treatment of Kirillov can be read as a critique of Nietzsche. Miller, "The Nihilist," 224. Lavrin sees Ivan's conversation with the Devil as proleptic critique of Nietzsche. Lavrin, "A Note," 167.

44. On this point see Mark Lilla, *The Stillborn God* (New York: Vintage, 2007), 18–39.

45. Stroeber believes that both thinkers draw on Jacob Boehm's mysticism of the will. Stroeber, "Dostoevsky's Devil," 27, 38. While there is much to be said for this argument, there are many more immediate sources for Nietzsche's notion of the will.

46. For a defense of Dostoevsky's position, see David Walsh, "Dostoevsky's Discovery of the Christian Foundation of Politics," *Religion and Literature* 9:2 (Summer 1987): 49–73.

47. *KGW* VI, 1: 276.

Joshua Foa Dienstag

Nietzsche's Pessimism in the Shadow
of Dostoevsky's

IT IS A SCENE CINEMATIC in its possibilities: Fried-
rich Nietzsche, impoverished and largely friendless, is living in a cheap
rooming house in Nice in the winter of 1887. He is nearly blind but it doesn't
stop him from perusing the town's bookstores. He doesn't buy very often—
both because he cannot afford it and because he moves so often that pos-
sessions are an encumbrance. But one day he comes across a recent translation of Dostoevsky's *Notes from the Underground*, which has been given the
French title *L'esprit souterrain*. One imagines him flipping the pages, at first
idly, then with increasing interest. Quickly, he decides he has encountered
something special, a kindred spirit. He buys the book and tears through it.
Then he reads everything else from Dostoevsky (in French) that he can get
his hands on, including *The House of the Dead* and *The Idiot*.

This much, and it is not very much, we know from Nietzsche's letters of
the period.[1] We know from further stray remarks in other letters and late writings some of what attracted him to Dostoevsky: his psychology, his analysis of
crime and criminality, and his image of Prince Myshkin as a holy "idiot," a term
Nietzsche applied to himself more than once in his last writings.

Here, however, I want to suggest a further point of identification that
may throw some light on what each writer considered central to his political
and cultural aims. As it happens, in the last months of 1886, just before
he encountered Dostoevsky, Nietzsche was engaged in a project of self-
examination and self-definition through a particular mechanism. His books
had, to this point, sold very poorly. Furthermore, his publisher, whom he had
initially met through their mutual admiration for Richard Wagner, had become more reluctant to support Nietzsche's work as the philosopher's alienation from Wagner had increased in the 1880s. Nietzsche had found a more
enthusiastic publisher, however, and in addition to printing his new books,
this firm had bought up the stock of remaining copies of his earlier works
and planned to reissue them.[2]

To support the reissue, Nietzsche was asked to write new prefaces for his previous writings. These would be printed up separately and then bound together with the existing unsold copies to form a new "second" edition. Nietzsche took to the project with enthusiasm and wrote a series of prefaces very quickly in the last months of 1886 even though he was moving around the cities of southern Europe at the same time in an effort to find a mild climate. The most famous of these prefaces is the "Attempt at a Self-Criticism" which was added to *The Birth of Tragedy* and which has formed a touchstone for Nietzsche commentators ever since. But the "Attempt" was not written in isolation. There were also new prefaces for *Human, All Too Human, Assorted Opinions and Maxims, Daybreak*, and *The Gay Science*, along with a large, new concluding section for the latter.[3]

Reading the prefaces collectively, as I will do in this essay, one gets the sense of an author taking the measure of his own efforts and coming to some conclusions, not exactly new in themselves, but now more clearly in focus. Foremost among these was a growing certainty about what Nietzsche would call the intellectual project he was engaged in. In the new section of *The Gay Science*, Nietzsche writes of a new kind of pessimism, a "pessimism of the future," as his "*proprium* and *ipsissimum*," that is, as "my own and my quintessence."[4] In the new prefaces, and the new portion of *The Gay Science*, he repeatedly refers to himself as a pessimist and refers to his philosophy variously as "Dionysian pessimism" and as "a pessimism of strength."[5]

It was as a self-conscious pessimist, then, that Nietzsche came across Dostoevsky's books and, I will maintain here, it was as a pessimist that he found an affinity with them. Indeed, in one of his notebooks from that period, where he made a list of the different kinds of pessimism, he created a special category of "Russian pessimism" whose only entrants are Dostoevsky and (curiously perhaps) Tolstoy.[6] While all of Dostoevsky's books could be said to contribute to that categorization, I think there is a case to be made for the specific pessimism of *Notes from the Underground*, with its unusual narrator and structure.

The very fact that Nietzsche created such a list indicates that, for him, the term "pessimism" by itself is very unspecific. Indeed, one reason for Nietzsche's previous hesitance in embracing the term was its popular identification with the work of Schopenhauer. While Nietzsche had certainly been powerfully influenced by Schopenhauer (after a similar encounter in a bookstore) in an earlier period, by the late 1880s he had come to think of his own views as deeply opposed to those of the most well-known pessimist in Europe. He defined his own pessimism, therefore, in contradistinction to that of Schopenhauer and others, including, ultimately, Dostoevsky.

If we are to relate Nietzsche to Dostoevsky through the category of pessimism, then, we must be careful to understand what varieties of pessimism we have in mind. Certainly it is not a word that Dostoevsky used very often or that appeared to have any special significance for him (although the *Notes* refers to an "optimism" to be rejected).[7] But if Nietzsche's usage is idiosyncratic, then we should not be surprised that he might have had in mind concepts and categories that earlier writers might have used under another name.

Above all, we must be careful to indicate that in calling Dostoevsky a pessimist, Nietzsche does not necessarily mean to imply anything about his psychological makeup or even that of his characters. "Pessimism," to Nietzsche, is not the mark of a depressive or a misanthrope. The narrator of the *Notes* may (or may not) be both of these, but if he is a pessimist, that is a philosophical designation, though certainly one with implications for how we go about our everyday life. Nor is pessimism something that necessarily indicates passivity or resignation. As we shall see, it is instead a path to activity and even liberation.

NIETZSCHE'S PESSIMISM

Another note from *The Will to Power* bears the title "Pessimism in art?" and ends with the sentence: "How liberating is Dostoevsky!"[8] But at first glance, the note does not support the earlier labeling of Dostoevsky as a "Russian pessimist." Instead it seems to suggest that the very idea of a pessimistic art is a contradiction in terms. "Schopenhauer is wrong," Nietzsche writes, to believe that tragedy teaches resignation. "There is no such thing as pessimistic art—Art affirms . . . The things they display are ugly, but *that* they display them comes from their *pleasure in the ugly*." This description of Dostoevsky's art as something that craves ugliness is something, as we shall see later, that is also, for Nietzsche, a crucial part of his definition of tragedy.

By itself, this passage is hard to square with Nietzsche's praise of pessimism and his identification with it in the 1886 prefaces. But it begins to make more sense when, instead of concentrating on the generalizations, we focus instead on its rejection of pessimism as popularly understood, that is, pessimism in Schopenhauer's sense. That the outcome of pessimism was political or cultural "resignation" was a conclusion widely (and rightly) associated with Schopenhauer. It was also one that Nietzsche was profoundly concerned to reject. And he believed that he was joined in this pessimistic rejection of resignation by Dostoevsky. To understand why we need to look more closely at the understanding of pessimism in the 1886 prefaces and elsewhere in his work.

Schopenhauer was a contemporary of Hegel, but unlike Hegel, his fame and influence only appeared at the end of his career. Although his major systematic work, *The World as Will and Representation*, appeared in 1819, it was not until the publication of his collection of aphorisms, *Parerga und Paralipomena* (literally "appendices and omissions"), in 1851 that his work began to be noticed. The 1870s and 1880s brought an intellectual vogue of pessimism, particularly in Germany, where Schopenhauer's perspective was endorsed and extended by figures such as Eduard von Hartmann, whose *Philosophy of the Unconscious* appeared in 1869 and was very popular.

Thus pessimism, as Schopenhauer had outlined it, was a concept with which Nietzsche's readers were certainly familiar, whether or not they had adopted it. This made Nietzsche's task of introducing those readers to his own brand of pessimism more complicated. The 1886 prefaces bear out the effort to disentangle his pessimism from that of his predecessors and contemporaries. Hartmann, in particular, is treated with scorn, but with Schopenhauer the story is more complicated.

This effort of disambiguation is on continuous display in "Attempt at a Self-Criticism." *The Birth of Tragedy* had introduced readers to a distinction between the "Apollonian" and "Dionysian" elements of Greek culture and it is still often remembered for those categories, which went on to have a long life in classical studies and in the field of literature. For the second edition, however, Nietzsche largely ignored this distinction and, indeed, ignored the Apollonian entirely. Instead, he added a new subtitle (actually an alternative title), "Hellenism and Pessimism," and he spent much of the "Attempt" explaining it.

Most of all, he apologized for confusing his audience, in the first edition, by trying "laboriously to express by means of Schopenhauerian and Kantian formulas strange and new valuations which were basically at odds with Kant's and Schopenhauer's spirit and taste!"[9] Those "new" valuations were in fact a variation on the wisdom embedded in Greek tragedy, a wisdom Nietzsche aimed to describe as a version of pessimism but—now—one at odds with that of Schopenhauer. In short, the first edition, he felt, had been on to something about pessimism, but had not expressed it clearly. Thus, in the "Attempt," Nietzsche continually denounces his own previous *style* as excessively rococo and romantic, and apologizes for a confusing *vocabulary*, but attempts to rescue the cultural and philosophical substance of his first book by isolating its pessimistic content.

What was this pessimism, then, that Nietzsche ultimately found "liberating" and like the work of Dostoevsky? To begin with, we must consider Nietzsche's view of tragedy, since the virtues of Greek tragic literature will also prove to be among the virtues of Dostoevsky's writing. Tragedy, Nietzsche believes, has been widely appreciated but not widely understood. Its real origin, he claims, is "the good, severe will of the older [meaning pre-

Socratic] Greeks to pessimism."[10] This is not intended as a claim about the Greeks' disposition, but about their beliefs concerning nature and the place of the human in nature.

If there is one thing we can know about the pre-Socratic Greeks, it is that they had not read Kant or Schopenhauer. Nietzsche regretted that he had tried to render Greek pessimism in Schopenhauerian language because this "older" pessimism did not have a philosophical origin at all. It rested instead on that element of Greek culture that Nietzsche repeatedly termed "Dionysian." And "philosophy," as we shall see later, was specifically created in opposition to the Dionysian.

Any attempt to define the Dionysian, or even to determine Nietzsche's definition, is certain to be controversial. Classicists and literary theorists have debated its meaning, both in this text and generally, for decades. On the one hand, it does not encompass all of Greek culture, and yet Nietzsche never sets very clear boundaries to it. Neither is it clear whether it refers to ideas, practices, or—if a mixture of the two—how they relate to one another. It is sometimes identified with the elite and sometimes with the demotic. About all that we can say without fear of contradiction is that it expresses itself most purely in tragedy and that its enemy is Socratic optimism.

Having stated all these caveats, I will venture that the term "Dionysian," in Nietzsche's vocabulary, is used both for a set of life-conditions that bound all human experience and for whatever forms of culture give expression to these boundaries. This means that the Dionysian is valuable both for its form of expression and for its "honesty" (a term Nietzsche uses quite a bit where others might use "realism" or "truth") about the world we inhabit. Tragedy is "Dionysian" both for what it says about the world and in its means of saying it.

What features of that world are important? Above all for the "older" Greeks, and for Nietzsche, it is the lack of order that we find in the world. The universe is not ultimately governed by anything: not by laws of nature nor by an idea, reason, or any divine power. Nietzsche is sometimes called a "naturalist" but this is only true if we do not equate the "nature" involved with the ordered world of modern physics (and certainly not the still-more-ordered world of Darwinian biology!). Nietzsche's "naturalism" consists mostly in his anti-supernaturalism, that is, his denial that there is any metaphysical system that truly governs the world.

Whatever remains in the absence of metaphysics can certainly be called "nature"—if one wants a word for it other than "world" or "being." But that does not mean that "nature" is systematic in any way. While the Greeks may have believed in their divinities, the important point, for Nietzsche, is that the conflicts between the gods prevented any kind of systematic ordering of the world. Greek theology, such as it was, was a description and explanation of natural disorder, not (as in Christian theology) a suppression of it. "Pessimism," he wrote in a note from the period, "is the consequence of knowledge of the absolute illogic of the world-order."[11]

This idea of worldly disorder is closely connected, for both Nietzsche and the pre-Socratics, to the idea that human life is time-bound. This connection is visible in *The Birth of Tragedy* but it was also developed in *Philosophy in the Tragic Age of the Greeks*, a short companion text to *The Birth* that remained unpublished in Nietzsche's lifetime. Many have heard of Heraclitus's claim that one cannot step into the same river twice and that "Everything flows; nothing stands still." In *Tragic Age*, Nietzsche connects this idea of "flow" with the flow of time, and pays considerable attention to the only known fragment of Anaximander: "Where the source of things is, to that place they must also pass away, according to necessity, for they must pay penance and be judged for their injustices in accordance with the ordinance of Time."[12] The world is disordered, then, because time destroys all things; nothing survives unchanged indefinitely.

Tragedy is "Dionysian," then, because it recognizes this condition of life and shows us what it means to live within its bounds. Nietzsche rejects the traditional view that the point of tragedy is to teach us some moral lesson or to "purge" us of some emotion in the manner of Galenic medicine. Nor does tragedy even exemplify some form of cosmic justice; just the opposite in fact: "The hero of the tragedy does not prove himself . . . in a struggle against fate, just as little does he suffer what he deserves. Rather, blind and with covered head, he falls to his ruin: and his desolate but noble burden with which he remains standing in the presence of this well-known world of terrors presses itself like a thorn in our soul."[13]

Tragedy is pessimistic in the sense that it is based on a view of the world as fundamentally disordered and disordering. It shows that there is no security in any institutions, in values, or even in the gods. It is educative only in the sense that it shows how it is possible to live within such a world. It does not promise a formula for success or happiness in life but rather reveals what strength is required not to give way to despair. Only later interpreters attempted to reinterpret tragedy as a forum for moral education.

It is well known that the main thesis of *The Birth of Tragedy* is that tragedy is first opposed and then destroyed by Socratic philosophy. But what is not normally emphasized is that the important feature of Socrates's philosophy, from Nietzsche's standpoint, is its *optimism*.

Socrates is most famous for proclaiming that he did not know anything. How could a philosophy without any fixed content be an effective opponent to tragedy? Because the content is not the point. Socrates defends no particular factual proposition with absolute certainty, but he has an unbounded faith in the progressive character of his method. There *is* something fixed in the world, he contends: the conclusions of sound reasoning. Even without knowing in advance what these will be, we know (he contends) that they exist and can be accumulated: "Who could mistake the *optimistic* element in the nature of dialectic, which celebrates a triumph with every conclusion . . . the optimistic element which, having once penetrated tragedy, must gradually overgrow its Dionysian regions and impel it necessarily to self-destruction."[14]

So even while asserting that he only knows that he knows nothing, Socrates (in the *Gorgias* and the *Republic* among other places) asserts both that happiness results from virtue and that virtue can be taught via dialectic. Nietzsche calls this the "Socratic-optimistic stage world"—a world where suffering is not only far from universal but *avoidable in principle* even if it is only avoided in practice by a knowledgeable few. "Socrates is the prototype of the theoretical optimist who, with his faith that the nature of things can be fathomed, ascribes to knowledge and insight the power of a panacea."[15]

In effect, Nietzsche's charge of optimism is a charge of dishonesty and arrogance. Socrates, after all, lived in the same world as Heraclitus and Anaximander; he experienced suffering as they did and witnessed its widespread nature. But in creating a "stage world" where such suffering did not have to occur, Socrates created a contrast between the world of the theatre and the world as it actually occurred. In some sense, of course, the stage world was more appealing: it promised a potential end of suffering, and even happiness, to those who would follow the dialectical method. But from Nietzsche's perspective, it was a retreat from the honesty of the original tragedians and it could not teach the strength necessary to cope with the world as we actually experience it.

Optimism is not weak—indeed, in its defeat of the entire Greek tragic culture, it proves quite strong. But it is *for* the weak in the sense that it most appeals to those who cannot bear the honesty of Dionysian pessimism.

When Nietzsche returned to *The Birth* in 1886, it was precisely these points that he chose to emphasize as the central lessons of the book. In the very first section of the "Attempt," he identifies the "big question" of the book as follows: "Is pessimism *necessarily* a sign of decline . . . ? Is there a pessimism of strength? . . . That of which tragedy died, the Socratism of morality, the dialectics, frugality, and cheerfulness of the theoretical man— . . . might not this very Socratism be a sign of decline . . . ?"[16]

Nietzsche aims here not just to resist the normal political and cultural calculations about pessimism but to reverse them. Pessimism, in the first place, is not a sign of bad character, nor a sign of individual weakness. It is only a form of honesty and reflectiveness. Moreover, pessimism is not really a function of individual character at all. Rather, it pertains to a culture and a set of institutions which individuals merely reflect. Thus it makes much more sense to refer to tragedy or Athens as pessimistic than it does to refer to Heraclitus or Anaximander that way. Individuals may certainly be cheerful or gloomy, but pessimism is properly speaking a cultural or philosophical term, not originally a psychological one.

More importantly though, it is not pessimism that brings about cultural decline. In Nietzsche's view, it is optimism that is both a symptom and a cause of Greek decline. Optimism here, though it appears to involve imagining a better future, in fact means a retreat from the actual present, from the real world to a fantasy "stage world." The irony, then, is that the tragedians were the realists in Greek culture and the philosophers were the fabulists.

Socrates, in effect, created pessimism as a matter of individual psychology when he created philosophy as an individual practice of optimism that anyone could adopt, however inexpertly. Earlier generations now appeared "pessimistic" only in contrast to a faith in progress that was grounded not in the real world of experience but in the stage world of imagination. That is why Nietzsche refers to Greek pessimism as "older" than optimism, rather than thinking of optimism and pessimism as two equal, opposite psychological dispositions, as we might today. They are neither equal nor opposite in his view in the sense that reality and fantasy are not equal and opposite. They are, however, cultural forms in opposition to one another: they cannot coexist for any length of time. While it was hardly predetermined that Socratic optimism would defeat pessimism, it is not surprising to Nietzsche that one or the other would have to go.

If real pessimism is once again possible in the West, it is only, according to Nietzsche, because Socratic optimism has run its (very long) course. Schopenhauer's pessimism, though it went part of the way to recovering the Greek sense of disorder in the world and the importance of time, was still fundamentally a philosophy in Socrates's sense of that word. It was a practice of reason that attempted to establish the universe as a comprehensible place that answered to cogent metaphysical descriptions.

It is a particular feature of the 1886 prefaces that Nietzsche attempts to disentangle his own pessimism from Schopenhauer's precisely around this point. Contemporary readers might have found it bizarre that Nietzsche claimed to be the "first" to "really experience" pessimism. But what he meant is clear enough in the preface to *Assorted Opinions and Maxims*, where he described his work as "the critique and likewise the intensifying of pessimism as understood hitherto."[17] Nietzsche claims to be a better and purer pessimist than Schopenhauer because his pessimism is not mixed up with Socratic rationalism. Such a combination has to be unstable.

Thus, although Nietzsche is loath to leave the title of philosopher to the Socratists alone, he takes care to recommend his writings in very different terms, not as truths nor as gateways to mastery, virtue, or happiness, but rather in the terms that one might recommend tragedy: "they are *pre-*

cepts of health that may be recommended . . . as a *disciplina voluntatis.* There speaks out of them a pessimist whose insights have made him jump out of his skin, but who has always known how to get back into it again, a pessimist, that is to say, well-disposed *toward* pessimism."[18]

To speak properly, then, a pessimist must adopt a style of speech that must appear rather strange from the perspective of modern philosophy. It is precisely such a mode of speech, I will contend, that Nietzsche read in *Notes from the Underground.* However fictional, Dostoevsky's text shares with tragedy the characteristic of displaying the world in all its limitations and ugliness. It does not put its characters on a stage, as it were, but uses them precisely to destroy its readers' illusions and to force them to confront the limitations of their world and themselves.

DOSTOEVSKY'S PESSIMISM

What does it mean to suggest that Dostoevsky shared Nietzsche's pessimistic perspective? It will be clear enough from the previous section why Nietzsche was more disposed to identify pessimism in works of literature than in works of philosophy. The very attempt to discern an order in the world gets political and cultural inquiry off on the wrong step for him. Modern philosophy makes this mistake, as it were, by habit. Literature may make it as well (Jane Austen?), but it is hardly committed to it in the same way. Nietzsche connects Dostoevsky not just to literature, however, but particularly to tragedy.

In the "Attempt," Nietzsche uses the same language that he used in one of his notes on Dostoevsky to ask a question about tragedy in general: "how should we then have to explain . . . the *craving for the ugly* . . . the image of everything underlying existence that is frightful, evil, a riddle, destructive, fatal?"[19] Like the tragedians, then, Dostoevsky displays, as many readers of his novels will agree, a craving for the ugly that marks the rejection of an optimistic worldview.

More particularly, however (for one could perhaps find many authors who share this craving), *Notes from the Underground* seems to be structured precisely to answer the question that Nietzsche is asking here. Where does a craving for the ugly come from? In the first section, the unnamed narrator gives as precise as possible an explanation for his existence; in the second, the tragic, ugly action that is the inevitable result of such an existence is played out in excruciating detail. Thus, in Nietzsche's terms, Dostoevsky is not just a tragedian but, like Nietzsche himself, a *theorist* of tragedy, an explainer of its origins. Even, perhaps, a better and more complete explainer of it than Nietzsche himself.

117

In the very first line of the new preface to *Daybreak*, Nietzsche refers to it as the work of "a subterranean man" (*einen Unterirdischen*; recall Dostoevsky's French title *L'esprit souterrain*). Whether or not this recently written passage was recalled to Nietzsche's mind when he picked up the *Notes*, the parallel metaphors indicate something much more than an accidental overlap of style. Indeed, the extended discussion of pessimism in this preface reads in many respects as an unwitting introduction to the *Notes*.

Nietzsche goes on for a long paragraph describing, in the third person, the author of his book as working underground, tunneling, digging. Then he says, "do not ask him what he is looking for down there, he will tell you himself of his own accord." He then describes the work of the book as "pessimistic even into the realm of morality . . . but why? *Out of morality!*"[20] It is hard to imagine a better description of the contradictions built into the voice and reasoning of Dostoevsky's narrator, who speaks in the first person and who is at pains to describe how his acute moral sensibility has made him into someone who behaves in ways that seem contemptible.

Notes from the Underground is, of course, a radical stylistic departure from the norms of nineteenth-century fiction, even by the standards set by Dostoevsky's other works. The first-person narrator, especially in the first section, engages in a kind of self-psychoanalysis that is not at all distant, in tone or content, from the autobiographical portions of Nietzsche's writings.[21] But this analysis is simultaneously a reflection on the human condition, a reflection that bears a close resemblance to Nietzsche's views on Greek pessimism.

We could begin at many points here, but perhaps the quickest way to the heart of the matter is to focus on the perspective the narrator opposes. At the beginning of chapter 7, he tells us about it very explicitly, stopping just short of the name "Socrates": "Oh tell me, who was it who first announced, who first proclaimed that man only does vile things when he does not know where his real interests lie? And that if he were enlightened, . . . he would indeed see his own personal advantage in goodness."[22] This is transparently the Platonic Socrates of the *Gorgias* and the *Republic*, not just because he believed these things but because he was (famously) the first to argue for them. Moreover, it is the very element of the Socratic perspective, as we have seen, that Nietzsche cast as the opponent of tragedy. It is a crucial element of Socratic optimism that all will do good once they come to full knowledge of their true interests.

But Dostoevsky's narrator calls this the perspective of a "child," a "sweet, innocent babe," and sets about refuting it. The refutation is complicated and contains many elements. But a core element of the refutation is that individuality and individual desire are the opponent of reason and interest: "it is possible to desire against one's own best interest, and sometimes one *positively should*."[23]

The refutation continues by countering Socrates's optimistic contention that reason can govern man and, indeed, that in his essence, man is a rational being: "Reason is a fine thing, there's no question about it, but reason is only reason and only satisfies man's rational faculties, whereas desire is a manifestation of the whole of life."[24] That reason cannot govern the world is a central contention of the tragic worldview.

But if this is the narrator's pessimistic line of thinking about the human condition, why is he so passive in the face of the desires he so manifestly feels? "Concerning the Wet Snow" is largely an internal document of inhibition. The narrator is assaulted by the most powerful feelings—pride and love—and is seemingly unable to act on them or able to act on them only in self-destructive ways. If he is so full of desire (and he is), why remain motionless in a chaotic world?

Here we must consider what Dostoevsky's narrator has said earlier about consciousness. While we might normally think of consciousness as the seat of action and decision-making, the narrator of the *Notes* maintains the opposite. A "normal person," he says, is "spontaneous." "A person of heightened consciousness," on the other hand, cannot be spontaneous.[25] He cannot react naturally but must reflect on his choices before acting. But as Dostoevsky has his narrator trace out, this reflection can easily become never-ending. There are an infinite number of things to consider, and the possibility that any action may fail in its purpose. Then, when it produces "inertia," consciousness can turn on itself and produce self-loathing. "To be too conscious is an illness, a genuine full-blown illness . . . even any consciousness at all is an illness."[26] The normal person can act without thinking, but the more conscious we become, the less likely we are to engage the world like this "normal person."

Dostoevsky explores this path of intellectual (over-)development in detail. But it is worth noting that Nietzsche had already suggested some of its main elements. In the new section of *The Gay Science*, written in 1886, a few pages before he declared Dionysian pessimism to be his quintessence, he wrote: "[A]ll becoming conscious involves a great and thorough corruption . . . Ultimately, the growth of consciousness becomes a danger; and anyone who lives among the most conscious Europeans even knows that it is a disease."[27] And he also connected this sense of a diseased consciousness to tragic indecision via the case of *Hamlet*: "[Hamlet has] gained knowledge, and nausea inhibits action; [he] feel[s] it to be ridiculous or humiliating that [he] should be asked to set right a world that is out of joint. Knowledge kills action; . . . Conscious of the truth he has once seen . . . he is nauseated." Again, the behavior and emotions of the narrator are anticipated.

I will hardly be the first to suggest that Dostoevsky's narrator is an underground Hamlet. But the point not to miss here is that this inhibition is not simply a character flaw but a result of the honest view of the world that pessimism affords us. Greek tragic characters (like Oedipus) are often plagued by doubt and indecision and this is, from Nietzsche's perspective, a plausible reaction to the world (and the psyche) as we find it. If Dostoevsky's excruciating honesty is inward-looking, as opposed to the more outward-looking narratives of Greek tragedy, it still has the "unstaged" quality that marks a direct encounter with the disordered, time-bound world Nietzsche outlines.

It should be noted as well that Dostoevsky makes clear, in his short preface, his intention that his portrait be taken as a kind of cultural analysis of modernity. Consciousness is not just a disease but a particularly contemporary one, or one that has only increased in strength and prevalence in the nineteenth century. For all of Nietzsche's attacks on Socrates, it is clear that he shares this judgment, as well as the concern that modernity, if it does not embrace pessimism, will turn to nihilism. Indeed, I believe that one of the things Nietzsche most appreciated about Dostoevsky is his explanation of this turn.

The narrator of the *Notes* is frustrated, at least initially, with his own inertia. But he also explains how, over time, the mind can perversely come to value it: "[B]itterness finally turned into some kind of shameful, accursed sweetness and then in the end into definite, serious pleasure! Yes into pleasure, pleasure! I insist on it . . . the pleasure of despair; but it's precisely in despair that you find the most intense pleasure."[28] Reveling in one's own impotence and inertia is pretty much the essence of nihilism—not just believing in nothing, but desiring it and taking pleasure in it. Both as a psychological and as a cultural matter, it is hard to understand how such a stance could be generated. Nietzsche often decried the nihilism that he saw on the horizon but he did not detail its origin as precisely as Dostoevsky does here.[29]

As a cultural matter, although it is often perceived as an outgrowth of pessimism, the *Notes*, like Nietzsche's work, casts nihilism as the outgrowth of Socratic optimism. First you come to believe the world is predictable; then you come to believe that your own actions are predictable. But once your life is predicted, it is put on stage and you become a spectator to your own life, inertial and apathetic. Lastly, you learn to love this inertia, and this is the point where you give up your individuality and humanity, as the narrator does, after previously insisting that he would not be bound by rationality: "[I]t's better to do nothing at all! Better conscious inertia. And so, long live the underground!"[30]

Neither Dostoevsky nor Nietzsche, of course, embraces this nihilism, but they do mean to diagnose it as the most prevalent cultural danger of the nineteenth century. And it can only be properly diagnosed from a pessimistic perspective. It requires the rejection of optimism in all its forms, even those that are most appealing.

THE WANDERER AND HIS SHADOW

The 1886 prefaces may have had some effect on Nietzsche's reception. Perhaps it was coincidence, but Nietzsche's obscurity began to lift in the late 1880s as the new editions began to circulate. A turning point was a series of lectures on his philosophy in 1888 by the Danish critic Georg Brandes, who was well known throughout Europe. As Nietzsche's mental state deteriorated in 1888, he engaged in a correspondence with Brandes. One topic among others was their mutual admiration for Dostoevsky. In one of his last sane letters Nietzsche wrote to Brandes: "I am grateful to [Dostoevsky] in a remarkable way, however much he goes against my deepest instincts."[31]

Nietzsche's gratitude is not hard to understand. Besides appearing as a kindred spirit and confirming Nietzsche's concerns about Socratic optimism, Dostoevsky provided a kind of fine-grained psychological account of the development of the nihilistic consciousness that exceeded all of Nietzsche's efforts in that regard. Yet here, alongside the gratitude, Nietzsche indicates a distance between himself and Dostoevsky—and suddenly, it seems, the distance is marked as a considerable one. What, after his consistent praise of the novelist in all his other notes and letters, could Nietzsche have had in mind?

To answer this question, I propose that we take one of Nietzsche's compliments and ask it as a question, that is, "How liberating *is* Dostoevsky?" Nietzsche's answer I think is, in effect: extremely liberating—and yet not quite liberating enough. The voice of *Notes from the Underground* may be that of a pessimist, but even if Dostoevsky's faith is hard to perceive in that book (in part because of the censor's deletions!), it would have been clear enough to Nietzsche from Dostoevsky's other writings, most of all *The Idiot*.

The liberation that pessimism offers is the liberation that comes from knowing that the world is not calculable. The narrator of the *Notes* rails against a world in which everyone is reasonable, not least because nothing unpredictable could happen in such a world. It would be stupefyingly boring. But worse than boring, the "Crystal Palace" that the optimists imagine would be a kind of prison of possibility. If all rational actions can be known in advance, and all humans are in essence rational, then nothing unexpected can ever happen and to act independently would be to err or to sin. But the pessimist rejects that image of the world—not just of man, but of the world—as a calculable whole. Whatever suffering results from this rejection, there is at least a compensation in terms of freedom. When Dostoevsky's narrator suggests that we *should* act against our interests, he suggests only that we act as free beings, whatever the costs. But to embrace such a stance without any compensation is to pay a very high price for liberation.

Just as Schopenhauer had rejected *nearly* all of Socratic philosophy, but had, in the end "come to a halt" before morality, it seems likely that

Nietzsche judged Dostoevsky to have embraced all of pessimism—except the hardest part. The world Dostoevsky depicted is indeed the world that Nietzsche sees: a disordered world in which human instincts and desires run up against an uncaring universe and suffering is an inescapable result. But there is a kind of Christian pessimism (Reinhold Niebuhr is another example) that can embrace just such a picture of this world so long as the solace of *another* world, better ordered than this one, is allowed as an intellectual possibility and an object of faith. Indeed, such a faith may allow one to explore the depths of free earthly existence with increased courage.

Nietzsche's gratitude to Dostoevsky seems genuine. There is no reason to doubt his statements that the Russian opened up psychological perspectives for him that he would have been unable to reach on his own. But for Dostoevsky, the depravity and injustice of this world were embraced in his fiction not only to destroy the illusions that humans have about themselves but also, indirectly, to point them away from this world and toward another. Many readers, at least of *Notes from the Underground* (though not of the other works), might be surprised to learn that the author of this existential book was also a Christian, but Nietzsche was not surprised. He was merely disappointed.

Having encountered a book that shadowed, and foreshadowed, so many of his own conclusions, Nietzsche was perhaps entitled to his disappointment. Even in the 1880s, pessimism in its purest form was not exactly a popular philosophy. The preface to *Daybreak* speaks of the pessimist's task as an inherently lonely one: "[H]e who proceeds on his own path in this fashion encounters no one . . . For his path is *his alone*—as is, of course, the bitterness and occasional ill-humor he feels at this 'his alone.'"[32] This passage captures both the perspective of the narrator of the *Notes* and Nietzsche's perspective in encountering that narrator—not a real person, not Dostoevsky, but a ghost, a shadow, someone to accompany Nietzsche without ever offering any real company. The pessimistic wanderer may remain alone but his shadow reminds him of what it would be like to have a companion. And it reminds him of the emptiness of that hope.

NOTES

1. See Friedrich Nietzsche, *Selected Letters of Friedrich Nietzsche*, ed. Christopher Middleton (Chicago: University of Chicago Press, 1969), 260 and following.

2. These details are drawn from Curtis Cate, *Friedrich Nietzsche* (New York: Overlook Press, 2005), chapters 33–35.

3. After *Human, All Too Human*, Nietzsche had published both *Assorted Opinions and Maxims* and *The Wanderer and His Shadow* separately. Now the two were bound together and issued as the "second volume" of *Human, All Too*

Human, which is how they usually appear today. So there was a new preface for each of the two "volumes."

4. Friedrich Nietzsche, *The Gay Science,* trans. Walter Kaufmann (New York: Vintage Books, 1974), 330–31.

5. Friedrich Nietzsche, *Daybreak,* trans. R. J. Hollingdale (New York: Cambridge University Press, 1982), 4; *Human, All Too Human,* trans. R. J. Hollingdale (New York: Cambridge University Press, 1986), 211–14.

6. Friedrich Nietzsche, *The Will to Power,* trans. Walter Kaufmann (New York: Vintage Books, 1967), 51.

7. Fyodor Dostoevsky, *Notes from the Underground,* trans. Jane Kentish (New York: Oxford University Press, 1991), 33.

8. Nietzsche, *The Will to Power,* 434–35.

9. Friedrich Nietzsche, *The Birth of Tragedy,* trans. Walter Kaufmann (New York: Vintage, 1967), 24. I will leave to one side here the question of Nietzsche's "Kantianism," which would require an essay of its own.

10. Ibid., 21.

11. Friedrich Nietzsche, *Werke: Kritische Gesamtausgabe,* ed. Giorgio Colli and Mazzino Montinari (Berlin: Walter de Gruyter, 1967), volume 3, book 3, 74.

12. Friedrich Nietzsche, *Philosophy in the Tragic Age of the Greeks,* trans. Marianne Cowan (Washington, D.C.: Regnery Press, 1962), section 4.

13. Nietzsche, *Werke,* volume 3, book 2, 38.

14. Nietzsche, *Birth of Tragedy,* 91.

15. Ibid., 97.

16. Ibid., 17–18.

17. Nietzsche, *Will to Power,* 255; *Human, All Too Human,* 209.

18. Nietzsche, *Human, All Too Human,* 210.

19. Nietzsche, *Birth of Tragedy,* 21.

20. Nietzsche, *Daybreak,* 1–4.

21. The 1886 prefaces collectively make up one such portion (*Ecce Homo* constitutes another) but the mixing of the philosophical with the autobiographical is a more-or-less continuous feature of Nietzsche's texts.

22. Dostoevsky, *Notes,* 22.

23. Ibid., 26.

24. Ibid., 28–29.

25. Ibid., 13.

26. Ibid., 10.

27. Nietzsche, *Gay Science,* 300. The disease of consciousness is an idea that also precedes Nietzsche in the pessimistic tradition. It is especially conspicuous in Rousseau's *Discourse on Inequality.* Whether Dostoevsky knew this Rousseau text I do not know, but the *Notes* makes reference to *Émile,* which contains similar themes. See my *Pessimism: Philosophy, Ethic, Spirit* (Princeton: Princeton University Press, 2006), chapters 1 and 2.

28. Dostoevsky, *Notes*, 11–12.

29. This theme, of course, appears in Dostoevsky's other major novels as well, but it is not clear to me if Nietzsche read either *Crime and Punishment* or *The Brothers Karamazov*.

30. Ibid., 37.

31. Nietzsche, *Selected Letters*, 327.

32. Nietzsche, *Daybreak*, 1.

Edith W. Clowes

Mapping the Unconscious in *Notes from Underground* and *On the Genealogy of Morals*: A Reconsideration of Modern Moral Consciousness

There *in its nasty, stinking underground* our offended, beaten, taunted mouse plunges right away into a state of cold, poisonous and, this is the main thing, everlasting spite. For forty years on end it will remember the offense down to the most shameful details, each time inventing new details, even more shameful, maliciously teasing and irritating itself.
—Dostoevsky, *Notes from Underground*

There in its vile, filthy underground our *rat*, offended and mocked, hides right away in its cold, poisoned, eternal spite . . . it will remember down to the most shameful details of the offense, each time adding still more shameful details, *irritated by its own depraved fantasy, inventing aggravating circumstances on the pretext that they could have happened, pardoning itself in nothing.*
—Dostoevsky, *L'esprit souterrain*

These cellar creatures full of vengeance and hatred—what do they do with that vengeance and hatred? Have you ever heard these words? Would you suspect, if you trusted their words, that you are in the company of people of resentment [*ressentiment*]?
—Nietzsche, *On the Genealogy of Morals*

125

FOR WELL OVER A CENTURY major critics and thinkers have recognized Dostoevsky and Nietzsche as great moral psychologists. Lev Shestov, the existentialist philosopher, thought of Dostoevsky and Nietzsche as intellectual "twins," both of them psychological thinkers, made so through their similar inner experience.[1] Sensitive to the hidden impulses of the psyche, as Shestov argued, these writers were the first to address the impact of psychological life on our moral values.[2] A parallel in their thinking, relatively ignored in recent critical commentary, is the peculiarly *spatial* quality of Dostoevsky's and Nietzsche's psychological modeling, the metaphors of the underground, which strongly affect how we imagine the psyche.[3] Although Nietzsche sometimes described the unconscious psyche as a natural space "under the earth" (*das Unterirdische*), both Dostoevsky and Nietzsche typically thought of it as a human-made, "un-natural" space "under the floor" (*podpol'e*) and in "the cellar" (*Keller*). These metaphors help to make palpable what has always been and will always be invisible. To both thinkers, these underground spaces are inhabited by subliminal drives, aggressive and malicious in the extreme. Dostoevsky's underground in *Notes from Underground* (1864) is the site of uncontrolled ill-will, desire, and arbitrary willfulness (*zloba, khoten'e, zhelanie, voliu*). Nietzsche's underground space in *On the Genealogy of Morals* (1887) is the breeding ground of feelings of "*ressentiment*" and "remorse." They often imagine these drives as rodents—a mouse, a mole, or even a rat, as in the 1886 French adaptation of *Notes from Underground* that Nietzsche read.[4] For both thinkers, the key point is that unconscious psychological phenomena become the motivation for moral feeling, consciousness, and action. This essay undertakes to show that, though Dostoevsky was among the first thinkers to conceive of moral consciousness as something human-made and based on subliminal psychological drives, he *is* the first that I have found to imagine the psyche itself as a human-made *space*. And although Hobbes, Locke, and later Kant were the first thinkers to claim the autonomy of moral value from religious belief, Dostoevsky and Nietzsche were among the first, if not the very first, thinkers to situate moral psychology in a nondivine space, to "map" it, as it were.[5] And, finally, while Freud famously created a visual model of the conscious and unconscious psyche in "The Ego and the Id" (1923), Dostoevsky and Nietzsche did so metaphorically decades earlier.[6] Dostoevsky's impact on Nietzsche, and through Nietzsche on Freud, could be greater than we have generally thought.

As intellectual-historical background for this discussion it will be helpful to describe the "spaces" of moral consciousness in European writing before Dostoevsky's *Notes from Underground*. Moral values and consciousness have traditionally been located in the high, bright places of the human body—the heart, the soul, the mind—and linked to the most elevated value,

the divine. In contrast, the "roots" of moral consciousness, for both Dostoevsky and Nietzsche, are paradoxically located in the lower places of human
nature and the human body traditionally labeled "bad" or even "evil," in the
lightless realm "under ground." The lowest realm under the ground or in the
basement of a building traditionally designates variously "hell," "death," or
"imprisonment." Now, in the modern imagination, underground space becomes an allegory for the psyche and specifically the unconscious, that part
of the mind that is inaccessible to verbal description. In Dostoevsky's and
Nietzsche's work we deal with the paradox of the unconscious become conscious in words, the "speaking unconscious."

Dostoevsky appears to have invented the image of the human-made,
moral-psychological underground. Before Dostoevsky, literature is full of
underground prisons, hells, pits, and caves. In Plato's *Republic*, the space
of blind, unthinking belief and behavior is an "underground den," the famous cave.[7] In contrast, Dostoevsky's underground is unnatural; it is part of
a human-made building—a dark site from which to watch and react to the
real effects of our idealized systems of reasoned thought and belief on the
"surface" of human psychological life. This insight, leading at first to seemingly immoral behavior (asserting one's power through revenge), and later
to a form of moral behavior (a feeling of owing and repaying a debt, and a
need to confess the "truth") is the opposite of Plato's bright, sunlit images of
enlightenment.[8]

Arthur Schopenhauer, among the first psychologically oriented philosophers, still juxtaposes the physical and the metaphysical—he characterizes
"will" not as primarily psychological, but rather metaphysical. It is a post-
Kantian "thing in itself" that exists outside of human perception.[9] Schopenhauer's concept of will makes it possible, however, for philosophy to build
a bridge to psychology and to criticize human psychology, particularly the
concept of the "I," the ego, and its motivations. Importantly for us, Schopenhauer describes existence nonspatially, certainly since, for him, space itself is
a "mask." The mind and consciousness are still viewed in terms, if not of "enlightenment," then of "light" and flashes of lightning descending from above:
"consciousness is, as it were, a lightning-flash momentarily illuminating the
night."[10] Among post-idealist philosophers, Ludwig Feuerbach's thinking anticipates modern religious psychology. Feuerbach is known for founding the
anthropology of religion. He argues in *The Essence of Religion* (1841) that
God is a projection of human inner nature. His discourse on human nature
occasionally uses spatial metaphors, though he uses horizontal rather than
vertical spatial relationships, for example, contrasting "inner" and "outer"
spaces.[11]

It is important to note that the typical, independently thinking, isolated, and often alienated protagonist of late-eighteenth- and nineteenth-

century European literature inhabits a high place, often a garret, a cheap rental space high under the roof. The higher space points to the dominance in the protagonist of reason and ideas, rather than subliminal drive. For example, in *Rameau's Nephew* (1762) Diderot was among the first of many writers to create an outsider, who lives in a garret. This protagonist descends to the streets and cafes to launch a critique of social mores.[12] "Underground" spaces do appear later, for example, in the urban landscapes of Eugène Sue's *Les Mystères de Paris* (1842–43), where Sue writes of "underground life" and uses underground spaces, for example, kitchens, cafes, and taverns. Victor Hugo in *Les Miserables* (1862), uses underground imagery to refer to political and economic realia of "the underground of the world" and "underground pioneers" (vol. 3), and "underground education" (vol. 5).

Russian literature has relatively few underground spaces before Dostoevsky. The late-seventeenth-century Old Believer Archpriest Avvakum writes in his autobiography of being imprisoned in a "pit," a kind of earthly hell, in which he undergoes a severe test of his faith. Aleksandr Pushkin's post-1825 poems to his Decembrist brothers in the Siberian mines certainly speak of the underground space of the mines as a punishment, in which their faith in an Enlightenment polity would be hardened. One of the Underground Man's well-known precursors, Ivan Turgenev's "Hamlet from Shchigrovsky District" (1848), features a nameless character defined mainly through the tone of his voice, speaking in the partial darkness. Still, the space of the monologue is above ground, in the bedroom of a manor house. And here surface aspects of civility and good manners still apply. In Chernyshevsky's utopian novel, *What Is To Be Done?* (1863), against which *Notes from Underground* was written, there is one basement space, imagined by the protagonist, Vera Pavlovna. In her first dream Vera Pavlovna is liberated from a "damp, dark cellar," to skip through a field.[13] This act, in good Platonic tradition, is one of enlightenment and empowerment. At the end of the dream she unlocks other cellars to free other young women.

Although *Notes from Underground* (1864) was published twenty-three years before Nietzsche wrote *On the Genealogy of Morals* (1887), Nietzsche did not know of Dostoevsky or his book until 1886 or '87, when he was working on *Genealogy*. And though Nietzsche had developed his own underground imagery much earlier, it has been persuasively shown that in some respects *Notes from Underground* helped him to shape the underground concept in *On the Genealogy of Morals*. Nietzsche had independently developed his own metaphors, for example, in *Thus Spoke Zarathustra* (1885), the human-made space of the cellar. Here he talks about taming the "dogs in the cellar" to characterize the angry disharmony of the adolescent psyche.[14]

The question of a creative appropriation by Nietzsche of *Notes from Underground* is complex. The remarkable parallels between the passages in

Notes from Underground and *On the Genealogy of Morals* have long since been noted and connected through the strange French adaptation of two Dostoevsky works, *L'esprit souterrain* (1886). Soon before writing *On the Genealogy of Morals*, Nietzsche stumbled upon Dostoevsky for the first time in *L'esprit souterrain* late in 1886 or early in 1887, at a bookstore in Nice, France.[15] He enthused about Dostoevsky, finding in him "a psychologist with whom I can get along."[16] This odd French cannibalization of Dostoevsky had two parts, part 1, titled "Katia," and part 2, titled "Liza." "Katia" was, in fact, a retitled but quite complete translation of Dostoevsky's early story "The Landlady" ("Khoziaika," 1847). However, "Liza," or part 2 of *L'esprit souterrain*, was an unreliable, badly mutilated set of excerpts from both parts of *Notes from Underground*. The original titles of Dostoevsky's two parts, "The Underground" ("Podpol'e") and "A Propos of Wet Snow" ("Po povodu mokrogo snega") were missing, and "Liza" was presented as the diary of the protagonist of "The Landlady," Vasily Ordynov. By attaching these writings to a fully developed character in a romantic tale, the nameless voice of *Notes from Underground* loses much of its auditory punch. Fabricated passages adapting "Liza" to the "Katia" section were added, substantially altering the quality of *Notes from Underground*.[17] Completely ignorant of the poor quality of the French adaptation, Nietzsche nonetheless found the second part to be a "stroke of psychological genius."[18]

It has been argued that Nietzsche's reading of *L'esprit souterrain* helped him to shape "under-earth" imagery in another work, the 1886 preface to *Daybreak* (1873), where Nietzsche sees his philosophical persona as something like a mole, an "underground person, drilling, digging, undermining."[19] That image emphasizes intellectual, psychological inquisitiveness, rather than the psychology of resentment that links *Notes from Underground* and *On the Genealogy of Morals*. It is important to point out that Nietzsche read *L'esprit souterrain* before drafting *On the Genealogy of Morals*, which was written in July 1887, and published four months later, in November. It is impossible, however, to substantiate any linear creative appropriation of *Notes from Underground* in *On the Genealogy of Morals*, since Nietzsche had earlier developed the imagery linking underground "cellar" spaces and what we can call the "moral unconscious," at least since *Thus Spoke Zarathustra* (1885). It is not a stretch, however, to assert that reading *L'Esprit souterrain* offered Nietzsche corroboration of his thinking and may well have turned his concept of the unconscious away from *visual* imagery and toward *auditory* imagery.

The critical commentary has more often than not overlooked the link between underground spatial imagery and the interaction of psychological impulses and moral consciousness. The first critic to address the underground setting as a metaphor for the psyche was Nikolai Antsiferov, who in his 1922 study *The Soul of Petersburg* remarked on the parallels between the "underground of the human soul" and the "underground of the city."[20] To Antsiferov's parallels between the psychological underground and architectural, urban underground spaces we can add that the underground is an "uncanny" metaphorical space—both familiar and foreign. The Underground Man inhabits it, even though he also reviles it. It is both "home" and a "strange space," alien to how we would like to view ourselves—as reasonable, noble, enlightened beings—a place where we conceal fantasy and experience unacceptable in ordinary social parlance. As such, the underground is a critical complication that characterizes the self-aware psyche of modern, urban, educated, self-reflective people.

It comes as a surprise that the inventor of the spatial concept of the "chronotope," Mikhail Bakhtin, never considered the underground as a chronotope. In *Problems of Dostoevsky's Poetics* (1929), Bakhtin discusses important aspects of the figure of the Underground Man, but without asking why the underground setting itself might be important. Bakhtin's crucial point is that the Underground Man is a voice with an attitude, not a fully realized character. He is not an actual protagonist but the "subject of consciousness and dreaming."[21] Thinking in terms of the chronotope, however, the underground is certainly a crucial, symbolically significant time-space ensemble that divulges an "image of human nature," as Bakhtin defines the chronotope, and one that makes the unconscious thinkable and palpable.

Regarding the underground space as the space of the unconscious—now strangely articulated in the figure of the Underground Man—we find that the unconscious becomes the crucial foundation (another spatial metaphor) for what we might call moral "pre-consciousness," leading to consciousness in a modern world without divine intervention. The "desire" for some overriding, authoritative system of moral value springs not from a superhuman power but from the complex of subliminal human instinct.

Dostoevsky's and Nietzsche's underground settings are important because they imply a radically different "image of human nature," to use Bakhtin's term. These cellar-type spaces lie under an allegorical "house," or system, of consciously held ideals, values, and opinions. As Joseph Frank and Russian critics before him have pointed out, Dostoevsky's underground is both psychological and ideological, situated, as it were, under the utopian construction of Chernyshevsky's Crystal Palace in *What Is To Be Done?*, which promotes rational egoism and its idealized image of a completely reasoned and educable human nature. Nietzsche's image is psychological, under the "house" of the conscious psyche, the ego and its valuative constructs. For both, but particularly for Dostoevsky, the underground is a space in which to observe what is commonly accepted as "good" human behavior, both admiring and resenting it: "I have the underground. And as long as I live and desire, let my hand wither, if I should

130

ever lay even one brick on that fundamental edifice [*kapital'nyi dom*]. Don't think that I long since rejected the crystal building just because I could not stick my tongue out at it" (*Notes* I:8).[22] The underground is rather that shifting space of desiring, from which the Underground Man (himself in many ways a rational egoist) reviles the metaphorical Crystal Palace of the rational, utilitarian social order, so beloved by Chernyshevsky, having once upon a time admired it. The very concept of the Crystal Palace represents the death of personal desire, the very thing that the Underground Man will valorize as the root of human nature.[23]

Even in the narrative portion of *Notes from Underground*, part 2, the underground remains a space of instinct and subliminal drive, as Vasily Rozanov noted, an "inner space" in one's psyche that forms over a lifetime (forty years), which one "carries" inside himself (*Notes* II:1). The Underground Man's interactions with the prostitute Liza are motivated by the unconscious desire to assert himself, to influence and control. His actions are continually—and most tragically with Liza—motivated by this "gloomy thought," accompanied by a less well-defined "nasty sensation of going into a damp, moldy basement" (*Notes* II:6). As he reflects on his underground, the Underground Man also links the inner underground to urban houses of ill repute, dives of debauchery that he visits: "I was terribly afraid of being recognized. I frequented the darkest places" (*Notes* II:1). It is important to note that even in his dark excesses, the Underground Man is morally conscious: he is abnormally aware of the moral turpitude of his thoughts, and he judges his attitudes and actions.

In contrast to Dostoevsky's underground, which is primarily a space of observing, criticizing, and self-criticizing, in *On the Genealogy of Morals* Nietzsche *also* explicitly sees the underground with all its skepticism as a creative space, a "dark workshop" where "ideals are made on earth" (*GM* I:13).[24] It is worth noting, as an aside, that the widely used Kaufmann translation of *On the Genealogy of Morals* omits the spatial aspect of the observer looking "down" and "under" in order to comprehend the psychological roots of moral feeling. A fuller translation of this passage would read: "Does anyone want to look down and under the mystery of how ideals are made on earth?" (*GM* I:13).[25] Importantly, Nietzsche focuses on a different set of senses from those emphasized in realist and scientific writing. While scientific empiricism and literary realism rely on sight and seeing, Nietzsche consciously turns to listening since sight works poorly in this dark space, a change in perspective quite possibly motivated by his reading of the French adaptation of Dostoevsky, *L'esprit souterrain*.

In *On the Genealogy of Morals* Nietzsche likens the whole psyche to a house with "doors and windows of consciousness" and the unconscious to a lower realm, an "underworld" (*Unterwelt*) of "utility organs working with and against one another" (*GM* II:1, 57E). Forgetfulness ("an active and in the strictest sense positive faculty of repression" (*positives Hemmungsvermögen*; *GM* II:1, 245G) lets us rest from often conflicting workings of the consciousness and the unconscious. Pursuing the architectural metaphor, Nietzsche compares the function of forgetfulness to a "doorkeeper, preserver of psychic order, repose, and etiquette: so that it will be immediately obvious how there could be no happiness, no cheerfulness, no hope, no pride, no *present*, without forgetfulness" (*GM* II:1, 58E).

Thinking about the underground as a chronotope, a time-space ensemble, prompts us to investigate the function within this space of concepts of time and change. Dostoevsky's and Nietzsche's underground spaces feature quite different concepts of time. Although the very fact of its coming into existence is a major event in the back history of *Notes from Underground*, Dostoevsky's underground is personal, seemingly timeless, eventless, and, in his words, "inert." Indeed, the Underground Man calls his perspective "conscious inertia" (*Notes* I:9). The editor of *Notes from Underground* and the Underground Man disagree about the nature of time in the underground. The editor sees the underground as an *evolutionary development* of *this* younger generation in the mid-nineteenth century. In the editor's view, the Underground Man "seems to want to explain the reasons for its (the underground's) appearance, and why it had to appear, in our milieu" (*Notes* I: footnote). In contrast, in the Underground Man's view, the underground is indeed inert. In his historical critique of the cruelty of Cleopatra, among other examples, he suggests that human nature generally does not change, that it is a constant, with which one must work—for the good or the bad. The one major change, implied in this critique, but made explicit in Nietzsche's essay, is that with time the cruel aspects of human nature have gradually been repressed and have turned inward, giving rise to the self-conscious self.

Nietzsche's underground, in contrast, is historical. As he suggests in the title of his book, the psyche has a "genealogy," and it has developed over eons. Nietzsche's goal is to sketch in allegories this long-term evolutionary shift, starting with the "blond beast," moving through various archetypal developments—the warrior-master and the priest-slave psychological formations—and now arriving in his own time at the complacent "last man."

The interaction between the underground psychological space and the faculty of language is another defining issue for understanding the nature of the underground. As Bakhtin points out, the Underground Man is a speaking voice. Dostoevsky's underground closely anticipates the Freudian "id," and particularly the Lacanian "Real," levels of the psyche which are inaccessible to direct verbal expression. In Dostoevsky's rendition, the underground is separate from language. It is a site of silent resentment, in contrast to Nietzsche's underground workshop, which is a space of ill-willed grumbling.

132

It is only *after* "being released" from the underground that the Underground Man starts speaking—and will not stop. Indeed, he insists that the underground or unconscious should remain wordless: "you know what? I am persuaded that our underground brother should be held in check. He can sit in silence in the underground for forty years, but if he gets out, he'll burst and then he'll just talk and talk and talk" (*Notes* I:8).

Language does function in Nietzsche's underground, though it is hardly intelligible. In this dark workshop one hears "malignant muttering and whispering" (46): "Weakness is being lied into something *meritorious*" ("*Die Schwäche soll zum* Verdienste *umgelogen werden*") (*GM* I:13, 47E; 237G). And yet this language is extremely difficult to perceive. The investigator (Nietzsche's speaking persona) has to sharpen his ears to hear the sense of the speaking voices. It is important to note that when both thinkers do speak of underground emanations, they speak in indirect terms, because, even for Nietzsche, the unconscious is inaccessible to direct verbal expression. Through simile (the organ stop) and allegory (mouse), in Dostoevsky's case, and human archetypes (blond beast, master-warrior, slave-priest, ascetic philosopher, and last man), in Nietzsche's case, they apprehend perceptions and behavior as the direct result of underground instinctive drives.

Although the underground-as-unconscious is mainly apart from language, Nietzsche famously develops the vocabulary of "*ressentiment*" to talk about the impact of the unconscious on "moral" consciousness and behavior. For Dostoevsky, however, the workings of the unconscious filter into consciousness through a subtler vocabulary of underground will and desire and the alliterative dispersal of the sounds of the Russian words for will and desire throughout the *Notes*. Though the Russian word for "free will" or "anarchic will," *volia*, has received a great deal of critical attention, the much less common word for willing that also contains the notion of desiring, *khoten'e*, and words with its related roots (*khot'*- and *khoch*-) are used in *Notes from Underground* much more often than *volia*.[26] In *Notes from Underground*, *khoten'e* appears twenty times; *khochu* or *khochet* (I want or he wants)—forty-five times; various other forms—*khotet'* (to want), *khotelos'* (I felt like), *zakhotelos'* (I suddenly got the urge), *okhota* (desire; urge)—seventy-four times. There are dozens of appearances of similar-sounding words—*khot'* and *khotia*—which, although having no meaning related to desiring (*khoten'e*), spread the sounds of desiring throughout the work. These sounds also extend paranomastically (through alliteration) to the very discomforting "*kho**khot**"* (guffaw) and "*kho**khot**at'sia*" (burst out laughing), which likewise have no connection in meaning but designate involuntary, jeering responses that make the Underground Man cringe. In contrast, "*volia*" (conscious will) appears eighteen times, and "*svoevolie*" (self-will) appears twice. It is certainly significant, however, that the "*vol'*-" root is ubiquitous, for example, in such words as "*pozvol'te*" and "*izvol'te*" (permit me) and "*dozvol'te*" (allow me). The repetitions of these roots (*khoch, khot'*, and *vol'-*) create a subliminal tapestry of "desiring" and "wanting" that asserts its edgy, unmanageable presence throughout *Notes from Underground* and is the very stuff of the unconscious.

The word *khoten'e* is a key word in Dostoevsky's vocabulary of the psyche. Relatively unusual sounding, it lacks the fields of meaning of *volia*, which is linked to issues of conscious judgment and action, self-will, willfulness, and arbitrariness. *Khoten'e* links more clearly to unconscious and involuntary desire. Although it appears in apposition to *volia* and *svobodnaia volia* (free will), *khoten'e* is also independently contrasted to "reason" or *rassudok*. Much deeper and more pervasive than reason, it becomes the nascent foundation, however shaky and unreliable, of the self. As the Underground Man famously says, "[R]eason, gentlemen, is a fine thing without a doubt, but reason is only reason and satisfies only human faculties of reason, but desiring [*khoten'e*] is the manifestation of all life, that is, all human life . . . and even though our lives in this manifestation often produce rubbish, at least it is still life, and not just the calculation of a square root" (*Notes* I:8). Desiring is the one aspect of human nature that we know will always exist. And even if it works at cross-purposes to the goals of reason, it is still more important than reason. Desiring is what differentiates a person from a tool or a cog in a machine: "What is a person without wishes, without will, and without desires but an organ stop?" (*Notes* I:8). And desiring can be for the good or the bad. If it is ignored, it will almost certainly be for the bad.

Underground desiring affects the practice of ideal values but does not *itself* represent value. The underground is in no way an ideal space or a "more true" space than any imagined, idealized space above ground. Awareness of the underground can lead to seemingly "truer" insights into human nature, though, as we know, the Underground Man does not let us believe in their truth for very long. The Underground Man does "try on" an idealization of the underground and immediately rejects that option:

> Better to live in conscious inertia. Therefore, long live the underground! I may have said that I envy a normal person to my last bit of spleen, even though in the conditions I now see him, I wouldn't want to be him (although I still won't stop envying him. No, no, the underground still is more advantageous!) There at least I can . . . Oh, even here I am fibbing! I'm fibbing because, just as I know that two times two is four, I know that it isn't the underground that is better but something entirely different, which I yearn for but can't find! The heck with the underground! (*Notes* I:9)

Although awareness of underground desires and drives (for example, the drive to power, to influence and control other people) can lead to a trenchant critique of any system of value, it is also corrosive and ultimately destroys all opportunity for human self-respect. It undermines any idealizing innocence, for example, a belief in true love. Here, following Schopenhauer, true love becomes merely the window dressing for an unconscious urge, in this case, the need to wield power over another person:

> "I couldn't even fall in love because . . . to love with me always meant tyrannizing and being morally superior. My whole life I could not even imagine to myself another kind of love . . . In my underground dreams I couldn't imagine love in any other way than as a struggle, I always began with hate and ended with moral conquest and then couldn't imagine what I should do with the subjugated object." (*Notes* II:10)

Both Dostoevsky and Nietzsche suggest a generalization about the underground: the "underground" is a subliminal space that exists in every person, a space of substantial importance, of authenticity, that is not just cheating or swindling (*naduvanie*) or a fake. The Underground Man concludes first by questioning just himself: "Why am I made with these kinds of desires? It can't really be that I'm made [*ustroen*] this way, just to draw the conclusion that my nature [*ustroistvo*] is really just a swindle?" (*Notes* I:10). He then suggests that everyone—and not he alone—faces the same quandary: "[T]he main point is that all this will produce the most unpleasant impression because *all of us have lost the habit of living* [*otvykli ot zhizni*], *we all are doing poorly* [*khromaem*], to a greater or lesser degree" (*Notes* II:10, emphasis added).

The Underground Man is sure that generalizing his own condition to all people will meet with tremendous resistance from his intended audience of "men of action," whom he imagines stamping their feet and shouting, "Speak for yourself alone and your miseries in the underground, but don't dare say 'all of us'"; to which the Underground Man retorts that he has taken to an extreme what other people out of cowardice have "not even dared to take half way" (*Notes* II:10). He argues that virtually everyone will be in deep denial of their own internal undergrounds, which in itself is a disturbing, destructive step: "We even have a hard time being people [*chelovekami*]—people each with our own, real, flesh and blood; we are ashamed of that, we consider it a scandal and try to adhere to some sort of impossible norm [*norovim byt' kakimi-to nebyvalymi obshchechelovekami*]. We are stillborn . . . Soon we'll think of a way to be born of an idea" (*Notes* II:10). If one denies one's inner, though unknowable, core—however horrifying that core might be—one relinquishes the basis on which to develop into more than just someone else's idea—one loses the potential to gain real personhood.

On the Genealogy of Morals concludes with a human archetype that can face his underground, contemplate it, and embrace it—the ascetic phi-

Edith W. Clowes

losopher. The crisis of the day, in Nietzsche's view, is the well-trained but unthinking "last man," who like Dostoevsky's imagined audience denies any connection to an unconscious. Nietzsche holds out the hope for the inner, autonomous development of a few strong, thinking, self-reflexive people. With the ascetic philosopher, "the animal being becomes more spiritual and acquires wings; *repose in all cellar regions*; all dogs nicely chained up; no barking of hostility and shaggy-haired rancor; no gnawing worm of injured ambition" (*GM* III:8, 108E, emphasis added). The moral-psychological space here is no longer an underground but the wide-open space of the desert. The desire for power and revenge has become conscious and has been acknowledged and addressed. In both these cases, Dostoevsky and Nietzsche have made the case that moral need—whether perverted or not—is located in the indispensable underground and is crucial to a productive modern moral consciousness.

Among the innovative aspects of Dostoevsky's and Nietzsche's concepts of the underground is the psychological function of turning one's aggressive, violent impulses against oneself and blaming oneself for one's earthly condition. For both writers, the sense of one's own weakness and inability to take revenge, hateful and ugly as it is, informs and deepens human reflexivity and ultimately moral consciousness in ways that contradict Enlightenment views of morality, from Locke and Kant to Chernyshevsky. Self-contempt and the inner act of deliberately undermining one's cherished ideal values, reevaluating the world and human behavior—however "sick" or "perverse"—these inner functions are crucial to the deepening of moral consciousness. As the Underground Man puts it, "in this cold, loathsome half-despair, half-belief, in the conscious burying of myself alive from grief, in the underground for forty years, *in all this poison of unrequited desires, turned inward*, in all this fever of indecision, firm decisions then retracted the next minute—was the essence of [a] strange pleasure" (*Notes* I:3, emphasis added). Nietzsche seems to echo the Underground Man's insight that, far from being at the opposite poles of moral value, as the utilitarians held, pain and pleasure are closely intertwined. Whether inwardly or outwardly directed, that "subterranean thing," cruelty and making another or oneself suffer as a form of pleasure, is a frequent motivation for "moral" behavior (*GM* II:6, 63E).

The Underground Man's self-loathing and Nietzsche's concept of "bad conscience" are quite similar. The underground realm for both writers has, in fact, served as the site of a human self-creativity that has made human nature itself more complex and profound, by making it self-reflective. Both argue that psychological constraints, which they express through ideological and social metaphors, have brought about human reflexivity. For the Underground Man it is the symbolic "wall," the inescapable "laws" of rational thought that established an authoritative, broadly accepted set of values based on a limited physiological and rational definition of human nature.

136

Nietzsche thinks of early, psychologically simpler people as being independent, akin to Rousseau's natural man. He compares the experience of violent urges being hemmed in, repressed, to being forced to live in an urban
environment, "enclosed within the walls of society and of peace" (*GM* II:16,
84E). The ultimate result is an awareness of oneself in one's social environment that can eventually lead to moral consciousness.

The Underground Man's deepened moral consciousness and en-
suing confession grow out of a life of gathering self-contempt and corrosive,
underground skepticism. After railing against the rational egoists, he turns
against himself and doubts his own veracity. No claim to "truth," even his
own claim, can be allowed to stand: "I swear to you, gentlemen, that I don't
believe a word I've just now jotted down! I mean, I believe it, if you like, but
at the same time, I don't know why, I suspect that I'm lying like a dog. 'So,
why did you write all that?' you ask. Well, what if I could put you into prison
[*posadil by*] for about forty years without anything to do, and came back to
the underground forty years later, to ask what had become of you? Can one
really leave a person alone for forty years?" (*Notes* I:9). While repeating the
themes of the underground's inertness, the Underground Man also suggests
that his life of observing his own inner motivations has altered him. Unlike
the simple "man of action," he can reflect on the quality of his own feeling
and thinking. Despite all the love of paradox and the self-contradiction and
the pleasure he takes in his own psychological pain, he has arrived at least at
the *perception* of a new level of honesty and truth.

Nietzsche compares the conditions for an emerging concept of bad
conscience to imagined prehistorical conditions that placed constraints on
people through forces of social conformity. In this situation instincts not
permitted to be discharged outward will turn inward, be "internalized" and
pointed at one's self, which brings about the appearance of the "soul" (84E).
Bad conscience is "man's suffering of man, of himself—the result of forcible
sundering from his animal past . . . a declaration of war against the old instincts upon which his strength, joy, and terribleness had rested hitherto"
(*GM* II:18, 85E). Bad conscience is the result of a person turning against "his
ancient animal self" ("*sein ganzes tierisches altes Selbst*"; *GM* II:18, 274G).
The pleasure in suffering, like the Underground Man's seemingly perverse
pleasure in dwelling on his psychological pains, is the beginning of moral
consciousness and of the deep alteration of human nature. This change, as
Nietzsche famously says, is "new, profound, unheard of, enigmatic, contradictory, and *pregnant with a future*" (*GM* II:18, 85E). In his view, this unconscious suffering of oneself is the function that brings out the "flower" of
new ideological formations. Here Nietzsche transforms Feuerbach's philosophical anthropological view that humans created gods as a powerful version of themselves into a subliminal psychological function, remarking:

This secret self-ravishment, this artists' cruelty, this delight in imposing a form upon oneself as a hard, recalcitrant, suffering material and in burning a will, a critique, a contradiction, a contempt, a No into it, this uncanny, dreadfully joyous labor of a soul voluntarily at odds with itself that makes itself suffer out of joy in making suffer—eventually this entire *active* 'bad conscience'—you will have guessed it—as the womb of all ideal and imaginative phenomena, also brought to light an abundance of strange new beauty and affirmation, and perhaps beauty itself. (*GM* II:18, 87–88E)

Why do spatial metaphors of the psyche matter? Although it is a cliché to assert that the place of the underground deepens and complicates our understanding of human nature, these "maps" of the psyche divulge a new orientation to the origins and nature of moral consciousness and draw attention to crucial problems in moral behavior. They make the psyche imaginable as a *human* space, replacing an age-old notion of the soul as the site of intervention of the superhuman in human life (through visions, dreams, voices, feeling, intuition). A "map" will show not just traditional vertical spaces of the psyche—"high" and "low," "above" and "below," "over" and "under"— but also the symbolic values embedded in these spaces as Dostoevsky and Nietzsche articulate them. They are both familiar and uncanny—both self and other. *That* the two see the unconscious as the motivator for moral consciousness—for the sense of moral need—has long since been viewed as their defining feature as modern thinkers. By comparing and contrasting *how* each thinker undertakes the project of mapping the underground, we have seen how both thinkers link moral consciousness and moral behavior to their unconscious ground in instinct and drive. Importantly, while these instincts may appear as "bad" and "destructive," they no longer are "evil" or "diabolical." They represent our only ground for moral behavior in the modern world, in which the divine no longer is viewed as creative agent but is, in contrast, created by people out of a psychological need for higher moral order.

The impact of Dostoevsky's and Nietzsche's verbal maps of the unconscious anticipate later spatial constructions of the psyche, particularly Freud's.[27] Freud in *The Ego and the Id* models the psyche as a generally circular, brainlike space with the very top designated as perceptible and knowable to the conscious brain.[28] An important parallel to Dostoevsky's and Nietzsche's verbal maps is Freud's emphasis in this model on auditory signals for access to the preconscious level of the brain. Whatever the linkage with Freud, Dostoevsky and Nietzsche both made the human unconscious with all its ancient animal baggage not only thinkable and imaginable, but connected to the highest aspirations of human moral consciousness.

NOTES

Translations in this chapter are the author's unless otherwise indicated. The chapter epigraphs are as follows:

F. M. Dostoevsky, *Zapiski iz podpol'ia*, http://az.lib.ru/d/dostoewskij_f_m /text_0290.shtml (accessed May 2011), I:3. "*Там, в своем мерзком, вонючем под-подполье, наша обиженная, прибитая и осмеянная мышь немедленно погружается в холодную, ядовитую и, главное, вековечную злость. Сорок лет сряду будет припоминать до последних, самых постыдных подробностей свою обиду и при этом каждый раз прибавлять от себя подробности еще постыднейшие, злобно поддразнивая и раздражая себя собственной фантазией.*" My translation, emphasis added.

Th. Dostoïevsky, *L'esprit souterrain*, trans. E. Halpérine and Ch. Morice (Paris: Plon, 1886), 169 (II:3). "*Là, dans son souterrain infect et sale, notre rat offensé et raillé se cache aussitôt dans sa méchanceté froide, empoisonnée, éternelle. Quarante années de suite il va se rappeler jusqu'aux plus honteux détails de son offense et, chaque fois il ajoutera des détails plus honteux encore, en s'irritant de sa perverse fantaisie, inventant des circonstances aggravantes sous prétexte qu'elles auraient pu avoir lieu, et ne se pardonnant rien.*" My translation, emphasis added to show additions by French adapters.

Friedrich Nietzsche, *Zur Genealogie der Moral*, in *Werke*, 5 vols. (Frankfurt: Ullstein, 1981), I:13. "*Diese Kellertiere voll Rache und Hass—was machen sie doch gerade aus Rache und Hass? Hörten Sie je diese Worte? Würden Sie ahnen, wenn Sie nur ihren Worten trauten, dass Sie unter lauter Menschen des Ressentiment sind?*" My translation, emphasis added.

1. Lev Shestov, *Dostoevskii i Nitsshe: Filosofiia tragedii* (http://www.vehi .net/shestov/nitshe.html, accessed May 17, 2011): "If people are not brought closer together through shared birth, life lived in shared quarters, or similarity of character—but through identical inward experience—then Nietzsche and Dostoevsky can without exaggeration be called brothers, and even twins."

2. The theme of the moral aspects of the Underground Man's monologue and their distortion through feeling is among the oldest of critical themes in the commentary. For example, the public intellectual Vasilii Rozanov in his 1894 essay *The Legend of the Grand Inquisitor*, noted the Underground Man's long observation of his own inner motivations as the source of his moral critique: "The Underground Man is a person immersed in the depths of his self [*ushed-shii v glubiny sebia*], who has grown to hate life, whose malicious critique of the rational utopian ideal is based on a precise knowledge of human nature, honed by isolated, prolonged observation of history and himself" (Vasilii Rozanov, *Legenda o velikom inkvizitore*, http://www.vehi.net/rozanov/legenda.html, accessed June 7, 2011). Lev Shestov in *Dostoevskii and Nietzsche: The Philosophy of Tragedy* (1902) equated the "underground" and "psychology." Shestov

considered Dostoevsky's underground to be one of his world-class creations, the "first gift that Europe gratefully received from Russia was Dostoevsky's 'psychology,' that is, the Underground Man." *Dostoevskii i Nitsshe: Filosofiia tragedii* (http://www.vehi.net/shestov/nitshe.html, accessed May 17, 2011). Although, in Shestov's view, Dostoevsky is horrified at the experience of the underground, as something within himself, familiar yet disturbing, he finds the underground to be the "path to the truth." Much later, Joseph Frank in his treatment of *Notes from Underground* sees both sides, both the psychological and the ideological. The Underground Man, in his view, is both a "moral-psychological type whose egoism Dostoevsky wishes to expose" and a "social-ideological one, whose psychology must be seen as intimately interconnected with the idea he accepts and by which he tries to live," which, indeed, is the very philosophy he also hates, Chernyshevsky's rational egoism. Joseph Frank, *Dostoevsky: The Stir of Liberation, 1860–65* (Princeton: Princeton University Press, 1986), 314.

3. Robert L. Jackson, *Dostoevsky's Underground Man in Russian Literature* (The Hague: Mouton, 1958), 29–31. Jackson sees the underground as a "fantastic, withdrawn, lonely, and troubled inner world of consciousness" (p. 29). He draws attention to the allegorical aspects of the underground and views *Notes from Underground* as an "internal drama" with characters being "fragments of personality" (p. 31).

4. Eric von der Luft and Douglas G. Stenberg, "Dostoevskii's Specific Influence on Nietzsche's Preface to *Daybreak*," *Journal of the History of Ideas* 52:3 (1991): 441–61. See especially the treatment of Nietzsche's mole, pp. 455–56.

5. In contrast, Voltaire in his *Encyclopedia*, vol. 12, claimed that "morality proceeds from God, like light; our superstitions are only darkness. Reflect, reader; pursue the truth, and draw the consequences"; http://www.gutenberg.org/files/35628/35628-0.txt, accessed June 6, 2011.

6. Sigmund Freud, *The Ego and the Id* (1923), trans. J. Riviere (New York: Norton, 1962). See the model presented on p. 14.

7. Plato, *The Republic*, Book 7, in *The Republic and Other Works*, trans. B. Jowett (New York: Anchor Press, 1973), 205.

8. Note, also, that for the sixth-century philosopher Boethius, who languished long in prison, philosophy and higher consciousness come down from heaven.

9. Arthur Schopenhauer, *Essays and Aphorisms*, trans. R. J. Hollingdale (Harmondsworth: Penguin, 1981), 56.

10. Ibid., 57.

11. Ludwig Feuerbach, "The Being of Man in General," in *The Essence of Religion*, trans. G. Eliot, http://www.marxists.org/reference/archive/feuerbach/works/essence/ec01_1.htm, accessed June 6, 2011. It is worth noting, in contrast, that Feuerbach does note the vertical quality of seeing for human cognition: "The eye that looks into the starry heavens, that contemplates the light that bears neither use nor harm, that has nothing in common with the earth and its

needs, this eye contemplates its own nature, its own origin in that light. The eye is heavenly in its nature. Hence, it is only through the eye that man rises above the earth; hence theory begins only when man directs his gaze towards the heavens. The first philosophers were astronomers."

12. Discussed in Joseph Frank, *Dostoevsky: The Stir of Liberation, 1860–65* (Princeton: Princeton University Press, 1986), 311.

13. Nikolay Chernyshevsky, *What Is To Be Done?*, trans. M. Katz (Ithaca: Cornell University Press, 1989), 129–30.

14. In *Thus Spoke Zarathustra*, Zarathustra uses "dogs in the cellar" as an image of the unconscious: "In the end all your passions became virtues and all your devils became angels. Once upon a time you had *dogs in your cellar*, but in the end they were transformed into birds and sweet singers." "Von den Freuden und Leidenschaften" *Also Sprach Zarathustra* in *Werke*, vol. 2, ed. K. Schlechta (Frankfurt: Ullstein, 1976), 302, emphasis added.

15. C. A. Miller, "Nietzsche's 'Discovery' of Dostoevsky," *Nietzsche-Studien* 2 (1973): 202–57.

16. Letter from Nietzsche to Overbeck, quoted in Miller, 205.

17. Miller, 207. This mistake of linking the speaker in *Notes from Underground* to Ordynov in "The Landlady" has its own history, launched by F. M. Borras in his introduction to the Bradda Books edition of *Zapiski iz podpol'ia* (Letchworth: Bradda, 1965). In his translation of *On the Genealogy of Morals* Walter Kaufmann mistakes *L'esprit souterrain* for "a French translation of that work [*Notes from Underground*]" (p. 128, ftn. 1). Recently Yi-Ping Ong makes the same mistake as Kaufmann but compounds it by claiming that Nietzsche had also already finished his final draft of *On the Genealogy of Morals* when he found *L'esprit souterrain*. See "A View of Life: Nietzsche, Kierkegaard, and the Novel," *Philosophy and Literature* 33:1 (April 2009): 167–83.

18. Quoted in Miller, 208.

19. For an argument for Dostoevsky's impact on this 1886 preface to *Daybreak*, see von der Luft and Stenberg, "Dostoevskii's Specific Influence."

20. Nikolai Antsiferov, *Dusha Peterburga* (Petrograd, 1922), 36, http://www.wmos.ru/book/detail.php?PAGEN_1=36&ID=4255, accessed June 3, 2011.

21. As Bakhtin puts it, the Underground Man "figures not as a person in real life but as a conscious, dreaming subject"; M. M. Bakhtin, *Problemy poetiki Dostoevskogo*, http://az.lib.ru/d/dostoewskij_f_m/text_0410.shtml, accessed May 15, 2011.

22. F. M. Dostoevskii, *Zapiski iz podpol'ia*, http://az.lib.ru/d/dostoewskij_f_m/text_0290.shtml (accessed May 20, 2011). Citations from *Zapiski iz podpol'ia*, hereafter abbreviated as *Notes*, will be given in the text, showing part and chapter. Translations are my own.

23. James P. Scanlan, "The Case against Rational Egoism" in *Dostoevsky the Thinker* (Ithaca: Cornell University Press, 2002), 57–80.

24. Friedrich Nietzsche, *On the Genealogy of Morals,* trans. W. Kaufmann (New York: Vintage, 1969), 46. Further citations from the English translation will appear in the text, with *Genealogy* abbreviated as *GM*, and showing part, chapter, and page number followed by "E." Page numbers followed by "G" are from volume 3 of the German original: Friedrich Nietzsche, *Zur Genealogie der Moral,* in *Werke,* 5 vols. (Frankfurt: Ullstein, 1981).

25. Nietzsche, *"Will jemand ein wenig in das Geheimnis* hinab- und hinuntersehn, *wie man auf Erden Ideale fabriziert . . . Hier ist der Blick offen in diese dunkle Werkstätte"* (*GM* I:13, 237G; emphasis added).

26. A recent consideration of *volia* is: Evgenia Cherkasova, "Kant on Free Will and Arbitrariness: A View from Dostoevsky's Underground," *Philosophy and Literature* 28:2 (October 2004): 367–78.

27. Henri F. Ellenberger, *The Discovery of the Unconscious: The History and Evolution of Dynamic Psychiatry* (New York: Basic Books, 1970), 277. This view is disputed by Daniel Chapelle, *Nietzsche and Psychoanalysis* (Albany: SUNY Press, 1993), 12–13. Alternatively, as recently as 1974, a broadly used German psychology textbook compares Freud's model of the psyche to the natural image of an iceberg, with six unconscious parts underwater and the seventh, conscious part visible and above water. For other work on Dostoevsky's moral psychology see Edith W. Clowes, "'Self-Laceration' and 'Resentment': The Terms of Moral Psychology in Dostoevsky and Nietzsche," in *Freedom and Responsibility: Festschrift in Honor of Robert Louis Jackson,* ed. E. C. Allen and G. S. Morson (Evanston: Northwestern University Press, 1995), 119–33. "*Nadryv*" has traditionally been called "self-laceration," or more recently "stress" (in the Volokhonskaia and Pevear translation of *Brothers Karamazov*), neither of which is satisfactory, in my view.

28. Sigmund Freud, *The Ego and the Id*, 14.

Ilya Kliger

Tragic Nationalism in Nietzsche and Dostoevsky

THIS CHAPTER STAGES a confrontation between Dostoevsky and Nietzsche on the terrain of what might be called the "historical imaginary." By "historical imaginary" I mean here a vision of the contemporary moment's place within a larger historical narrative, a vision that contains the moment's diagnosis and, in the same gesture, projects its cure. In the account that follows, each author brings something to the encounter: Nietzsche, his elaborate understanding of the tragic, with its historico-philosophical resonances; Dostoevsky, his tangled nationalism and its complex novelistic refractions. Put another way, an encounter with Dostoevsky will render more pronounced in Nietzsche's early thought the role of a certain nationalist imaginary in locating the place of the tragic in modernity. Nietzsche's work on tragedy, in turn, will illuminate crucial aspects of Dostoevsky's novelistic poetics.[1] Ultimately, then, this chapter seeks to make visible the outlines of tragic nationalism as a species of modern historical imaginary, capable of both representing and—imaginatively—overcoming the dire condition of modern life.[2]

NONSYNCHRONOUS HISTORIOGRAPHIES

In the 1870s, Nietzsche repeatedly describes the modern age as hasty, mindless, broken up into isolated, self-seeking individuals; in short, as "the age of atomic chaos."[3] These are familiar topoi of what Georg Lukács has called "romantic anticapitalism," a position that condemns "a society based on money and competition" for separating "individuals into egotistical monads that are essentially hostile or indifferent to each other."[4] As Robert Sayre and Michael Löwy point out, Lukács uses the phrase for the first time in connection with Dostoevsky, whose writings indeed provide countless examples of such condemnation. Perhaps the best-known and the most vivid of these is formulated by the Elder Zosima's mysterious visitor in *The Brothers Karamazov* (1880): "For all men in our age [of aloneness (*uedinenie*)] are separated into units, each seeks seclusion in his own hole, each withdraws from the

143

others . . . He accumulates wealth in solitude . . . and does not see, mad-man as he is, that the more he accumulates, the more he sinks into suicidal impotence."[5]

As is usually the case with romantic anticapitalism, however, the vision of the unhappy present is opposed by some alternative, some new and genuine togetherness. Thus, for Zosima's visitor "man's true security lies not in his own solitary effort, but in the general wholeness of humanity"; man's true mission is not accumulation of wealth but "the act [*podvig*] of brotherly communion."[6] Similarly, Nietzsche speaks of "moments and, as it were, sparks of the brightest, most ardent fire in whose light we no longer understand the word 'I,'" and of an integration "into a powerful community, one that, to be sure, is not held together by external forms and laws, but by a fundamental idea."[7]

A certain kind of unification, then, is a crucial element in the historio-graphic imaginaries of both authors; its metaphysical and ethical stakes are high. But what sort of unification, and what are the means for its achieve-ment? Here it is worth pausing for a more detailed account.

In his notebooks from 1861, Dostoevsky glorifies the feat whereby the highly developed individual sacrifices itself for "the all" and "[returns] to immediacy, the masses."[8] Dostoevsky's choice of words here invokes a cer-tain philosophy of history, broadly shared among the Native Soil journalists (*Pochvenniki*) contributing to the Dostoevsky brothers' journal, *Vremia* (*Time*, 1861–63). In the language of one of the journal's intellectual leaders and its chief literary critic, Apollon Grigoriev, "immediacy" refers to the uncon-scious tribal life of a people, a life undisturbed by contact with foreign cul-tures and thus lacking both the means and the need for self-reflection. It is this life, with its unique and unrepeatable ideals and forms, that constitutes the essential core of a people and the seed from which its history sprouts forth. Invariably, however, the era of immediacy in the life of a nation is re-placed by a period of reflection; doubt, analysis, critique set in, undermining the foundations of communal life. Only toward the end of this second devel-opmental stage is early "tribal" immediacy recovered, reaching conscious ar-ticulation in the work of artists, poets, and intellectuals. Such people create "in the name of the ideals inherent in [their people] and not of those [they] had made up [themselves]."[9]

Returning to Dostoevsky's vision of unification, we can see the stan-dard historico-philosophical tropes acquire a different resonance. Dosto-evsky does not speak of sublation or synthesis; he speaks of the precipitant sacrifice of the self, the plunge that takes one from the lonesome pinnacle of reflection back to the sea of undifferentiated togetherness: for "it is clear that the highest willfulness is at the same time the highest abnegation of one's will . . . In what consists the ideal? In reaching the full power of consciousness and development, in becoming fully conscious of one's 'I'—and in giving it *all* up, willfully, for *all*" (*PSS* 20, 192). There is no talk here of the passing of the national-historical baton from the common people to the intelligentsia, but rather of the sudden collapse of the intelligentsia back onto the common people.

Writing in a less ecstatic and metaphysical voice, Dostoevsky often addresses the problem of unity with reference to one of the most burning issues of the time, the matter of "the people's education [*narodnoe obrazovanie*]." The standard Native Soil line on this issue consisted in asserting that the spread of literacy and general knowledge among the newly emancipated peasants would grant them broader access to the social and cultural life of the country. In certain respects, Dostoevsky, too, embraces this vision. He writes: "We just recognized that we were separated by purely external circumstances. These circumstances did not allow the masses to follow us and thus to bring into our activity *all* of the powers of the Russian spirit."[10] Yet nagging in the background is a question: if the common people simply re-enforce the ranks of the educated elites, will not Russia as a whole, without a remainder of communal "immediacy," enter into the modern world, so ruefully decried for its descent into universal "aloneness" (*uedinenie*)? This is, after all, if not always the conscious goal, then at least the actual outcome of most nationalist campaigns for the education of the people: the creation of a robust and mobile middle class capable of functioning in a capitalist society, the production of "industrial man."[11] A true "romantic anti-capitalist," Dostoevsky inevitably recoils from this vision. He repeatedly assures us that nothing like this would happen, that there is not, nor can be, a separation of estates in Russia, and that the intelligentsia, being one with the people, cannot make of them anything they're not. The people's education thus acquires a tautological status: its urgent work is to unify what is already inseparable. If its task were anything else, it would be the wrong kind of education: instead of genuine unity, it would achieve only synthetic and homogeneous atomization. But to posit the unity of the intelligentsia and the people in the face of its obvious disunity is to court paradoxical consequences.

One example—found in Dostoevsky's article "Bookishness and Literacy" ("Knizhnost' i gramotnost'"), from 1861—will suffice for our purposes here. The striking premise of this article is that the literary works that are most distinctively Russian, most representative of the common Russian people, are utterly inaccessible to them. It is of course possible to imagine, Dostoevsky argues, that a truly "popular" poet might arise from the peasant milieu and reflect it beautifully in the language of the illiterate or semiliterate peasant himself. Such a poet would certainly be easier for the common people to understand. And yet he would not express the *essence* of the people nearly as well as Pushkin, thoroughly Westernized and completely incomprehensible to the peasant. How could that be right? Isn't Pushkin, according to the Dostoevsky of *Vremia*, the poet of alienation *par excellence*?[12] Are we to suppose that alienation, the modern condition of rootlessness, is an essential feature of the very immediacy of the Russian people? Is unity, in the case of modern Russia, achieved precisely in separation? Or, in the metaphysical language of the notes: is the sacrifice of the reflective self to the immediacy of the masses performed precisely at the pinnacle of this self's sovereignty?

These questions must await further elaboration below, but it is clear already at this point that, instead of neutralizing the paradox of unity-in-separation, Dostoevsky's account of the people's literacy reproduces it. Instead of simply adopting the standard nationalist response to the emancipation—educate, mobilize, modernize!—Dostoevsky struggles with it. The historical nonsynchrony of the intelligentsia and the people, the direct outcome of the institution of serfdom, is for him a source of horror and salvation at once. The status of the Westernizing elites is correspondingly ambiguous. On the one hand, he refuses to agree with those in the Slavophile camp who take the Russian upper classes to be a wholly foreign phenomenon: the Russian intelligentsia is, for Dostoevsky, Russian enough.[13] But at the same time he cannot fail to acknowledge "the depth of the abyss separating our European-style civilized society from the people."[14] In short, what Dostoevsky appears to posit, by contrast with the more linear vision of national development from immediacy to reflection through education into the realities of modern life, is a paradoxical principle of unity-in-separation, a principle that internalizes (rather than denies) the nonsynchronous predicament of the contemporary Russian moment.[15]

One of the less conspicuous passages of *The Birth of Tragedy* (1872) reads, in a recognizably "Dostoevskian" manner: "This so questionable culture of ours has as yet nothing in common with the noble core of our people's character. On the contrary, all our hopes stretch out longingly toward the perception that beneath this restlessly palpitating cultural life and convulsion there is concealed a glorious, intrinsically healthy, primordial power."[16] The culture of which Nietzsche speaks here, modern European culture broadly understood, is the culmination of a long modernity that begins with the death of Attic tragedy and the triumph of Socratic optimism in philosophy. What Nietzsche calls the Socratic-Alexandrian age, characterized by individualism, rationalism, blind faith in science, and cowardly failure to face existence in its naked horror and beauty, reigns, more or less comfortably, from the death of tragic culture to the day of the composition of *The Birth of Tragedy*. But all along, underneath the shallow surface of this culture (one that is, incidentally, foreign—"Romanic," "Western," "French") the primordial substratum of the German character nonsynchronously keeps alive.

Much of Nietzsche's thought (early as well as late) can be understood as an attempt to answer the question: What is to be done in the face of the abyss separating the false and feeble civilization to which all writing and re-flection belong from the true, robust source of life so gloriously on display in archaic societies, particularly that of the Greeks? One of his earliest attempts to answer this question, to envision bridging the gap, involves, just as it does in Dostoevsky, the highly topical concern with the question of education for a genuine German culture (*Bildung*).

At first glance, his 1872 lecture series "On the Future of Our Educa-tional Institutions" might appear to be no more than a restatement of the basic principles of the classical German discourse on *Bildung* from the late eighteenth and early nineteenth centuries. Thus, one recent commentator sees the lectures as presenting a critique of "the disastrous status quo of an increasingly specialized education system" and a defense of the concep-tion of education as "*Bildung* in the sense of an aesthetic and philosophical self-cultivation, thus reiterating the ideological program of the nineteenth-century *Bildungsbürgertum*."[17]

It is indeed possible to detect a Humboldtian dimension to the lec-tures, especially when it comes to mistrust of the state and critique of spe-cialization. But there is at least one crucial and telling difference: though there is certainly much talk of *Bildung* here, little or no mention is made of *Bürgertum*. Instead, the public in Basel heard a lot about *das Volk* and *der Genius*. The main "action," the drama of true culture, unfolds in Nietzsche's lectures between these two:

Thus education of the mass cannot be our goal: rather education of the in-dividual, selected human beings, equipped for great and lasting works . . . That which one calls education of the people is to be reached in a direct way, for instance through a universally compulsory elementary instruction, only wholly externally and crudely: the authentic, deeper regions in which the great masses generally meet with culture, there where the people nourishes its religious instincts, where it further composes in its mythological images [*Bildern*], where it keeps up its faith in its custom, its right, its home soil, its language, all these regions are hardly, and in any case only through acts of de-structive violence, to be reached in a direct way: and in these most serious things truly to advance the education of the people only means so much, to ward off these acts of destructive violence, and to maintain that wholesome unconsciousness, that sound sleeping of the people, without which counteref-fect, without which remedy no culture [*Kultur*], with the consuming tension and excitement of its effects, can endure. [Those who speak of the educa-tion of the people] destroy the roots of those highest and noblest educational forces [*Bildungskräfte*] which burst forth out of the unconsciousness of the people, which have their motherly vocation [*Bestimmung*] in the begetting of genius and then in the proper education [*Erziehung*] and cultivation [*Pflege*] of the same.[18]

All this could not of course be farther from Humboldt's vision of the nation as a community of free and fully realized individuals in which it is the duty of *all* to achieve "the highest and most harmonious development of his powers to a complete and consistent whole."[19] Nietzsche's conception of culture is not democratically diverse but two-tiered and hierarchical. He appears to treasure the very archaic properties of the people that the proponents of the "education of the masses" desire to supplant with the superficial, rationalist, and individualistic modern civilization. This erasure is, according to him, neither feasible nor desirable. As one commentator points out, what Nietzsche objects to here is the kind of education that would be made available to the greatest possible number of citizens with the purpose of producing numberless bourgeois.[20] Middle-class morality, willy-nilly democratic politics, and positivist epistemology—these are the rotten fruit, in 1872, of the noble Humboldtian seeds from 1791. They are not the values of a true culture, but they are the only ones available to modernity pure and simple, uprooted from its "native soil" (*Heimatsboden*).

Nietzsche's true culture, then, relies on and feeds off social and historical stratification. What matters for it is an ability to endow the unconscious and mythopoetic powers of the people with a well-defined shape of a great person or work. The logic here is evidently reminiscent of Dostoevsky's: it is precisely where the people are most themselves—most confident of their religious ideals, most unreflective of their native way of life— that they are closest also to high artistic culture. And it is at its highest—in the figures of great meaning-giving, image-making powers (e.g., Wagner, Pushkin)—that culture is able to give voice and shape to the unconscious life of the common people.

For Dostoevsky, the concept of the *narod* has a very particular, though also a confusingly dual, referent: the common people (*prostonarod'e*), and the Russian nation as a whole (*narod*), for which the former often stand synecdochally. Nietzsche's *Volk*, on the other hand, is a somewhat more rarefied, though also dual, category. In addition to invoking the German nation (as contrasted with the French, Romance, Latin, in short, foreign elements), it also approaches something altogether metaphysical, serving as a catachretic name for a kind of natural flux of creation and destruction. This is the primordial "All" in which, according to the maxim of one of Nietzsche's favorite pre-Socratic philosophers, Anaximander, all existing things are condemned to perish "for they must pay penance and be judged for their injustices, in accordance with the ordinance of time."[21] In this view, culture is what ensures, through the mediation of the genius (artist, philosopher, saint),[22] the preservation in images and symbols of the essence of the people and with it, of the genuine experience of life itself.

To inquire into what that experience might be, in specific social terms, is to confront the darker aspects of Nietzsche's early thought on culture. For the position of the great man vis-à-vis the people is not merely that of increased articulation; it is also the position of lordship. In speaking of the Greeks' special talent for true culture, Nietzsche does not shirk from dwelling on the institution of slavery as its real socioeconomic foundation. The Greeks, Nietzsche says, "regarded [slavery and labor] as a necessary indignity, of which one is ashamed; hidden in this feeling is the unconscious knowledge that the true goal needs these prerequisites, but that here lies the terrible and predatory quality of nature, the sphinx presenting the torso of a beautiful girl with the intention of glorifying the artistic freedom of cultural life."[23] The point here is not simply that artists and philosophers need to lead the life of contemplative leisure in order to produce their works. Worse: culture needs cruelty itself, for its own sake; it feeds off suffering; alternatively, it loses touch with what is most essential about life. "Hence the cruel reality of culture—insofar as it builds triumphal gates on enslavement and destruction."[24] All true beauty and meaning has terrifying origins; all genius is an ability to give voice and image to blind, unarticulated pain; all culture must internalize exploitation. Otherwise, like its modern "autonomous" avatar, it becomes superficial and false by forgetting its origin and impulse.

Like *obrazovanie* in Dostoevsky, then, Nietzsche's *Bildung* is a strange sort of middle term. Intended to mediate between the isolated individual and the communal whole, between the deep archaic past and radical modernity, it produces no middle ground between them—neither transitional stages of development, nor civil society, nor the third estate—but promotes instead an odd vision of immediate unity-in-separation: between antiquity and modernity, community and the individual, reflection that produces stable images and blind creative-destructive nature.

UNIFICATION AND (AS) FORM: CHARACTER

How can this unity-in-separation be characterized more precisely? At least in the early 1870s, when speaking of the true men of culture, Nietzsche has foremost in mind Schopenhauer and Wagner, the exponent of tragic metaphysics and the practitioner of tragic art. The tragic dualism implicit in the figure of the human-beast of the sphinx applies also to them. Schopenhauer, like Anaximander long before him, is the philosopher of tragedy because he refuses to avert his eyes from the creative-destructive workings of the

primordial Will underneath the veneer of well-proportioned, socially sanctioned forms and representations.[25] In Wagner, as in Aeschylus, "the creative, innocent, bright side remained faithful to the dark, uncontrollable, and
tyrannical one."[26] The fidelity of the great men of true culture to the darker,
less tractable sides of existence, even as they create coherence in thought
and in image—this fidelity is what characterizes them as properly tragic.

"The tragic idea," we read in Nietzsche's notebooks from 1869 to
1870, involves "absolute submission to the Olympians out of the most terrible knowledge." And a little further down: "Everything excessive must be
given a voice."[27] Indeed, in the terms of Nietzsche's early work, it is precisely
tragedy that gives voice to excess. Out of the mixture of the Dionysian horror
and ecstasy at the sight of the primal creative-destructive unity of life, tragedy produces calm and lucid Apollonian images. What makes tragedy the
form particularly fit for the task is that it has its roots in the throng of Dionysian worshipers, who, at the height of ecstatic oblivion, imagine themselves
to be transformed into geniuses of nature, satyrs. Thus is formed the proto-
phenomenon of tragedy, the chorus. Nietzsche insists that dramatic action
and character "masks" were nothing other than Apollonian objectifications,
in individuated images, of the ecstatic worship of the Dionysian chorus.[28]
"The choral parts with which tragedy is interlaced are, as it were, the womb
that gave birth to . . . the entire world of the stage, the real drama" (*BT* 65).

The tragic form itself is thus nonsynchronous.[29] On the one hand, on
the level of character and plot as it were, it relies on the more recent and
more measured Apollonian vision of individual action with closer links to
fifth-century Athenian culture. But at the same time, it contains powerful
vestiges of primordial Dionysian worship (*BT* 65), which presupposes precisely the nonreality of individuals and measure, the oneness of all humans
and their ultimate union with the creative-destructive flow of life. We should
be careful, however, not to give in to the lure of a simple dichotomy, linking the chorus with Dionysus and the individuated hero with Apollo. Such
a view would badly misrepresent Nietzsche's account. Though a creature of
Apollonian individuation, the hero is also, simultaneously, beyond individual
measure: his "overweening pride and excess are regarded as the truly hostile
demons of the non-Apollonian sphere, hence as characteristics of the pre-
Apollonian age—that of the Titans" (*BT* 46).

The Apollonian protagonist is thus both Apollonian and Dionysian.
He belongs nonsynchronously both to the Titanic past and to the Olympian
present. Correspondingly, he belongs to two ontological and representational
orders: the Will and appearance, unrepresentable ground and its representation. Put another way, the hero carries within him a piece of the chorus,
a kind of choral substratum, and in the very act of standing apart, elevates
the Dionysian principle to the heights of artistic poignancy and visibility (*BT*

131). The hero's separateness from the chorus does not take the form of alienation pure and simple. Instead, it functions as a kind of condensation, so that looking at the tragic hero on stage, the audience "[does] not see the awkwardly masked human being but rather a visionary figure, born as it were from their own [that is, the chorus's and the audience's] rapture" (*BT* 66). This is how we should understand Nietzsche's claim that "the Greeks simply *could* not suffer individuals on the tragic stage" (*BT* 73).

The Birth of Tragedy itself only hints at the association between the chorus and the archaic primordial spirit of the people. Thus, we are comforted, says Nietzsche, by the thought that "in some inaccessible abyss the German spirit still rests and dreams, undestroyed, in glorious health, profundity, and Dionysian strength, like a knight sunk in slumber; and from the abyss the Dionysian song rises to our ears" (*BT* 142). The notebooks, as well as the subsequent essay on "Wagner in Bayreuth," leave few doubts about the association: "Among the Greeks, the beginnings of drama go back to the unfathomable expressions of folk impulses [*Volksleben*] . . . Nor are such conditions entirely remote from the life of the German people, except that they never experienced such a flowering: at least I see the St. John's and St. Vitus's dancers, who used to wander singing and dancing from town to town in enormous and constantly increasing masses as nothing other than such Dionysian movement."[30]

Now, such "a people" is not something idyllic; and unity with it, with the ecstatic throng of Dionysian revelers, does not entail pacification. It is not a prodigal son's penitent homecoming, nor the result of the sort of social integration we find in the form of the *Bildungsroman*, whose hero, having "sowed his wild oats" as Hegel famously says, is at last "educated into the realities of the present."[31] Nietzsche reminds us that we are talking here of satyrs and not of shepherds with flutes (*BT* 61). The hero's unification with the chorus is identification precisely with what is most extreme, least measured, and least contemporary in him. In temporal terms, it consists not in circling back to the past, nor in giving up on it in the process of educating oneself into the "realities of the present." Rather, the proper tragic attitude to the past is one of framing and flaunting it, of staging its insistence, of giving it voice and shape.

In the 1860s and '70s Dostoevsky repeatedly invokes a world-historiographical persona that can be seen as a counterpart to Nietzsche's Dionysian German knight. It is the Russian epic hero, *bogatyr'*. In an 1873 entry to the *Diary of a Writer*, entitled "Vlas," we find the story, supposedly true, of an eponymous young peasant who comes close to shooting the Eucharist on a dare but, at the last moment, has a sudden vision of Christ on the cross and collapses. Everything about the story seems to fascinate Dostoevsky: the dare itself, the personality of the hero, the social conditions under which such an act is thinkable. "Our epic hero [*bogatyr'*] has awakened," he comments, "and is stretching his arms; perhaps he will have the urge to go on a spree, to dash off somewhere beyond the limit [*makhnut' cherez krai*]."[32] As always, Dostoevsky's greatest interest lies with this *bogatyr'*'s inner experience of the event. He guesses that at some pivotal moment, the young peasant is overcome by "an urge to go beyond the limit, an urge for the sinking sensation one has when one has come to the edge of an abyss, leans halfway over it, looks into the bottomless pit itself, and . . . throws oneself headlong into it like a madman."[33] And again, in a properly nationalist register: "this whirlwind, this fateful maelstrom of violent and momentary negation and destruction of self that is so typical of the Russian national character at certain fateful moments in its existence."[34] Thus, true Russianness is associated with something dangerously vigorous, shockingly self-transcendent, insistently beyond measure.

Dostoevsky initially develops this manner of characterizing the common people in a number of passages in his *Notes from the House of the Dead* (1862). Here, the first-person narrator—a nobleman condemned to hard labor for the murder of his wife—attempts to come to terms with the existence of what he calls "the desperate people" (*reshitel'nye liudi*) among his "common" fellow prisoners.[35] Such people, says the narrator, might live for a long time under persecution, meekly suffering insults and mistreatment year after year, until, suddenly, they can stand it no longer. Then, it is as if such a person "leaps out of measure" (*vyskakivaet iz merki*), "as if, having once crossed the line that for him was sacred, he begins to revel in the fact that for him there is no longer anything sacred, as if he had an overwhelming urge to transgress all at once against every law and authority, to enjoy the most unbridled and boundless freedom, and to enjoy the sensation of terror which he can't help but feel toward himself."[36]

But this is not all. What strikes the narrator even more is that in committing the most terrible crimes, and often long afterward, the criminal can display a certain swagger and tell his story with terrifying affected braggadocio. "And with what subtlety they preserve their self-esteem, how indolently off-hand their story sometimes is! What studied conceit is manifested in the tone, in every word of the narrator! And where did these simple people learn all this?"[37] In other words, these criminals manage not only to transcend all measure, not only to break all laws, including the laws of reasonable self-preservation, but also to re-stage that transcendence, to flaunt it before others, affecting pride at having served as a vehicle for such an overwhelming transgressive force. This, then, is where the greatest mystery lies: the crimes are committed in delirium, but they are appropriated, acknowledged as one's own, with a lucid mind and in a coherent language.[38] Thus the narrator concludes by asking where the common people could have learned this attitude, this self-congratulatory swagger. The question implies that this is not something we can expect of them. The terrible crimes are one thing, the elemental powers of the people are suited to that, but the affected self-esteem—that is something too reflexive, almost too perverse, something more readily attributed to members of the aristocracy or the intelligentsia than to the common people themselves.

With this, then, we come to the question: who is this Dostoevskian *bogatyr'* really, in concrete socio-historical terms? Recalling "Vlas" we should observe that the entry is explicitly framed as a case study in Russian futurology. Now that Russia has been on the course of social reforms for ten years, where is it going, what will become of it? According to Dostoevsky, the answers to this question are increasingly to be looked for among the newly freed peasants. It is ultimately by unpuzzling the enigma of the common people that we will be able to gain insight into the future of Russia as a whole: "Our Russian destiny will not be finally resolved by Petersburg. And therefore every *new* feature, even the smallest, that serves to characterize these 'new people' may be worthy of our attention."[39]

It is worth dwelling here for a moment on Dostoevsky's characterization of Vlas as "a new man." "New people" is a historico-generational category, popularized by Nikolay Chernyshevsky's 1863 novel *What Is To Be Done? Tales about New People* and referring to the politically radical and socially underdetermined intelligentsia, the so-called *raznochintsy* (literally, "people of diverse ranks") emerging to the foreground of Russian civic life in the early 1860s. Sociologically, then, referring to the peasant Vlas as a "new man" produces a polemical misnomer: enough with the radical intelligentsia as the progressive force of history. What matters, by contrast, what is of genuine interest, is the common people—how they think, how they act, where their tendencies point. But this change in status brings with it serious consequences for what might be called the history of consciousness or "Spirit": as "new people" the peasants can no longer stand for pure immediacy. Like the criminals from the *House of the Dead*, they don't merely act, but also stage themselves acting.

There are other places in Dostoevsky where this sort of conflation between the popular-archaic and the very modern appears. One vivid example comes from a fictional entry in the *Diary*, "The Meek One" (1876). There, having finished the sad tale of his wife's suicide, the first-person protagonist exclaims: "Oh nature! People are alone on the earth—that's the trouble! 'Is there a living man on the field?' the Russian warrior [*bogatyr'*] cries. I too, though not a warrior [*ne bogatyr'*], cry out and no one answers."[40] A disgraced officer and longtime pawnbroker, the narrator in "The Meek One" is indeed no *bogatyr'*. And yet at the moment of desperation, he is allowed as it were to ventriloquize the very spirit of the people. The alienated *raznochinets* channeling Russia's *bogatyr'*, a young peasant as a "new man"—a nebulous conceptual space appears to be developing here, within which one social category can flow into the other and the two can be confused.

Yet another striking instance of such deliberate conflation can be found in Dostoevsky's contribution to *Vremia* from 1861, entitled "A Series of Articles on Russian Literature." Here, Peter the Great himself, together with the modernizing section of the Russian population (i.e., the intelligentsia), is identified with Dostoevsky's favorite *bogatyr'*, Ilya Muromets, who "sat on the stove" for thirty years, until he felt his strength ripen within him, got up, and walked off to perform miraculous deeds. "In any case," writes Dostoevsky, "in the person of Peter we see an example of what a Russian can resolve to do when he develops for himself a total conviction and begins to feel that time has come and the new forces have ripened within him. And it is frightening to conceive the extent to which the Russian man is free in spirit, the extent to which his will is strong! Nobody has ever torn himself from the native soil the way he has sometimes had to, or veered to the side so sharply following his convictions."[41] The logic is by now familiar: it is precisely at the moment of extreme separation and rootlessness that the Russian people approach their essence, are at their most national and immediate.

Thus we have here something like Dostoevsky's "national ontology," elaborating a nonsynchronous (monstrous) fusion of the modern "new man" and the archaic epic *bogatyr'*. This ontology can be regarded as an imaginary resolution of the contradictions implicit in understanding the intelligentsia as one with, and simultaneously separate from, the *narod*. In literary-historical terms, this particular resolution allows Dostoevsky to continue his investigation of the narrative enigma of the common people in the realm of the realist novel by substituting the more novelistically fit alienated member of the intelligentsia for the immediate collectivity of "the *people*."[42] According to the logic of such a substitution, a highly individuated (alienated, rootless) intelligentsia hero is called upon to render vivid, through a kind of novelistic catachresis, what is at bottom unrepresentable (the spirit of the common people, the chorus) while, at the same time, encoding this unrepresentability in its representation. What he must vividly embody, in other words, is something indefinite, boundless, beyond measure, but in embodying it, he must not cover it up altogether. Borrowing Nietzsche's evocative expression from the early *Notes*, we might say that such a hero serves as a "fluttering veil" over the elemental existence of the people. Dostoevsky's ability to novelize "the people," then, relies precisely on the (Nietzschean) tragic paradigm within which separateness is conceived in terms of representational individuation or condensation rather than in terms of social alienation pure and simple. Risking scandal, we might say that just as Nietzsche's Greeks could not tolerate individuals on the tragic stage, so Dostoevsky could not bear individuals in his novels.[43] This, in turn, would encourage us to think beyond the standard vision of the Dostoevskian hero as a socially alienated *intelligent* possessed of (and by) an idea.[44]

Perhaps the most dramatic case in point here is *Crime and Punishment*, where the enigmatic status of the "new man" Raskolnikov opens up a field of narrative experimentation, onto which various visions of Russia's proper historical path can be projected.[45] The crime is committed almost unintentionally, "as if someone had taken him by the hand and pulled him almost wholly mechanically: as if a piece of his clothing had been caught in the cogs of a machine."[46] A number of accidents accompany the hero's dazed journey to the place of the crime and bring him back unnoticed, at once ensuring his success and divesting him of agency, so that in the end the event is posited as thoroughly mysterious, soliciting understanding and re-narrativization. Who was it, after all, who killed the old pawnbroker? And how exactly did it happen?

Much of the novel, then, can be read as a series of emplotments weaving into, out of, and around each other, each associated with a character (or a set of characters) and each corresponding to a prominent contemporary vision of the historical shape of the Russian nation as a whole. Thus, to the vision of precipitant now-time of the crime or the great deed (guiding Raskolnikov himself) corresponds the radicals' conception of revolutionary time in which the violent overthrow of the current state of things in Russia will be sudden and decisive. To the no less precipitous hagiographic time of conversion (associated with the saintly prostitute Sonya) corresponds Russia's religious regeneration under the influence of a recently emancipated peasantry invested with the messianic purpose of leading the nations of the world into a new age of universal brotherhood in Christ. The homogeneous empty time of a career (proffered by the lawyer Luzhin) finds its historiographic analog in the degraded Western European vision of progress as mechanistic accumulation. And, finally, the developmental temporality of *Bildung*, advocated by the detective-mentor Porfiry Petrovich, corresponds to the "German-romantic" and nationalist ideology of the organic unfolding of the national spirit.

Meanwhile, the protagonist himself is not decisively positioned on the side of one of these historiographical shapes. Rather, persisting in his enigmatic status, he serves as the narratological condition for the possibility of any national-historical shape being tried out to begin with. As such, he delineates precisely the nonsynchronous generic space where the *new man* blurs into the *bogatyr'*, where the rootless member of the intelligentsia is one with—or simply "is"—the people.

Raskolnikov is of course not alone among Dostoevsky's protagonists to arise out of the convergence of the "new man" and the *bogatyr'*. Prince Myshkin too is an enigmatic figure whose very individuation involves a mystery, a lack of measure and definition, as well as a socio-historical ambiguity. Myshkin belongs to three historiological dimensions at once. As an evidently Christlike figure ("Prince Christ" in the notebooks to the novel), he invokes Christian soteriology, the sacred history of humanity organized around key "kernel" events such as creation, the fall, incarnation, resurrection, and apocalypse-redemption. As an offspring of an old noble family, mentioned in Karamzin's canonical account of the history of the Russian state, he belongs to the essential Russian past, predating the cultural separation between the educated upper classes and the common people. Finally, as a newcomer from Switzerland, educated far from the native soil, he is, back in Russia, a rootless stranger and a *novyi chelovek* (new man) characterized by socially inappropriate behavior and shockingly "democratic" manners.

The first two mytho-historical dimensions combine to produce Dostoevsky's master-fantasy of the specifically Russian Christ. This is the figure supposedly carried in the soul of the common Russian people through the ages and into modern times.[47] Within the third historical dimension, that of modernity itself, Myshkin is given to us as a typical rootless individual. This vision of the protagonist is best articulated by the purveyor of acceptable and humane common sense, Evgeny Pavlovich. According to this version, Myshkin is a well-meaning but supremely idealistic and, in social terms, irresponsible member of the intelligentsia, with "conventionally democratic" tendencies, bookish ideas, and naively progressive sympathies.[48]

At the end of the novel, Evgeny Pavlovich accuses Myshkin of having abandoned a society girl, who loved him and whom he was about to marry (Aglaya Epanchina), for a fallen woman (Nastasya Filippovna). He produces a detailed explanation for Myshkin's actions: he was new to Russia; he was struck upon arrival by Nastasya Filippovna's beauty; "add nerves, add your falling sickness, add our nerve-shattering Petersburg thaw, add that whole day in an unknown and almost fantastic city, a day of encounters and scenes, a day of unexpected acquaintances . . ." Evgeny Pavlovich still goes on, and when he concludes, Myshkin replies to this overwhelming additive logic with the simple, "Yes, it was almost so."[49] The "almost" here points to the fact that Evgeny Pavlovich's list of causes does not in the end add up to a full explanation, to an exhaustive emplotment. As Nancy Ruttenburg points out, this "almost" is related to Myshkin's use of the expression "*ne to*" ("not quite that"), which "stands in, as a negative signifier, for that which cannot be named or performed, that for which 'an image' does not yet exist."[50] What it is that is guiding Myshkin's actions we never truly find out, but this "almost so" can be read here precisely as the principle of their representation: the socially sanctioned explanations are always only *nearly* correct. The veil flutters and lifts every time Myshkin displays his characteristic lack of the sense of measure, every time he "exaggerates" (*preuvelichivaet*).

To be sure, some of this has been captured by Mikhail Bakhtin's classic analysis of "unfinalizability" in Dostoevsky. According to Bakhtin's view, Dostoevsky represents human beings as ineluctably unfinished, open-ended creatures, resisting all externally (and, in fact, internally) imposed determinations. The Underground Man's "word with a loophole," Myshkin's evasive "almost so," the persistent mystery of Raskolnikov's or Stavrogin's (or Versilov's, etc.) identity, and an entire fictional world of actions performed contrary to expectations—all testify to the unavoidability of Bakhtin's conclusions. But Bakhtin's dominant, though for the most part implicit, manner of historicizing this "dialogic" revolution in novelistic form grounds it firmly in a certain logic of modernity, the heroic logic of capitalism in which "everything solid melts into air." Thus, he cites with approval the opinion of Otto Kaus that "Dostoevsky is the most decisive, consistent and implacable singer of capitalist man. His art is not the funeral dirge but the cradle song of our contemporary world, a world born out of the fiery breath of capitalism."[51] And he concludes one section of his 1929 *Problems of Dostoevsky's Art*: "All this is a most profound expression of the social disorientation of the classless [*raznochinnoi*] intelligentsia, which feels itself dispersed throughout the world and whose members must orient themselves in the world one by one, alone and at their own risk."[52]

Now Bakhtin's vision of the Dostoevskian human being in constant flux, unfixed by social determinations and collective institutions, fits into a long tradition of tracing the hero in Dostoevsky to the condition of intelligentsia rootlessness. Yet the above discussion of the workings of a certain (tragic) "nationalist imaginary" in Dostoevsky's poetics of character tends to detect in it a more archaizing vision, in which the staging of the hero's repeated de-individuation, the rendering visible of his being "beyond-measure," posits him (or her) as only provisionally extricable from the choral substratum of the Russian people.[53] On this account of unfinalizability, modern isolation, rational skepticism, and open-ended biography can be found on only one side of a kind of tragic Möbius strip. The other side (which is the very same side, of course) presents us with archaic frenzy, implacable fate, and the state of possession by the unrepresentable collective transcending the measure of the individual.

UNIFICATION AND (AS) FORM: PLOT

These considerations bring us to the question of plot. For if the most extreme modern alienation is linked in Dostoevsky's protagonists with the most extreme rootedness in the archaic; if apparent social isolation, psychological self-centeredness and metaphysical individuation coincide with deep-seated unity with the folk, psychological loss of self, and metaphysical dissolution in the eternal All-One; and if all this is there *to begin with*, not as the outcome, but as the very principle of character construction—then what happens with plot; what is it there for; what, if anything, does it accomplish?

Again, Bakhtin's remarks provide a fruitful starting point. If we take unfinalizability seriously, then what sort of an ending can meaningfully justify a beginning and a middle? According to Bakhtin, no such finality exists in Dostoevsky; what we have instead is "a conventionally literary, conventionally monologic ending."[54] Dostoevsky's plotting as such is, in Bakhtin's view, only of secondary importance. Its task is to make the hero "collide with other people under the unusual and unexpected conditions precisely for the purpose of *testing* the idea and the man of the idea."[55] It is there to open up the space of the dialogic situation, which is in principle never to be finished.

Bakhtin writes *Problems of Dostoevsky's Art* (1929) in the shadow of Vyacheslav Ivanov's highly influential and explicitly Nietzschean interpretation of Dostoevsky as a tragic novelist. In some respects Bakhtin's reading is indebted to Ivanov; in many it is not. One of the ways in which Bakhtin seems to depart from Ivanov most radically is in his understanding of the function of plot in Dostoevsky. For Ivanov, one of the central aspects of Dostoevsky's tragic poetics is the circular movement of some of his narratives, staging separation from the choral community, the suffering of individuation, and at last, ecstatic return:

> The consciousness of the sacred realities of being was, to begin with, native to Raskolnikov; and only for a time did his vision of them become dimmed . . . The experience of love, being an experience of mystical realism . . . , helped him, in the person of Sonya, to resurrect in his soul "the visions of the early pure days."[56]

This is perhaps a legitimate reading of *Crime and Punishment*, but it is far from being consistently Nietzschean. It appears rather that in foregrounding the centrality of the polyphonic chorus in Dostoevsky, Bakhtin reaches back to Nietzsche over the head of his most influential Russian interpreter.

Indeed, Nietzsche's insistence on the primacy of the Dionysian chorus coincides with a resolute denigration of dramatic plot. As far as Nietzsche is concerned, the key to the tragic effect is not the drama itself, but *pathos* (what we might call "passion," or suffering a fate); and the adequate expression of *pathos* is the choral song.[57] "The concept of 'drama' as 'action' [*Handlung*]," Nietzsche writes, "is very naive in its roots: the decisive factor here is the world and the habit of the *eye*."[58] In other words, plot is for Nietzsche on the side of vision (Apollonian appearance), while what achieves *pathos* is music in its capacity to contain "the universal forms of all conditions of desire" and thus to be "more intelligible to us than any single action."[59] Unlike plot, which refers us to a particular situation or event, music evokes in us the affect of the universal situation of desire and becoming. We might say then that drama is an externalized Apollonian expression of music, just as the tragic hero is an individuated Apollonian expression of the chorus. And just as the hero exists in order to point beyond himself, through *pathos*, to the unindividuated experience of Dionysian unity, so also dramatic plot, by placing the hero in situations appropriate for the expression of *pathos*, serves to adumbrate the choral-musical parts of the play.

By contrast with Ivanov then, nothing like the cycle of unity, separation, and return matters for Nietzsche's conception of tragedy. Still less does the tragic rely on the spiral shape of development. Rather, what we have is a pulsating rhythm of action and pathos: "In this way two worlds which more or less alternated were kept side by side, so that the world of the eye disappeared when the world of the ear began and vice versa. The action served only to lead to the suffering, and the *outpouring* of the *pathos* again made a new action necessary."[60]

This downgrading of the functions and capacities of plot has consequences that reach beyond the merely technical descriptions of an old genre. At stake for Nietzsche is the central question of theodicy—how is suffering to be justified?—and "tragedy" is his name for a justification that would not involve the plotted coherence of sacred history (or updated versions of it in progressivist or Hegelian philosophy). If suffering and dissonance cannot be framed by a meaningful before and a weighty after, then it indeed cannot be thought of as a consequence of the fall or as a promising *felix culpa*. Suffering, then, cannot be emplotted as expiation or purification; disharmony cannot be justified as a momentary stage in the trajectory affirming harmony. And, in the Hegelian inflection, the "labor and suffering of the negative" can no longer "pay off" in the completed System.

For Nietzsche, tragic pain, like musical dissonance, is (dis)pleasurable in itself. Both tragedy and dissonance "play with the sting of displeasure, trusting in their exceedingly powerful magic arts; and by means of this play justify the existence of even the 'worst world.'"[61] In this respect at least it is possible to draw a direct line of descent from Nietzsche's early work on tragedy to his late formulation of the Eternal Recurrence. Nietzsche himself calls attention to this fact with the title of the section that follows his first elaboration of that "doctrine" in *The Gay Science: Incipit tragoedia*. Indeed, one of the key corollaries of the thesis that "every pain and every joy and every thought and sigh and everything unutterably small or great in [our lives] will have to return . . . all in the same succession and sequence"[62] is that "the present must absolutely not be justified by reference to a future, nor the past by reference to a present" and that "becoming is of equivalent value at every moment."[63] Plot—insofar as it makes meaning out of a before and an after, insofar as it presupposes that succession and sequence can vary and are thus signifying—is an enemy of the sort of immanentist thinking that gives assent to every moment of becoming. To reject plot, then, is in a sense to reject the very project of placing value on the world that is itself the condition for the possibility of valuation.

Of course for Nietzsche, the Eternal Recurrence of the Same is not merely a statement of fact, but also a staging of a trial. How will one respond when confronted with the hypothesis? Will one recoil in horror or give joyful assent? And what does such an assent, a plotless "confirmation and seal"[64] of becoming, look like? One of Nietzsche's responses to this question— admittedly, an early one and one rife with Schopenhauerian dualisms—is tragedy itself, insofar as it manages to posit the suffering of an individuated hero as always already (and eternally) redeemed by the womblike presence of the chorus and the sound of its compassionate song.

Dostoevsky's position on the role of plotted coherence in redemption is probably still more complicated. One look at the epigraph to *The Brothers Karamazov* is enough to see how powerfully the teleological paradigm of sacred history is at work in his writing. Thus, from the Gospel of John: "Verily, verily, I say onto you, Except a corn of wheat fall into the ground and die, it abideth alone: but if it die it bringeth forth much fruit." As if in a preemptive reply to Ivan Karamazov's "rebellion," suffering and death are here posited as necessary steps on the way to fruition. But it would be wrong to stop here, for the rebellion is not so easily dismissed and, with it, numberless passages that question precisely the logic whereby the past can be justified with reference to the present and the present with reference to the past. Examples of such questioning abound, and they are well known: from the Underground Man's insistence that to predict is to kill, to Captain Snegiryov's refusal to accept the money intended to rectify a terrible insult, and finally, rising to the level of a genuine critique of theodicy, to Ivan Karamazov's (and Alyosha's) refusal to take part in universal harmony if it is to be bought with a single child's tear.

It is in fact possible to see, in Dostoevsky's poetics of plot, a genuine tension between these two tendencies: an acceptance and at the same time a rejection of emplotment as a fundamental mechanism for making meaning out of a sequence of events. This acceptance and this rejection, together with the corresponding constructions of character (the intelligentsia ideologue uprooted from the people versus the tragic hero serving as a catachretic crystallization of the in-itself unrepresentable popular element), in fact do not simply vie for dominance in Dostoevsky's narrative world; they sustain each other as well. And they can be said to belong to different levels of generic sedimentation—one to the realist problematics of the modern novel of alienation and socialization, the other to the tragic-nationalist logic of simultaneous unity-in-separation.

Indeed, the two novels we have considered in some detail, in addition to the tragic characterological dynamic, possess a more "contemporary" generic appearance. *Crime and Punishment* is a proto-detective novel about the consequences of social dislocation, initially conceived as a novel about alcoholism. *The Idiot* is an idiosyncratic *Bildungsroman* about a foreign-educated young man's attempts to find a home in contemporary Russian society. As "realist" novelistic treatments of contemporary life, these novels represent the consequences of fragmentation, loss of unity, and alienation, centering on the hero's rootlessness and foregrounding the problematics of societal integration.

From this point of view, the plot of the novel, elucidating the biographical unfolding of the hero's path through the social world, is of vital importance. Much depends on how and where the novels begin and still more on how and where they end. But at the same time, and on a deeper generic level perhaps, we could say that the question of rootlessness and its neutralization is a moot question, since the principle of the hero's tragic character-construction itself presupposes unity with, as much as separation from, the choral substratum of the people. And thus understood, that separation itself is not so much a matter of social isolation as the result of a condensed representation, a making visible of forces that are unrepresentable directly. From this perspective, the "novelistic" plot can be seen as subsidiary, framing or staging moments of the hero's transcendence of measure (*pathos*) rather than working to stabilize his individuality through social determination.

Thus, returning to *Crime and Punishment*, we would have to understand the plot of the novel as, in a certain sense, nonsynchronous, with the choral substratum of the hero's non-individuated existence enduring alongside attempts to individuate and define him through coherent narration. In the case of *Crime and Punishment*, this choral substratum—the place where, within Dostoevsky's historical imaginary, the *raznochinets* and the *narod* are one—is the space of the enigma itself, the space into which the hero returns again and again, breaking out of the multiple emplotments that individuate him as a "someone" in the social world: hagiography (Sonya's: go to the crossroads, fall on your knees, kiss the earth, etc.), the *Bildungsroman* (Porfiry's: have patience, let life take over and carry you to the shore, proceed gradually, step-by-step, etc.), the plot of a career (Luzhin's: get a position in the office, advance through the ranks), the biography of a Napoleon-like great man (Raskolnikov's own: kill the old lady, take her money, and use it to become the benefactor of humanity), the detective plot (Zamyotov's: the criminal has left enough clues and will be discovered), and so on.

The two layers of the text thus posit two distinct—in fact diametrically positioned—points of maximal integration or completion. As a hero of a realist novel about contemporary life, as a rootless member of the intelligentsia, Raskolnikov is most at one with his world in Sonya's (the people's) embrace in the epilogue. From this point of view, the moment of the crime is the height of Raskolnikov's individuation, his separation from the community. But understood in light of a tragic nationalist imaginary of unity-in-separation, the crime is precisely the moment when what is least individual, what is precisely "beyond measure" in him, becomes visible. Thus, the narrator comments that Raskolnikov's first blow is delivered with "a strength that is not his own." Having lost the resolve to commit the crime, he is unwittingly directed to follow through by his own future victim, Lizaveta; and he is carried to the place of the crime "as if by an alien force." His choice of the murder weapon is significant as well. As his fellow prisoners from the common people observe: "What did you take up an axe for; it's no business for a gentleman."[65] In an odd restaging of the fruitful conflation between the intelligentsia and the *narod*, the peasant Vlas, in the manner of a "new man," plans to shoot a gun at the Eucharist, while the rootless Raskolnikov wields the common people's weapon of choice. At the risk of overstating my case, I would suggest that Raskolnikov is here nothing but the vehicle whereby the Russian people purges itself of the evil seeds of capitalism in the figure of the old pawnbroker. The domain of equivalence, exchange, and competition is thus not only bypassed but eradicated in an ecstatic murderous embrace between the overweening individual and the body politic—not, to be sure, in a kind of totalitarian swallowing of the individual, but precisely through his hubristic inflation beyond all measure.

A parallel dynamic suggests itself when we recall that throughout much of the novel, while Raskolnikov wanders the streets of St. Petersburg, the authorities already have the presumed murderer in custody. This is Mikolka, the peasant, who incurs the suspicions of the police by being in the wrong place at the wrong time and acting strangely in the aftermath of the murder. At a dramatic moment in Raskolnikov's interrogation, just as he seems ready to break down and confess, Mikolka pushes his way into the investigator's office and confesses instead, substituting himself for Raskolnikov and allowing the novel to continue. What is further curious about Mikolka in relation to Raskolnikov is that, as the novel reminds us several times, he is a religious schismatic (in Russian, a *raskol'nik*), as it were realizing the metaphor of the protagonist's name. In short, we can observe the logic of mutual substitutability between the novelistic hero traversing the narrative in full visibility and the representative of the common people, Raskolnikov's common double, who only appears in glimpses, momentarily uncovered by the Nietzschean flutter of the veil.[66]

The special interest of *The Idiot* for investigating the relationship between the realist and the tragic conceptions of plot lies in the fact that the novel creates the horizon of expectations associated with the paradigmatic realist novelistic sub-genre, the *Bildungsroman*. Here we have a young man of good family but poor means, in fact, an orphan, an idealist, brought up in Switzerland—the land of democracy, Rousseau, and the idyll—where he spent his time primarily among children. He arrives in Russia and lands directly in the salon of a representative aristocratic Russian family. A Russian Rastignac, he is at once seductive and discomfiting, and it appears at least initially that the central question of the novel will be how this innocent provincial-foreigner is going to fare in the world of good society, organized around the Epanchin family, and by extension, in contemporary Russia as a whole. About two-fifths into the novel, this suspicion is reinforced as we begin to detect the development of a potential courtship plot between Myshkin and the youngest and most beautiful Epanchin, Aglaya. Much of what is at stake throughout on the level of plot is whether or not Myshkin will be able to behave properly in a society that values order, decorum, elegant moderation, and good breeding above all. He repeatedly and, by the end, flamboyantly, fails to do so.

Thus the pulsating rhythm of the plot is evident: socializing individuation is repeatedly interrupted by the image of the hero as beyond measure; action repeatedly culminates in *pathos*. These moments of *pathos*, however, bare the incompleteness of the world of decent society itself, revealing it to be no more than a surface layer, the tip of the social iceberg. What scandalizes most about Myshkin is his mysterious link to the nether world. This world coagulates around the figure of the "kept woman" Nastasya Filippovna and her passionate suitor and representative of the *narod*, the schismatic Rogozhin. If order and propriety are the basic principles of the upper social world, the world below (which is the "common" world since Rogozhin brings with him the dregs of society: drunks, adventurists, petty criminals, etc.) oozes with dark destructive passion, where love and hate, vitality and morbidity, become indistinguishable.

Having retreated to the background at the end of part 1, this world continues to operate in a subterranean manner, with Nastasya Filippovna and Rogozhin making sudden appearances that frighten, disgust, perplex, outrage, and, perhaps worst of all, implicate the good members of the broader Epanchin circle. The underworld is perpetually "beyond measure"; it makes no sense, it threatens from within, and it manipulates. One of Nastasya Filippovna's main intrigues involves getting Aglaya to marry Myshkin, working with, and not against, the momentum of Myshkin's *Bildungsroman*. There is an uncomfortable sense, in other words, that the two worlds—the nocturnal world beyond measure and beneath visibility and the diurnal world of coherent social forms—are tightly stitched together. And Myshkin himself, this *Bildungsheld cum* tragic hero, is the thread.

Things are still more complicated, however, since it would not be entirely accurate to say that Myshkin keeps bringing scandal and disorder into the world of dignity and calm. The Epanchin family itself, we are told, is eccentric, somehow improper, devoid of measure and tact.

> These people, or at least the more reasoning members of the family, constantly suffered from one nearly general family quality, the direct opposite of those virtues [of orderly propriety and practicality] we have discussed above. Without fully understanding the fact . . . , they occasionally suspected all the same that in their family somehow nothing went the way it did with everyone else. With everyone else things went smoothly, with them unevenly; everyone else rolled along the rails—they constantly went off the rails. Everyone else became constantly and decorously timid, but they did not."[67]

Lizaveta Prokofyevna and Aglaya in particular lack a sense of propriety, of "decorous timidity." Like Myshkin himself, they constantly "exaggerate." They are susceptible to hysterical fits; their behavior is perpetually puzzling, "setting riddles."[68] In other words, the social world into which Myshkin, in his capacity as a hero of a *Bildungsroman*, is supposed to be integrated turns out to be the world of scandal, unhinged and "beyond measure." Myshkin's "failure" to achieve *Bildungsoman* finalization thus corresponds to something objective: there is no stable, well-ordered system into which he could be integrated. And it is precisely this lack of stability and decorum that makes it specifically *Russian*. Evgeny Pavlovich calls it "Russian originality";[69] Myshkin himself calls it "Russian passion" (*strastnost'*).[70]

Much like the socio-ontological makeup of the novel's protagonist, the social world into which he is placed is two-tiered. Just as the veneer of the "new man" serves to conceal and reveal the popular-religious dimension encoded in Myshkin's "archaic," Christological associations, so the socially proper and novelistically appropriate Epanchins internalize the barely representable depths of underworld commonness. To notice this perpetual (or, to put it somewhat paradoxically, static) instability is also to measure the complexity and genuine eccentricity of the problematics of plot in Dostoevsky.

CONCLUSION

Crime and Punishment and *The Idiot* (as well as Dostoevsky's other late novels we do not have the time to consider in detail) internalize the dilemma of unity-in-separation against a common horizon of what I have termed "tragic nationalism."[71] Each produces a distinct characterological and narratological configuration, but both are subject to a stratified representational logic: historically nonsynchronous (combining the ultramodern with the deeply archaic) and socially hybrid (productively conflating members of the educated elite with the common people). As such, this is the very representational logic that Nietzsche ascribes to Attic tragedy: the hero's unity-in-separation with the chorus.

The problems that Dostoevsky and Nietzsche saw themselves as confronting were analogous. They found themselves in the midst of a fragmented and therefore feeble modernity, "looking back" at what they saw as a living source of strength and unity in the people. And the question arose, how it might be possible to bring these two together, to give voice to the people, and to intellectuals—life. For both Dostoevsky and Nietzsche—or rather for the "tragic-nationalist" vision constructed somewhere at midpoint between them—the problem is historical in nature. Its acknowledgment is fundamental to a proper grasp of modernity. The separation (between the past and the present, the people and the cultured elite) is extreme, and only if we take that extremity seriously can we conceive of an adequate solution. This solution seems no longer capable of reducing the two poles of the opposition to the privileged one (as is common in both the modernizing and the archaizing "Enlightenment" solutions still current in the 1860 and '70s in both Germany and Russia), nor of producing a dialectical synthesis between them (as in the Hegelian and Native Soil models). Rather, it envisions a representational logic whereby the extremes of modern alienation can be deployed as the means for giving shape to an imponderable archaic unity. This logic is articulated in Nietzsche as a relation between the hero and the chorus and enacted by Dostoevsky in the sleight of hand that constitutes the generic kernel of his late novels: the substitution of the novelistically fruitful member of the intelligentsia for the *narod*, a substitution that allows the tragic-hero-beyond-measure to give shape to the (choral) substratum of the common people.

Understood as a symbolic form for making sense of the paradoxical dynamic of unity-in-separation, Dostoevsky's hero can thus no longer be comprehended by the accepted formula of "social rootlessness plus modern idea." The argument here would suggest instead that the sort of rootlessness we find in Dostoevsky is a realist-novelistic instantiation of a deeper generic field within which it is inseparable from the most extreme form of rootedness. It is the prominence of the hero's link to the choral or popular substratum that accounts for Dostoevsky's specific elaboration of the central realist problem of individuality and social belonging. In this elaboration, the act of sacrificing the reflecting "I" to "the immediate" is performed not at the *chronological*, plotted end but at the *logical* beginning, as the principle of the character's construction itself.

Reading Nietzsche as Dostoevsky's unwitting Aristotle allows us to confront his thought on tragedy with a like-minded, or like-imaged, novelistic complement, no less congenial perhaps than the dissonances of Wagner's music. It is well known that Nietzsche admired Dostoevsky in the capacity of perhaps the greatest psychologist of modern decadence and nihilism. There is no evidence that he ever thought of Dostoevsky as actualizing his hopes for a new tragic culture. And though he reports having felt a special affinity with some novelists (e.g., Stendhal, Dostoevsky himself), there is no evidence that he believed the novel form to be a worthy vessel for such culture. The parallels in their conceptions of the hero and of plot, however, are striking. And if they help to elucidate something about Dostoevsky's poetics, they are no less clarifying about Nietzsche's project, allowing us to embed it more thoroughly in the historical moment and to see in it an instance of tragic nationalism—a decidedly modern form, a species perhaps of "romantic anticapitalism"—confronted by a specifically modern set of problems and particularly sensitive to modernity's nonsynchronous predicament.

NOTES

1. My examples here will be confined primarily to Dostoevsky's two novels from the 1860s, *Crime and Punishment* and *The Idiot*.

2. This approach to genre as affording an imaginary solution to actual sociohistorical contradictions originates with Fredric Jameson's influential extension of Lévi-Strauss's conception of the function of myth in primitive societies. See Jameson, *The Political Unconscious: Narrative as a Socially Symbolic Act* (Ithaca: Cornell University Press, 1981), 79. It has been more or less explicitly taken up by such theorists of the novel as Franco Moretti, Nancy Armstrong, and Margaret Cohen. For a brief overview of these developments, see Cohen, *The Sentimental Education of the Novel* (Princeton: Princeton University Press, 1999), 19. Other approaches to understanding the relationship between the two authors here at issue include exploring the admittedly intriguing details of Nietzsche's reading and reception of Dostoevsky (see C. A. Miller, "The Nihilist as Tempter-Redeemer: Dostoevsky's 'Man-God' in Nietzsche's Notebooks," *Nietzsche Studien* (1975): 165–226); positioning the two side by side within a single philosophical tradition (see Lev Shestov, *Dostoevskii i Nitsshe: Filosofiia tragedii* [Moscow: Graal', 2001], and Walter Kaufman, *Existentialism: From Dostoevsky to Sartre* [New York: New American Library, 1975]); as well as comparing and contrasting their visions of a particular historical or psychological phenomenon (see Robert Louis Jackson, "Counterpoint: Nietzsche and Dostoevsky," in *Dialogues with Dostoevsky* [Stanford: Stanford University Press, 1993]; Edith W. Clowes, "Self-Laceration and Resentment: The Terms of Moral Psychology in Dostoevsky and Nietzsche," in *Freedom and Responsibility in Russian Literature: Essays in Honor of Robert Louis Jackson*, ed. Elizabeth Cheresh-Allen and Gary Saul Morson [Evanston: Northwestern University Press, 1995], 119–33; and René Girard,

"Superman in the Underground: Strategies of Madness—Nietzsche, Wagner, and Dostoevsky," *MLN* 91 [1976]: 1257–66). Most previous attempts to understand the tragic dimension of Dostoevsky's novels have focused on their predilection for dramatic dialogue, temporally condensed action, and the disastrous outcome. Implicit in them is thus a generalized conception of tragedy, a kind of trans-historical formal paradigm with stable characteristics. See, for example, Konstantin Mochulsky, *Dostoevsky: His Life and Work*, trans. Michael Minihan (Princeton: Princeton University Press, 1967), 289–313; Steven Cassedy, "The Formal Problem of the Epilogue in 'Crime and Punishment': The Logic of Tragic and Christian Structures," *Dostoevsky Studies*, vol. 3 (1982): 171–90. By linking Dostoevsky to the contemporary and specifically Nietzschean conception of the tragic, I hope to avoid this methodological pitfall, to endow "tragedy" with more historical as well as more philosophical content and thus to understand what specific problems it was called upon to stage and resolve. The most philosophically formidable and historically inflected discussion of the tragic form in Dostoevsky and Nietzsche still belongs to Vyacheslav Ivanov, whose reading of Dostoevsky as the creator of novel-tragedies becomes important for the later section of this essay.

3. Friedrich Nietzsche, *Unfashionable Observations*, trans. Richard T. Gray (Stanford: Stanford University Press, 1995), 199.

4. Robert Sayre and Michael Löwy, "Romantic Anti-Capitalism," *New German Critique*, no. 32: 55.

5. Fyodor Dostoevsky, *The Brothers Karamazov*, trans. Richard Pevear and Larissa Volokhnosky (New York: Farrar, Straus and Giroux, 2002), 303.

6. Ibid., 303–4.

7. Nietzsche, *Unfashionable Observations*, 213.

8. Dostoevsky, *Polnoe sobranie sochinenii v tridtsati tomkh*, ed. G. M. Fridlender (Leningrad: Nauka, 1972–90), 20:192–93. Translations from the complete works edition are mine. Henceforth, references to this edition will be abbreviated *PSS* and provided in parentheses in the body of the text.

9. See Grigoriev, *Literaturnaia kritika* (Moscow: Khudozhestvennaia literatura, 1967), 373; my translation. The three stages are obviously reminiscent of Hegel's stages of "Immediate Spirit," "Self-Alienated Spirit," and "Absolute Spirit" in *The Phenomenology of Spirit*.

10. Dostoevsky, *PSS* 19:14.

11. Ernest Gellner, *Nations and Nationalism* (Oxford: Blackwell Publishing, 2006), 35.

12. Dostoevsky, *PSS* 19:9–16.

13. Ibid., 19:14.

14. Ibid., 19:6.

15. On the concept of nonsynchrony, see Ernst Bloch's original elucidation in *The Heritage of Our Times*, trans. Neville Plaice and Stephen Plaice (Berkeley: University of California Press, 1990), 97–103.

16. Nietzsche, *Birth of Tragedy and the Case of Wagner*, trans. Walter Kaufmann (New York: Random House, 1967), 136.

17. Emden, *Friedrich Nietzsche and the Politics of History*, 114.

18. Friedrich Nietzsche, *On the Future of Our Educational Institutions*, trans. Michael W. Grenke (South Bend: St Augustine's Press, 2004), 66–67.

19. Wilhelm von Humboldt, *The Limits of State Action*, ed. J. W. Burrow (Cambridge: Cambridge University Press, 1969), 10.

20. Nietzsche, *Prefaces to Unwritten Works*, trans. and ed. Michael W. Grenke (South Bend: St. Augustine's Press, 2005), 30.

21. Cited in *Philosophy in the Tragic Age of the Greeks*, 45.

22. These are the three possible instantiations of genius mentioned in "Schopenhauer as Educator," in *Unfashionable Observations*, 213.

23. Nietzsche, *Writings from the Early Notebooks*, ed. Raymond Geuss and Alexander Nehamas, trans. Ladislaus Löb (Cambridge: Cambridge University Press, 2009), 69.

24. Ibid., 33.

25. Nietzsche, *Unfashionable Observations*, 205.

26. Ibid., 266.

27. Nietzsche, *Writings from the Early Notebooks*, 20.

28. Nietzsche, *The Birth of Tragedy*, 56. Later references to this edition will be abbreviated *BT* and provided in parentheses in the body of the text.

29. On nonsynchrony as the historical condition for the development of the tragic form, see, for example, Jean-Pierre Vernant and Pierre Vidal-Naquet, *Myth and Tragedy in Ancient Greece*, trans. Janet Lloyd (New York: Zone Books, 1990), 27.

30. Nietzsche, *Writings from the Early Notebooks*, 10.

31. G. W. F. Hegel, *Aesthetics: Lectures on Fine Art*, Vol. 1, trans. T. M. Knox (Oxford: Clarendon Press, 1988), 593.

32. Fyodor Dostoevsky, *A Writer's Diary: Volume 1, 1873–1876*, trans. Kenneth Lantz (Evanston: Northwestern University Press, 1994), 168 (*PSS* 21:41).

33. Ibid., 161 (*PSS* 21:35).

34. Ibid.

35. Dostoevsky, *PSS* 4:87.

36. Dostoevsky, *Memoirs from the House of the Dead*, trans. Jessie Coulson, ed. Ronald Hingley (Oxford: Oxford University Press, 2008), 129 (*PSS* 4:88).

37. Ibid., 130.

38. Nancy Ruttenburg writes: "It is no longer a matter of just the evil deed itself, which one might imagine is committed out of 'delirium' or 'possession,' but of a seamless and unapologetic integrity of act and agent." The suggestion I am making is that this integrity is precisely a tragic one. See Ruttenburg, *Dostoevsky's Democracy* (Princeton: Princeton University Press, 2008), 120.

39. Dostoevsky, *A Writer's Diary: Volume 1*, 160 (*PSS* 21:34).

40. Dostoevsky, *The Eternal Husband and Other Stories*, trans. Richard Pevear and Larissa Volokhonsky (New York: Bantam Books, 1997), 294.

41. Dostoevsky, *PSS* 18:55–56. The association between Peter I and Ilya Muromets appears already in Belinsky's article on "The Sketches of the Battle of Borodino" from 1839. Here, too, the giant figure of Peter is compared to the power of this epic hero, while the latter's biography (with its thirty years of immobility, followed by great deeds) maps onto the history of the Russian people. For further insightful discussion of the motif of the sleeping peasant in pre- and post-Reform Russia, see Aleksei Vdovin, "Literaturnyi kanon i natsional'naia identichnost': 'Chto ty spish', muzhichek?' Kol'tsova i spory o russkosti v XIX veke" (The Literary Canon and National Identity: Kol'tsov's 'Why do you sleep, little peasant?' and Debates about Russianness in the Nineteenth Century), in *Acta Salvica Estonica IV: Trudy po russkoi i slavianskoi filologii, Literaturovedenie, IX*, ed. A. V. Vdovin and R. G. Leibov. Vol 4: Khrestomatiinye teksty: russkaia pedogagicheskaia praktika i literaturnyi kanon XIX veka (Tartu: University of Tartu Press, 2013), 139–62.

42. Another instance of productive conflation between the description of the popular and the vision of the rootless hero can be found in Dostoevsky's notes toward "Life of a Great Sinner," an unrealized project in the shadow of which Dostoevsky's last three (and arguably last five) novels were written: "This is simply the type of a wheeler-horse, unconsciously troubled by the power peculiar to him as a type, the power that is absolutely immediate and lacking in foundation. Such wheeler-horse types often become [rebels like] Sten'ka Razin or [sectarians, like] Danilo Filippovich, or they go all the way to [the peasant sectarianism of] Khlystovstvo and Skopchestvo" (*PSS* 9:128); my translation.

43. In this connection see Nikolay Berdyayev's observations on Dostoevsky's "Dionysianism" in "The Revelation on Man in Dostoevsky's Art," in *Sobranie sochinenii* (Paris: YMCA-Press, 1989), 3:77–78.

44. The formula seems to have been developed by Boris Engel'gardt in his "Ideologicheskii roman Dostoevskogo," in *F. M. Dostoevsky: Stat'i i materialy*, ed. A. S. Dolinin (Leningrad: Mysl', 1924), 85–86. It is cited with approval by Lidiya Ginzburg as well as Mikhail Bakhtin. See Ginzburg, *O literaturnom geroe* (Leningrad: Sovetskii pisatel', 1979), 83; Bakhtin, *Problems of Dostoevsky's Poetics*, trans. Caryl Emerson (Minneapolis: University of Minnesota Press, 1984), 24–25.

45. I have argued this at greater length in "Shapes of History and the Enigmatic Hero in Dostoevsky: The Case of *Crime and Punishment*," *Comparative Literature* (Summer 2010).

46. Dostoevsky, *Crime and Punishment*, trans. Richard Pevear and Larissa Volokhonsky (New York: Random House, 1992), 70.

47. Dostoevsky, *PSS* 8:35.

48. Dostoevsky, *PSS* 8:481.

49. Dostoevsky, *The Idiot*, trans. Richard Pevear and Larissa Volokhonsky (New York: Random House, 2003), 580 (*PSS* 8:481–82).

50. Ruttenburg, *Dostoevsky's Democracy*, 18.

51. Mikhail Bakhtin, *Problems of Dostoevsky's Poetics*, trans. Caryl Emerson (Minneapolis: University of Minnesota Press, 1984), 19.

52. Ibid., 281.

53. To be sure, there are also other, more archaizing tendencies in Bakhtin's text, especially when taken in a complex with his early philosophical manuscripts and in dialogue with his close friend and interlocutor, the literary historian Lev Pumpiansky. For an account of these, see Ilya Kliger, "Dostoevsky and the Novel-Tragedy: Genre and Modernity in Ivanov, Pumpiansky, and Bakhtin," *PMLA* 126, no. 1 (January 2011): 73–87.

54. Bakhtin, *Problems*, 39.

55. Ibid., 105.

56. Vyacheslav Ivanov, *Sobranie sochinenii* (Brussels: Foyer Oriental Chrétien 1987), 4:431.

57. Nietzsche, *Writings from the Early Notebooks*, 18. For Nietzsche, the supreme achievement of the art of tragedy, its early Aeschylean instantiation, is almost altogether plotless. And Aristotle's insistence on complete action can only be understood in light of his historical position as a codifier of an already degenerate form. It is perhaps this Aristotelian tradition, along with a commitment to a certain soteriological narrative arc, that tempted Ivanov away from the strictly Nietzschean problematic.

58. Ibid., 28–29. Compare Bakhtin (at p. 7): "It follows that ordinary pragmatic links at the level of the plot (whether of an objective or psychological order) are insufficient in Dostoevsky's world: such links presuppose, after all, that characters have become objects, fixed elements in the author's design; such links bind and combine finalized images of people in the unity of a monologically perceived and understood world."

59. Ibid., 11.

60. Ibid., 12.

61. Ibid., 143.

62. Nietzsche, *The Gay Science*, trans. Walter Kaufmann (New York: Random House, 1974), 273.

63. Nietzsche, *The Will to Power*, trans. Walter Kaufmann and R. J. Hollingdale (New York: Random House, 1967), 377–78.

64. Nietzsche, *The Gay Science*, 274.

65. Dostoevsky, *Crime and Punishment*, 576.

66. A still further coincidence, testifying to the imaginative conflation between the *raznochinets* Raskolnikov and the common people has to do with the use of the topos "to say a new word [*novoe slovo*]," which articulates both Dostoevsky's expectation of the newly emancipated peasants (see, by way

of comparison, *Occasional Writings*, 230) and Raskolnikov's expectation of himself.

67. Dostoevsky, *The Idiot*, 327.

68. Ibid., 332.

69. Ibid., 334.

70. Ibid., 546. The motif of the violation of decorum may admittedly be conceived as melodrama, and Dostoevsky has often been accused of drawing on that lurid register. There are important ways, however, in which this is, strictly speaking, inaccurate. Dostoevsky's representation of sharp contrasts and scandalous situations thoroughly lacks the explicit bipolarity of villainy-innocence, without which the genre of melodrama is unsustainable. Instead, ambiguity and mutual contamination are everywhere, and the dynamics of a scandalous outbreak serve only to confirm it. There is nevertheless a logic according to which the temptation to see Dostoevsky's work as melodramatic becomes understandable. This has to do with the link between melodrama and tragedy. Following George Steiner, Peter Brooks sees melodrama as the outcome of the decline of tragedy, itself caused by "the loss of an operable idea of the Sacred" (*The Melodramatic Imagination*, 82). Yet it should by now be clear that in Dostoevsky, the idea of the sacred is very much alive, alighting on the body of the nation, the "God-bearing people," and thus embedding the novelistic plot in a concrete historical problematic, while melodrama tends to treat essential conflict in a rarefied manner as metaphysical (Good vs. Evil).

71. Of course the nationalist problematic does not inform Dostoevsky's post-Reform novelistic work alone. Consider this well-known passage from Tolstoy's *War and Peace* (1865–69): "Where, how, and when had this little countess, brought up by an émigré Frenchwoman, sucked this spirit in from the Russian air she breathed, where had she gotten these ways, which should have been long supplanted by the *pas de châle*? Yet that spirit and these ways were those very inimitable, unstudied Russian ones which the uncle expected of her. As soon as she stood there, smiling triumphantly, proudly, and with sly merriment, the fear which had first seized Nikolai and all those present—that she would not do it right—went away, and they began to admire her." Tolstoy, *War and Peace*, 512.

War and Peace is a contemporary of *Crime and Punishment* and *The Idiot*, and though it is a historical novel, its concerns are understandably similar to theirs. From the beginning to the end, it is obsessed with the characteristically post-Reform problematic of the relationship between the Westernized elite and the people. The description of Natasha's dance casts this issue in the form of a question. And the question has no answer. Or, better perhaps, the question contains within itself a response and is thus a pseudo- or a rhetorical question: where did she get it from the Russian air she breathed? This short-circuiting is indicative of Tolstoy's tendency to resolve the problem of separation by fiat. It is just the case, in his world, that some belong to the people, and others don't. We find no unrepresentable core here, and no privileged vessel of representation to be discovered precisely at the furthest distance from that core. No dualism of the sort that dominates the imaginaries of Dostoevsky and Nietzsche, but a differentiated field of socially varied characters all marked as "Russian" (and Natasha's dance is of course the prime exhibit) and opposed only to the no-less-varied world of those who cannot be graced with such a designation. Tolstoy's characters display external signs of belonging or not belonging to the people: they speak bad French or bad Russian, they are uncalculating or careerist, over-flowing with innocence and life or debauched and barren. What Tolstoy is here staging, in other words, is not a tragic unity-in-separation, but (an epic?) unity in diversity: Andrey Bolkonsky, Captain Tushin, Platon Karataev, Field Marshal Kutuzov belong to different socioeconomic classes and occupy more or less piv-otal positions in the plot, but they are all united in their Russianness.

Dmitri Nikulin

The Gods and Demons of Dostoevsky and Nietzsche

IT IS THE FALL OF THE YEAR 1869, and Dostoevsky and Nietzsche are thinking and writing about apparently very different things. (They do not know of each other's existence, but eighteen years later Nietzsche will accidentally pick up a French translation of two of Dostoevsky's novels and will immediately recognize a touch of the genius of psychological depiction.)[1] Nietzsche is a brilliant classical philologist who becomes increasingly disappointed with the petty precision of textual criticism. This year he begins writing *The Birth of Tragedy*, a literary reflection on the role of ancient literature in the constitution of modernity. Nietzsche decides that tragedy comes out of communal choral musical performance. But now tragedy is dead, which seems to signify history as a bleak, rationally chartered implementation of thinking, rather than a joyful and bawdy celebration of life. Dostoevsky is a military engineer trained in mathematics who finds its precision stifling and keeps drawing Gothic windows in the margins of his manuscripts as a way of rendering the dry mathematical beauty appealing to the senses. In his search for liberation from the current unbearable social and political conditions, he turns to the study of human desperation in the hope of its transformation and overcoming by the ahistorical and otherworldly. This year, Dostoevsky publishes *The Idiot*, which portrays a "positively morally beautiful person" who strangely enough turns out to be a complete stranger to the world. This foreigner to any country, who is more of an ideal human type than a real person, will reappear in a dramatic collision with other characters in his last novel, *The Brothers Karamazov*. Yet, most surprisingly, although Dostoevsky and Nietzsche come out of very different contexts and sets of problems that define their thinking, their character types remarkably share many of the same features.

173

And neither iambs nor amusements please me.
—Archilochus, fr. 215 West

German philosophy of the twentieth century, from Cassirer and Heidegger to Gadamer, Hannah Arendt, and Hans Jonas, owes many of its achievements to the classical philology of the nineteenth, which combines the precision of textual readings with broader historical reconstructions and hermeneutic insights. Nietzsche is exemplary as a representative of this philologico-philosophical approach: in 1867 he published a substantive study of the Theognidean fragments;[2] two years later, an essay that reconsidered Homer's place in classical philology;[3] and the same year he decided to rewrite the whole history of Greek literature in a way that would also vindicate German philosophy and even mythology, the spirit of which his friend and later fiend embodies in his innovative operas. However, the idea of understanding the moderns in an encounter with the ancients as allowing for an external comprehensive look at oneself is not original but goes back at least to Charles Perrault's *querelle des anciens et des modernes* (quarrel of the Ancients and the Moderns) and flourishes in the Romantics, who also meant to come to self-understanding as inscribed into the history of the movement of thought and writing, with all its continuity and ruptures, from antiquity onward.

Later, in 1886, in the self-critical and penitential palinodia, Nietzsche recognized the weakness and bias of his original reconstruction in *The Birth of Tragedy*, which he called a "weird and poorly accessible book" (*wunderliches und schlecht zugängliches Buch*; *GT* 1, 11).[4] In the original work, he famously attacks the image of antiquity as the monolithically beautiful "other" of modernity. Nietzsche's complication of the view of antiquity, however, is itself rather simplistic: in his reconstruction, the essentially beautiful and serene obtains its double in the apparently ugly and unruly.

THE APOLLONIAN AND THE DIONYSIAN

Nietzsche's rethinking of the meaning of antiquity and the history of its literature is propelled by the play of opposites that appear unbridgeable, mutually exclusive and complementary, and thus contradictory. It is Apollo and Dionysus that become mythological personifications of the opposite principles of thought and life for Nietzsche. In his interpretation, Apollo, the divinity of light, is the foreteller and nunciate of the future, seen as a beautiful illusion in dreams (*GT* 1, 26; 10, 72). As such, he is the embodiment of passivity, which is represented in and as the image and concept, *das Bild und der Begriff*, of *what is*, contemplated in and by reason (*GT* 9, 67; 6, 51). Apollo, therefore, stands for cognition and self-cognition based on moderation and measure (*Maass*;

GT 4, 40; 9, 70), which is the principle of individuation (*GT* 1, 28; 16, 103). Indeed, everyone has to apply and interpret the prophesied in dreams to oneself, and thus turn into a unique recipient and guardian of such knowledge. The uniqueness and self-deification become, then, the source of satisfaction and "cheerfulness" (*Heiterkeit*; *GT*, *Attempt at Self-Criticism* 1, 11; *GT* 17, 115).

Dionysus, on the contrary, is the best-kept secret of ancient *Weltanschauung* for Nietzsche. The "other god" is the principle of life, insuperably powerful and joyful, displaying himself in intoxication, ecstasy, and sexual licentiousness (*GT* 1, 28; 2, 30; 7, 56). As such, Dionysus is represented as the sublime terror translated into the dissolute joy of the annihilation of the individual and the destruction of the principle of individuation (*GT* 2, 33; 16, 103). Instead of moderation and measure, exorbitance becomes the truth (*GT* 4, 41). Contrary to the Apollonian maxim "nothing in excess," the Dionysian precept is "everything in abundance." Reason and nature, then, are considered as opposites without reconciliation: in modern understanding imposed onto antiquity, reason becomes disembodied in nature and nature becomes irrational and thus can be known only to the extent that it is considered devoid of any thought. For Nietzsche, reason becomes the Apollonian plastic and is opposite to the Dionysian music; the seen is opposed to the heard. The Apollonian theoretical optimism of the cognition of being comes in stark contrast to the Dionysian practical pessimism of striving toward nonbeing. Rather than remaining an isolated individual who fasts eternally with water, one joyfully dissolves oneself into nothing, in a violent communal celebration with wine (*GT* 3, 35). For Kant, phenomena are knowable, but things in themselves are accessible not to reason, but only in practical action. Nietzsche interprets this distinction as the opposition between the knowability of the Apollonian appearances and the noncognizability of the Dionysian things in themselves. For Nietzsche, it is Kant who, without even having noticed it, thus restores if not the balance, then at least the opposition of the two gods.

Nietzsche makes a weak attempt to "deduce" the Dionysian, rather than just recognize it as a "fact." For if it is a "fact," then it could be thought of either as historical or as normative, similarly to the "state of nature," which was considered the historical condition of humans in Hobbes but only a normative way of describing their current state in Rousseau. Nietzsche suggests that since the Apollonian is the principle of individuation, of producing an individual, it takes us out of the Dionysian universality (*Allgemeinheit*) and makes us delight in an individual (*GT* 21, 137)—primarily, in oneself. The resulting Apollonian illusion liberates us from Dionysian excess. In a sense, Nietzsche himself wants to become the priest of Dionysus and, by trampling on the illusion of orderly thinking and rational argument, to bring us back to the life that suspends thought and apparently no longer needs reason. The Apollonian and the Dionysian thus mutually affect each other (*GT* 4, 41), insofar as the two are both mutually complementary and exclusive. The initial move beyond the primary unified universality comes from the necessity to *see* the world, to perceive it in its distinct concreteness and deceptive beauty, as an infinite series of individualized phenomena, which all turn out to be an Apollonian illusion. Therefore, the Dionysian originally engenders the Apollonian. However, once one is no longer satisfied with the illusory, one needs to transcend both the world and oneself in the world, which means that the seen and the individual must be destroyed (*GT* 24, 150). The Apollonian, then, must also produce the Dionysian (which, apparently, is the task Nietzsche sets out for himself in his book). Therefore, the Dionysian is both the precondition and the aspired-to end result of the reconstructed historical development, primarily seen in art. But the Dionysian as the task to be achieved is not a Hegelian sublation of an original thesis in the triple motion when, through a series of logical transformations, the thesis turns into the now enriched synthesis. Rather, the end is a complete oblivion of the existent in an ecstatic dreamless inebriation of the unreflective reproduction of the same.

Here, the picture of antiquity represented as the Apollonian "other" gets complicated by the original yet forgotten Dionysian, which appears as the not recognized "same" of modernity. So Nietzsche uses the dual force of the Apollonian and the Dionysian not for the sake of the understanding or rethinking of ancient literature and art but for the purpose of a reflective reconstruction and justification of modernity, of which he finds Wagner's music to be its alleged apex.

NIETZSCHE AND THE ROMANTICS

In doing so, Nietzsche draws largely on the broad tradition of German Romanticism, which also finds its way into Hegel's lectures on history and aesthetics. However, Nietzsche's attitude toward the Romantics is ambiguous, since, on the one hand, he criticizes the Romantic straw man of antiquity as univocally beautiful and Apollonian. Yet, on the other hand, Nietzsche is incapable of an *epoché*—a truly skeptical aesthetic suspension of judgment in his own understanding of antiquity—and thus reads ancient literature through the prism of the modern Romantic one. Thus, he interprets Goethe's Faust as an ultimate development of the figure of the Apollonian optimistic theoretician (*GT* 18, 124). In the understanding of music, Nietzsche also remains very much under the spell of the Romantics, which is evident in his own early musical compositions of 1862 that show the strong influence of Schumann.[5]

Among the Romantics' genuine insights into, and prejudices against, antiquity is the already mentioned attitude of taking it as the "other" of modernity, where antiquity appears in a reconstructed (either progressive or regressive) development toward modernity. In Hegel, antiquity, which itself goes from Greek to Roman, is predated by the broadly conceived "Oriental" stage in history and art (for instance, in sculpture and epic),[6] which in Nietzsche appears only later in the figure of Zoroaster-Zarathustra.[7] In fact, Nietzsche's preference for the Dionysian over the Apollonian is an intentional reversal of the "Oriental" Mazdaic opposition.

It is also noteworthy that Nietzsche demonstrates the same set of prejudged opinions toward ancient literature that are spelled out in August Schlegel's famous lectures on dramatic art and literature of 1808, which were known to Nietzsche.[8] Here, Schlegel establishes three historical oppositions: First, that of tragedy to comedy as two complementary dramatic genres, in which the latter is considered inferior to the former.[9] Comedy, then, is a decline and degradation of tragedy, or at least a depiction of subjectivity that abandons the substantial and shows itself in and as comic characters who comprise the democratic people. These are the characters whom Hegel in his *Lectures on Aesthetics* considers egoistic, vain, arrogant, irreligious, poorly educated, garrulous, quarrelsome, and boastful (as also does Aristophanes in his comedies).

Second, Schlegel affirms the superiority of Old Comedy over New Comedy, arguing that the Nea (New Comedy) of Menander and Terence is just "the old tamed down."[10] The loss of the boisterous and licentious paradise of tragedy due to the destructive forces of Apollonian optimistic inquisitiveness is Nietzsche's idée fixe, which makes him recognize the alleged superiority of tragedy not only over comedy but over any other literary genre. This is the reason why he does not spare sarcasm in his philippics against New Comedy, which for him only stresses the banality of everydayness against the sublimity of heroism, as well as the vulgarity of the crafty slave as the main comic character standing against the aristocratic chivalry and heroism of tragedy (*GT* 11, 76–79). The New Comedy of Menander and Philemon, then, appears a particularly odious and degenerative genre, since it marks the suicide of tragedy already committed by Nietzsche's nemesis Euripides, the first "sober" poet of "the aesthetic Socratism," who embodies the "non-Dionysian spirit" (*GT* 11, 76, and pages following; 17, 113). The Nea for Nietzsche is but a hopelessly optimistic and dialectical bourgeois drama, *"bürgerliche Schauspiel"* (*GT* 14, 94), employing petty familial characters. Nietzsche's inability to understand and appreciate the originality and true modernity of New Comedy comes from his suspicion of dialectic, which for him is the ultimate form of the Apollonian "syllogistic" rationalization of the unrationalizable raw Dionysian musical flux of life (*GT* 14, 95–96, and others). In fact, Nietzsche misses a most obvious point, namely, that comedy is a celebration of life, whereas tragedy is a celebration of death. To this very day, under the influence of the Romantics and Nietzsche, we are unable to fully appreciate the originality and subtlety of New Comedy, which is probably the only ancient literary genre that survives nowadays, due to its historical translation through the reading of Roman comedy but also because of the sheer modernity of the Nea. And yet, New Comedy presents a most subtle depiction and analysis of human conflict and of the possibility of its resolution that comes with a carefully calculated—truly Socratic and dialectical—movement from the initial problem through complications to the resolution, which is a joyful, yet not banal, good ending. Moreover, the main comic character, who appears in a socially subordinate and subjected position, is indeed the real thinker and political actor, who allows for the movement of comedy toward its end. This comic thinker is paradigmatically represented by the figure of Socrates.[11]

The third historical opposition established by Schlegel is between Greek and Roman drama in general, and comedy in particular.[12] Nietzsche, however, does not condescend to mention Roman poetry and drama, not even the great and utterly modern tragedy of Seneca and comedy of Plautus and Terence, which were directly inherited, read, and performed in their original language through centuries and imaginatively transformed into the modern drama of Shakespeare and Molière, the drama which for Hegel crowns the development of aesthetics. For Nietzsche, Roman literature is too much the "same," hopelessly and undeniably Apollonian.

The duality of the two opposite principles in Nietzsche thus appears to be a quasi-mythological appropriation of the Romantic and idealistic dichotomy into opposites, the moving force of that same Socratic dialectic that he so studiously criticizes and vehemently denies throughout his life (compare the section "The Problem of Socrates," in *Twilight of the Idols*). In particular, Friedrich Nietzsche's personified "divine" duality seems to arise out of the spirit of Friedrich Schiller, to whom Nietzsche keeps referring, always with approval, as someone who finds poetry in a musical mood, thus probably imagining Schiller as his alter ego or at least a precursor (*GT* 5, 43; 7, 54–55; 8, 58; 20, 129; 22, 144). One of the first theoreticians of modern literature and art, Schiller indeed tends to think in terms of opposites, which allows him to both detect and classify aesthetic phenomena. Thus, Nietzsche explicitly refers to and uses Schiller's distinction between elegy and idyll as the genres rooted in sadness and joy (*Trauer* and *Freude*; *GT* 19, 124). The well-known division of poetry into naive and sentimental is also mentioned by Nietzsche (*GT* 3, 37).[13] Less known is Schiller's distinction between fear and joy, *Furcht* and *Freude*: fear or awe is the principle of immobility and respect for the existing limits, whereas joy is the principle of creation and transgression.[14] One can easily interpret fear as standing for cognition that remains within the rationally accepted and discovers the new only within the confined, whereas joy stands for life that always moves on and produces the new. Fear and joy, then, exactly replicate Nietzsche's Apollonian and Dionysian principles. The duality of opposites, which in Hegel and Schiller serves as a heuristic and classificatory tool[15] and in modern ethics stands for the moralistic opposition between good and bad, thus becomes "divinely" personified in Nietzsche and turns into the device of a mythological rethinking of modernity through the opposition to its "other" of (re)constructed antiquity.

NIETZSCHE'S HISTORY OF ANCIENT LITERATURE

Nietzsche's Romantic story of the loss of life (of Dionysian tragedy) and the hopeful regaining of it (in new music, drama, and myth) necessitates the neo-mythological personification of abstract and unmediated opposites as ancient gods.[16] Yet the rigid schematism deprives them of their complex mythological and often contradictory traits and thus turns them into rational constructions necessary for a rather arbitrary reconstruction of the history of ancient literature. With Nietzsche, deliberate "strong readings" in the history of thought become a fashion and almost a norm.

Examples of such (often intentional) misreadings in Nietzsche are plentiful. He follows the traditionally accepted division of Greek literature into epic, lyric, and drama, and takes the decline of tragedy, already apparent in Euripides, as receiving its full expression in prose. For Nietzsche, this process comes to fruition in rational "syllogistic" and dialectical thought, whose main protagonist, Socrates, destroys myth (compare *GT* 23, 140) by critical and argumentative thinking that aspires and dares to *correct* being. Socrates thus undergoes a strange transformation from a passionate Dionysian flute-playing satyr, which he is in Plato (*Symp.* 215a–216c), into a cold and detached Apollonian thinker.

EPIC

Since Nietzsche attempts to derive the Dionysian from the Apollonian, epic for him is an Apollonian enterprise and as such precedes Dionysian tragedy.[17] Homer, therefore, is an Apollonian poet (*GT* 5, 42), a "dreamer" similar to the plastic artist in being immersed in the contemplation of images. However, since the Apollonian for Nietzsche arises by individuation from the universality of the Dionysian, the Dionysian and the Apollonian, on the one hand, stand in a quasi-historical logical progression. But on the other hand, they also appear as two opposite forces or principles underlying the development of literature and culture. The very account and understanding of such development, then, itself turns into a carefully calculated Apollonian theoretical enterprise, which Nietzsche strives to convert into a violent and ecstatic Dionysian one.

179

LYRIC

The problem with giving an account of Greek lyric is that it encompasses a wide variety of different poetic genres. Among them, one usually distinguishes elegy, iambus, and melic, which can be further subdivided by the generations of lyric poets. And yet, Nietzsche chooses just one poet—Archilochus—to bear the weight of this very diverse tradition and makes him the incarnation of the Dionysian spirit who "frightens us by his cries of hatred and disdain, by drunken blazes of desire" (*GT* 5, 43). However, in doing so Nietzsche misses a crucial difference between epic and lyric, namely, that epic poetry is to a great extent improvised and oral (and thus, "Dionysian," contrary to Nietzsche's claim), whereas lyric poetry is carefully calculated and written (thus "Apollonian").

Since Archilochus proclaims in his poems both love *and* scorn for the unfortunate daughters of Lycambes, by one of whom he was spurned, the poet embodies the primary *contradiction* (*Urwiderspruch*; *GT* 5, 44). Archilochus, who both loves and hates at the same time (*GT* 5, 45), thus displays the *mens diducta*, or "split soul," later exemplified also in Anacreon and Catullus (in the famous "*odi et amo*," "I hate and I love," Carm. 85). The lyric poet therefore personifies the Romantic and idealistic contradictory opposition, which Nietzsche ascribes to the restless Dionysian nature. Yet the duality within the uneasy lyric poet might signify the presence of *both* Dionysian and Apollonian principles in him, so that the "primordial" contradiction is in fact the result of the struggle of unmediated opposites.

What Nietzsche does not want to mention is that Archilochus is the originator of iambus, which is not only a specific poetic meter but also a way of mocking and criticizing one's opponents in acrimonious verses (even pushing them to suicide, as in the case of Lycambes's daughters). In Aristotle's account, lampoons or blameful songs give rise to iambus, which in turn produces comedy, as epic originates tragedy (Aristotle, *Poet.* 1448b27–1449a6, 1449b4–5). In this way, comedy comes out of the spirit of the down-to-earth iambic mockery. At the very heart of iambic poetry are agonistic verbal battles, personal attacks, and scoffs, all of which include explicit allusions to the favored topics of eating, drinking, and sexuality as the celebration of life in all its physically available forms.[18] These features are later incorporated into Old Comedy and become especially prominent, although refined, in New Comedy. Nietzsche, however, does not want to recognize them as comic but rather as Dionysian and tragic, which makes him reject outright and entirely disregard the great Nea. Neither the iambs nor the pleasures of comedy delight the suffering Nietzsche, who fancies himself a Bacchic follower of Dionysus but is in fact a despondent, overly reflective Alexandrian philologist choked by the noose of the abstract opposites.

Another problem with Nietzsche's Archilochus interpretation is the account of music, the inebriating "spirit" of which apparently gives rise to tragedy. For on the one hand, Nietzsche recognizes that lyric introduces the popular song into poetry, which for him reflects the fact that in lyric language imitates and follows music, so that poetry is produced by, and organized around, the rhythmic structure of the melody (*GT* 6, 48–49). In a sense, this claim reflects the broader Romantic interest in the genre of song, *Lied*, which intended to reflect and draw upon the "spirit of the people" and became highly refined in Schubert. But on the other hand, Nietzsche takes no notice of the important distinction between monodic and choral lyric, between the monodic lyric of Alcaeus and Sappho and the choral lyric of Stesichorus and Ibycus. The monodic lyric simply does not fit within the Procrustean bed of Nietzsche's interpretation, according to which, first, the Dionysian primarily shows itself in the chorus singing and, second, the lyric poet is identical with the impetuous Dionysian musician (*GT* 5, 43; 6, 49).

Thus, Nietzsche chooses to become the proponent of the orgiastic flute at the expense of ignoring the harmonious lyre. However, the opposition between the Apollonian serene lyre (perceived as "native") and the Dionysian ecstatic flute (perceived as "foreign") is traditional and central to ancient Greek culture and music.[19] This distinction is established already in the early lyric, which the author of the *De musica* attributes to Terpander, in the case of the lyre (*cytharoedic nomos*), and to Clonus, in the case of the flute (*aulodic nomos*; *De musica* 1133A).[20] Yet at the same time, contrary to his literary inventions, Nietzsche himself composed for piano, which is an awkward contemporary string version of the Apollonian lyre. He simply ignores the great polyphonic noninstrumental music of the Franko-Flemish School, particularly of Ockeghem—and the "mathematical" Bach is magically transformed into a Dionysian composer (*GT* 19, 127).

But the best-kept secret is Theognis, who is probably the key to the understanding of Nietzsche's entire work. Although Nietzsche knew Theognis very well and wrote a competent work on the *Theognidea*, he never mentions the poet in *The Birth of Tragedy*. For Theognis does not fit within Nietzsche's rigid opposition and refutes the idea of a lyric poet being a faithful attendant of Dionysus. Quite to the contrary, Theognis considered himself a follower of Apollo (1–4), even if his poems were sung accompanied by a flute (241–43). And yet, several central themes in Nietzsche appear to come straight out of Theognis. Thus, the poet's antidemocratic polemics (846–47); the contempt for the *kakoi*, the vulgar "many" (233–34, 319–22); the scornful rejection of the democratic belief in Enlightenment (437–38); the defense of the values and morality accessible only to the "noble" (27–36, 233–34)—all these topics become Nietzsche's leitmotif since the *Genealogy of Morals*. Moreover, Theognis is also famous for his moralistic gnomes.[21]

The *gnōmē*, literally, "thought" or "judgment," translated into Latin as *sententia*, is an energetic hortative statement. It is an old literary device, already found in Homer's poems (at least by his later readers, who are never tired of extracting quotations from Homer) and is mastered by Theognis. Sententiae progressively play a central role in Nietzsche's later works, including *The Gay Science*, *Böse Weisheit*, *Beyond Good and Evil*, and *Twilight of the Idols*. However, being intimately familiar with Theognis's gnomes,[22] Nietzsche is very reluctant to recognize the influence of the elegiac poet who is too much of the "same" for him and defies his interpretative scheme.

DRAMA

Finally, Nietzsche's reconstruction of drama appears equally willful, not only in his prejudiced rejection of Euripides and New Comedy. If tragedy indeed comes out of the cult of Dionysus, namely, from the dithyramb (*GT* 4, 42; compare Aristotle, *Poet.* 1448a14–16), then Nietzsche's account of it lacks any detail and finesse. Thus, for instance, he fails to mention Arion as being the first to turn dithyramb into an ordered genre that later became tragedy.[23] Besides, probably deliberately, Nietzsche omits mentioning that dithyramb, originally a choral hymn praising Dionysus, was sung by a large chorus. Later, in Bacchylides, it was structured as an antiphon or dialogue between the chorus and a single singer. This means that dialogue is already present and embedded in tragic dithyramb. Drama, therefore, is the narrative explained in and by action (properly, "drama") complemented by dialogue—in contrast to epic, where action is narrated by the author (compare Aristotle, *Poet.* 1448a20–24). But for Nietzsche, in tragedy the chorus is rigidly opposed to dialogue, because the former is deemed Dionysian, whereas the latter is Apollonian (*GT* 9, 64).

A CRITIQUE OF NIETZSCHE: APOLLO AND DIONYSUS

Yet the biggest problem with Nietzsche's rendering of the Apollonian and the Dionysian is his intentional suppression of the dual nature of each god.[24] That each one comprises opposite sides within himself is obvious in the extant myths. Thus, on the one hand, Apollo is the keeper of harmony and the leader of Muses (*Mousagetēs*; compare Homer, *Il.* 1.603–4); he is identified with the sun, the source of life and the metaphor for cognition. Through his oracle, Apollo prophesies the will of Zeus in order to help people (compare *Hom. Hymn* 3.131–32, 179 and pages following). He is also the protector of herds (Apollodorus III.10.4) and a skilled physician capable of curing disease (Aristophanes, *Aves* 584).

But on the other hand, the very same sun can burn and can be pernicious, which is suggested by one of the etymologies of Apollo's epithet Phoebus or "radiant" (coming from *phobos*, "fear"). When turning to the world with his other side, Apollo appears as "night-like" (*Il.* 1.47) and turns into a destroyer (from *apollumi*, "to destroy")[25] who can also cause a disease and put terror in people (*Hom. Hymn.* 3.447). In such a capacity, he sends a plague to Troy and curses a raven, turning it from white to black (*Il.* 1.9–10; Apollodorus II.5.9; III.10.2). Even before Apollo is born, it is feared that he will be too "reckless" or "wicked" (*atasthalos*; *Hom. Hymn.* 3.67). Since one of his attributes is a bow, which he gives to Hercules (Apollodorus II.4.11), Apollo shoots arrows (*Il.* I.43–52; "far-shooting," *Hom. Hymn.* 3.215, and others), with which he kills his adversaries and also produces lightning (Apollodorus I.9.26). The rays of the sun, of course, can not only give life but also slay the living and thus can become deadly arrows. Therefore, Apollo is also a *killer*: he is a "mouse-killer" (Smintheus); he kills Python in Delphi (Apollodorus I.4.1), the sons of Niobe (Apollodorus III.5.6), the Cyclopes (Apollodorus III.10.4), and even his own lovers—Coronis (Apollodorus III.10.3) and (accidentally, by discus) Hyacinth (Apollodorus I.3.3).

The duality of the sun god is captured in the duality of bow and lyre, which is the other common attribute of Apollo: when born, he asks for a lyre *and* a bow (*Hom. Hymn.* 3.131; compare *Il.* 1.603–4; *Hom. Hymn.* 3.201; Apollodorus III.10.2). Both are string "instruments," but the one celebrates the harmony of the existent, while the other destroys it. A famous story tells of Apollo's musical competition with the satyr Marsyas: Apollo's victory signifies the apparent triumph of the harmony-asserting lyre over the barbaric flute that disfigures the face of the player. And yet, it ends in a most atrocious act of Apollo flaying Marsyas (Apollodorus I.4.2; Diodorus 3.58.3; Pausanias 1.24.1; Aelian, *Var. hist.* 13.21; Ovid, *Fasti* 6.695–710).[26] It is quite remarkable that Nietzsche chooses to ignore the myth, which might be important for his own purpose, since it clearly suggests an opposition between two modes of music represented by the two instruments, one of which is Apollonian and the other Dionysian. But Apollo the slayer does not fit his own myth.

In turn, Dionysus is ecstatic and can even cause insanity. As such, he is associated with inebriation and always appears in the presence of wine and vine (Apollodorus I.8.1; III.5.1). Yet he also shows his other side, gentle and playful. Thus, a fragment of the Homeric hymn to Dionysus refers to the story about Dionysus fetching Hephaestus to Olympus not by force but by making Hephaestus happy while drunk (*Hom. Hymn.* 1C). And as a child, Dionysus is often depicted as cheerfully playing with a satyr.[27]

Therefore, contrary to Nietzsche, the duality is intrinsic in both Apollo and Dionysus, so that the two are inextricably connected and each contains the other in himself. No wonder that Apollo sometimes even bears the same epithets as Dionysus ("ivy"), and Dionysus is taken for Apollo (compare *Hom. Hymn.* 7.19) and in Hellenistic times loses much of his ecstatic appearance, often depicted very much like Apollo, as a beautiful and joyful young man. The new mythology created by Nietzsche misses the ancient myth, because his modern myth-making that is meant to substitute for rational dialectical thinking still embodies and uses the same unmediated abstract opposites that this very thinking is originally based on.

> Reason is a scoundrel, but foolishness is direct
> and honest.
> —Dostoevsky, preparatory notes for *The Brothers*
> *Karamazov, PSS* 15:232

The works of Dostoevsky and Nietzsche share a number of themes and topics,[28] such as skepticism, pessimism, and nihilism that lead to the desperation of the "Underground Man" (Lev Shestov), the force of evil (Simona Forti), the psychology of the *homo christianus* (C. A. Miller), the problem of God's existence (Janko Lavrin), the tension between "god-man" and "man-god" (Nel Grillaert), and the moral rebel and the superman (Edith Clowes and Nel Grillaert).[29]

The division between the Apollonian and the Dionysian is markedly present in Dostoevsky's main characters, despite his lack of awareness of such presence. However, what Nietzsche does out of the necessity of his reconstruction of the history of literature and art, when a modern writer is obliged to see himself through the eyes of the assumed cultural other, Dostoevsky does out of the necessity of his reconstruction of human psychology in moments of collisions and catastrophes, when a modern hero perceives herself through the words and actions of others.

It is worth noting that one of the first significant modernist novels, Andrey Bely's *Petersburg*, is based on the consciously accepted and intentionally redressed opposition between the Apollonian and the Dionysian.[30] The two main characters of the novel, the father Apollon Apollonovich Abveukhov and the son Nikolai Apollonovich, become Apollo (which is evident from the name) and Dionysus. The story is of a failed patricide, where the son becomes involved with an incognito terrorist who distinctly bears Nietzsche's features (the eyes and moustache, which are also attributed to a saint and a madman; *Petersburg*, 27, 624, 628). The section in which the nervous and excited Nikolai Apollonovich is described winding up the mechanism of a bomb meant to kill his father and thus turns into a "suffering Dionysus" is called "Dionysus" (*Petersburg*, 181–83). Apollon Apollonovich, on the contrary, is an embodiment of the purely rational "geometrical" and calculating Apollonian spirit, who also appropriately keeps an alabaster statue of Niobe, whose children were killed by Apollo and Artemis, in his house (*Petersburg*, 40). He sees and traces his surroundings as geometrical cubes, spheres, straight lines, and angles, all mutually balanced and symmetrical, which he eventually externalizes by a "cerebral game" (*Petersburg*, 17–21, 26–27). However, both of Bely's characters are in fact very Nietzschean in that, being rather schematic, they lack the depth and mutual inclusion of their mythical counterparts.

Traces of antiquity are always lurking in the background of Dostoevsky's writings, the image of which is to a great part informed by Bové's classicism, which surrounded Dostoevsky from his childhood. One cannot miss the triumphant yet intimidating presence of Peter Klodt's *Apollo quadriga* on the façade of the Bolshoi Theater. But literary "ancient" reminiscences in Dostoevsky often come from the Romantics. Thus, at a crucial moment of his conversation with Alyosha, Dmitry Karamazov quotes a translation of Schiller's "Das Eleusische Fest" (The Eleusinian Festival) at length, which invokes Ceres and Proserpina (*PSS* 14:68). He also refers to Ulysses from Tyutchev's rendering of Schiller's poem (*PSS* 14:362; and compare 14:176). At another climatic moment of the novel, one of his interlocutors mentions Pyrrho and recites Batyushkov's epigram referring to Sappho (*PSS* 14:382). The nonliterary presence of antiquity is felt in the novel, often in unexpected ways: thus, a gymnasium teacher bears the name of Dardanellov; the vexing question among the gymnasium boys, all of whom know Greek and Latin, is who was the founder of Troy; they write a caustic "classical" epigram to the marriage of their classics teacher; a doctor gives Ilyusha's father impossible advice to send the dying son to Syracuse; and in the preliminary materials Dostoevsky even mentions Plato as one of the sources (*PSS* 14:464, 496–98, 505; 15:204).

DOSTOEVSKY'S GODS

The distinction between the Apollonian and the Dionysian in Dostoevsky comes out of the "logic" of characters' interactions and struggles.[31] Yet this distinction in Dostoevsky is more complex and perhaps more refined than in Nietzsche, because the Apollonian and the Dionysian in Dostoevsky are not mutually exclusive opposites remodeled as literary devices; rather, each presupposes and bears the other within itself.

The figures of Apollo and Dionysus are paradigmatically represented in *The Brothers Karamazov*'s characters of Alyosha and Dmitry. In Dostoevsky, we have a series of both "strange" literary coincidences that point in the direction of such an identification, as well as the structural features of the characters that reflect certain "archetypes" of human characters. The coincidences begin with the names: both sets of names begin with an "A" and a "D" (and all are of Greek origin). Besides, Dionysus and Apollo are half-brothers: the two have the same father (Zeus) but different mothers (Semele and Leto). Such are also Dmitry and Alyosha: the same father (Fedor Pavlovich) but different mothers (Adelaida Ivanovna and Sofia Ivanovna). Both are also not properly educated, since neither completed the course at gymnasium (*PSS* 14:11, 20). But gods do not need education: they already know (moral) truths by heart and from the heart.

The "archetypal" similarities with the Greek gods, however, are even more conspicuous. Aleksey-Apollo is an embodiment of beauty, primarily moral but also physical (*PSS* 14:24). Light and bright, serene and fair (*PSS* 14:19), he strives toward the "light of love" and himself radiates human goodness. The dearest remembrance of his childhood, that of his mother, comes with the image of slant rays of light (*PSS* 14:18). The Apollonian character embodies for Dostoevsky the ideal humanness of the one who loves others "for nothing," for no reason at all (*PSS* 14:320) and is in turn loved by everyone (*PSS* 14:19). He is the personification of honesty "by nature," which shows itself both in the readiness to forgive others, as well as in the fearlessness based in the hope and trust in the ultimate goodness of people and in the world beyond their apparent baseness and corruption (*PSS* 14:19, 25).

Alyosha's "clarity," seen in its moral and physical purity, has a clear and intended similarity in Dostoevsky's "positively beautiful man" Prince Myshkin in the *Idiot*. Such "clarity" is translated into chastity (*tselomudrennost'*, literally, "the wholeness of wisdom"), which makes both erotically very attractive to women yet at the same time prevents them from being attracted to women. Rather, Alyosha is afraid of women, knows them "very little" and is "unfit to be a husband" (*PSS* 14:94; 15:21). And Myshkin acknowledges of his physical impotence, which for Lukács, according to Agnes Heller, meant the incapability of loving at all. Yet the incapacity or unwillingness for physical love might mean not only the latent homoeroticism of the Dostoevskian Apollo but perhaps—and even more so—the incapacity to act at all. And if Apollo is indeed a personification of rational deliberative thought (Alyosha always thinks and deliberates within himself, *PSS* 14:18), then this thought is not reflective—it is not the thought of itself about oneself, but about others. Alyosha can and does reach out for others, and is thus capable of love. This thought is the right moral judgment: "You are an angel on earth. You will listen, you will judge, and you will forgive . . . ," says Dmitry about Alyosha (*PSS* 14:97). "Apollonian" thought, then, is profoundly ambiguous in that, despite its intrinsic goodness, it *does not and cannot act*. It is the right judgment that does not translate into action. It is the thought that intends to, yet in the end does not, help others. It is the thought that understands and even foresees disastrous consequences of the actions of others and yet cannot prevent them and save others from destroying themselves and their loved ones.

On the contrary, Dmitry-Dionysus exemplifies all the qualities associated with Bacchic frenzy: the propensity toward debauchery and violence, cruelty and rage (*PSS* 14:100; 15:94, 153; and others). It is difficult to fathom what he is thinking: pensive and gloomy, he is of "abrupt and irregular mind" (*PSS* 14:63, 417). Rather, he is moved by outbursts of "passions," which become especially apparent in his drunken escapades that often display uncontrollable impulses (*PSS* 14:75, 110). Grief and yearning, anxiety and jealousy define his "Dionysian" mood, which often abruptly turns from deep melancholy to uncontainable hilarity and exuberant and frantic laughter (*PSS* 14:142, 344). Anger is the major driving force in him, which leads to the violation and temporary suspension of moral norms, as becomes manifest in his drinking, gambling, spending and appropriating money; in breaking social conventions and customs associated with family life and marriage; in fighting duels, beating up other people and eventually threatening to kill the father and the lackey Smerdyakov (*PSS* 14:11, 69, 128, 176, 458, and others). Rogozhin, the Dionysian character from the *Idiot* who acts in much the same way and is also a "half-brother" to Myshkin (once they exchange the crosses they wear, God becomes their "father"), ends by actually killing his lover (*PSS* 8:504).

Unseemly in appearance, Dmitry considers himself among the chthonic "underground men" (*PSS* 15:31). Similar to Dionysus, who is perceived in antiquity as an originally "Oriental" deity, Dmitry is associated in the book with Siberia (to which he will go in exile after being accused of murder) or America (to which he might flee), perceived by the readers as foreign and "Oriental" countries (*PSS* 15:10, 34, 5). Most remarkably, Dmitry's self-description is Dionysian: when drinking, he quotes from a poem of Apollon Maikov and explicitly compares himself to Silenus, which comes as a pun: "*ne Silen, a silën*," or, "I am not Silenus but I am strong" (*PSS* 14:98).

Drunkenness, sublimated to being "drunk in spirit" (*PSS* 14:368), is Dmitry's abnormal "normal" state, which for Nietzsche is the essential Dionysian modus operandi. Only in this state is the hero detached from the ordinary, when for a few brief moments he becomes capable of looking into the abysmal joy beyond everydayness, which otherwise remains inaccessible to him. "I will be cheerful, I will laugh," says Dmitry when being accused of murder and seeing no way out (*PSS* 14:418). The obscure Dionysian delirium and furor, ecstasy, and "edge" or "tear" (*isstuplenie, nadryv*) motivate Dmitry to act often against his own will and regret the impossibility of exercising any control over his actions.[32] But any rational calculation is suspect; in pecuniary matters, it amounts to sheer baseness (*PSS* 14:443). And yet his impulsive irrational spontaneity at times arouses deep sympathy for him (e.g., during the process), because others see his "hot heart" (*PSS* 14:10 and pages following; 15:90) as a manifestation of sincere, even if impure, intentions that aim at an unreachable and thus other-worldly utopian happiness and its celebration, as opposed to the cold rationalization of the "petit-bourgeois," down-to-earth, goal-oriented reason. Being drunk and being good, then, entail each other (*PSS* 14:188). "I love life," recognizes Dmitry (*PSS* 14:366), by which he means life at the extreme, the one that Nietzsche and his later followers (e.g., Hesse in *Steppenwolf*) yearned for. Dmitry, therefore, embodies the "heroic" and "angry" part of the soul, which dominates the actions of the Dionysian character and is associated in Plato with the heart, in contradistinction to the "rational" part (of Ivan's *Zweckrationalität* or "instrumental rationality") and the "vegetative" part (of the father Fedor Pavlovich's lust). Yet the lack of self-control unavoidably leads to eventual self-destruction, which, however, provokes pity and compassion from others. Perhaps this is something that Dostoevsky and Nietzsche share—the idea of the impossibility of the productive creativeness of the reflective mind (of the Apollonian) and the inevitability and constructiveness of the destruction brought about by life (of the Dionysian).

Yet both Alyosha-Apollo and Dmitry-Dionysus have and cultivate "the other within," absent in Nietzsche's schematic depiction of the two gods. This "other" shows not only through their mutual *philadelphia*, or brotherly love for each other (*PSS* 14:96), but also through the palimpsests of the Dionysian in Alyosha and the Apollonian in Dmitry, which at times become evident and readable again. Thus, Alyosha is surrounded by a quasi-Dionysian retinue (*vataga*) of boys who often pick on passers-by with tricky dialectical questions (*PSS* 14:471–77). At the very end of the novel, after the funeral of Ilyusha, one of the boys, Alyosha enthusiastically addresses his beloved "boys" almost in the form of a paean. And yet, his invocation of the restitution of life and the salvation of the dead through memory is more reminiscent of a Dionysian dream (*PSS* 15:195–96). Moreover, serene and conscientious Alyosha, ready to accept and forgive everyone, cannot halt a spontaneous outburst against the landlord in Ivan's story who hunts down a boy who accidentally harmed a dog. "Shoot him!" says Alyosha in a calm and thus even more frightening and resolute rage (*PSS* 14:221). A strongly "Dionysian" radicalism is evident in Alyosha: deeply pious, he rebels against hypocritical rules of behavior, and drinks vodka and eats sausage after the death and unseemly physical decay of his beloved spiritual leader *Starets Zosima* (*PSS* 14:309). In fact, according to A. S. Suvorin's testimony, in the planned continuation of *The Brothers Karamazov*, Dostoevsky intended to make Alyosha, who at a certain point wanted to become a monk, into a revolutionary and a regicide (*PSS* 14:17; 15:485–86). This intention became almost oracular, in that Alexander II was killed by an idealistic young man in March 1881, one month after Dostoevsky's death and in the same year that the novel was published as a book for the first time. It comes as no surprise, then, that Alyosha shows his Dionysian side when calling on Ivan not to be afraid of *life* and to love life beyond and above any logic (*PSS* 14:210).

Dmitry, on the other hand, is essentially a simple-hearted and innocent man (*PSS* 14:332) who strives toward an ultimate "harmony" and calm beyond and above passions and calamities of the world. Apollo is always lurking in the background—for example, when, "devouring space," Dmitry flies in his (Apollonian) chariot toward his fate and love (*PSS* 14:370). Besides, as Friedlander suggests, the prototype for the character of Dmitry was Apollon (!) Grigoriev, a famous poet and literary critic who died of delirium tremens (*PSS* 15:404). And even Dmitry's vision of himself as he should and will be (the one "of tomorrow") is that of the "golden-haired Phoebus," to whom he wants others to drink a glass (*PSS* 14:366, 370)!

DOSTOEVSKY'S DEMONS

One can trace a further important distinction that is altogether missing in Nietzsche. Not only "gods" but also "demons" play a crucial role in the intricately woven tissue of characters' interaction in Dostoevsky. These are the other two brothers, Ivan and the illegitimate half-brother Smerdyakov, whose connection to the three brothers Karamazov is widely known yet never explicitly recognized by them.

If indeed Dostoevsky's novels are "polyphonic"[33] in that all characters are independent voices simultaneously sounding in the texture of the novels, this means that there is no single character who would be at the center of the plot. In this respect, Dostoevsky's novels are also "polycentric." Ivan is one of such centers, although he also stands out among other characters of the novel. The middle brother (four years apart from each other brother), he is not a "middle" or mediator between the brothers and does not reconcile them as opposites, the way the Aristotelian "subject" or *hypokeimenon* would mediate and reconcile opposites. Ivan is *different*. He is the "stranger" among the brothers. Unlike Dmitry and Alyosha, Ivan does not exemplify either a self-contained thought or a spontaneity of life. He represents—or even, in a sense, *is*—an *educated* and *cultivated* self-reflective thinking. Unlike the other two brothers, he graduates both from a gymnasium and a university: Ivan is a "learned" and "proud" "man of letters" (*uchenyi, gordyi*; *PSS* 14:15–16), a writer and a journalist (the profession Nietzsche detested; *GT* 20, 130).

Yet unlike his two brothers who are "integral" persons, Ivan is a split mind (which is what "schizophrenia" literally means) who has neither an immediate (moral) knowledge nor is engaged in an unreflective action. This mind mirrors itself in the pamphlet Ivan writes about the church court, which, strangely enough, is praised by both opposing parties. This mind also produces a paper advocating that the state turn in a church, which Ivan clearly does not support himself (*PSS* 14:16, 57–58). Ivan is a "theoretical" mind that never comes to a definite conclusion that fully satisfies it, which is why it is in constant anguish (*toska*; *PSS* 14:241). For this reason, Ivan's brothers call him a "tomb," a "riddle," a taciturn "sphinx" (*PSS* 14:209; 15:32). Ivan embodies thinking that is reflective and yet cannot reconcile with and within itself and thus is dialectical, profoundly paradoxical and eccentric (*PSS* 14:65). Ivan is literally torn by opposite thoughts, strivings, and intentions and finds no way of bringing them together, which in the end of the novel leads to his full mental demise, one that amounts to death or at least a coma. Yet, on the other hand, the attempt to notice or reflectively trace and give an account of madness escapes the divided mind, which Ivan understands, asking Alyosha if it is possible to observe how one becomes insane (*PSS* 15:38). Apparently, such an observation is unreachable for the reflective consciousness that takes its very reflectiveness as the sign of proper functioning and sanity. And although Ivan has the face of a dying man (*PSS* 15:115), only others can see it. Because Ivan's mental and probably also physical death follow from the impossibility of coming to terms with himself, such a death is an intended but not intentional suicide, unlike the suicide of Ivan's "double," Smerdyakov, which is intentional but not originally intended.

Irredeemably torn within his own mind without a hope of bringing it together, Ivan is incapable of reaching out for others, which is why he is incapable of love that is a suspension of the self for the sake of other. Neither Ivan nor Smerdyakov loves anyone (*PSS* 14:114). Ivan cannot love and yet, because he is deeply paradoxical and attempts to think the impossible, despite all odds, he loves Alyosha (*PSS* 14:124). As we know from Zosima's homily, the incapacity to love *is* hell. Hence, Ivan lives in hell and only his mental and physical destruction allows him to escape from hell—or, who knows, perhaps allows him to sink even deeper into hell.

Ivan's inability to love is not only the result of his unhappy torn mind but also follows "theoretically" from his main "thesis" that if there is no immortality, then everything is allowed (*PSS* 14:65, 240). For if immortality means reaching out for and being with others in some state of uninterrupted communication, then, if there is no immortality, there is no love. This means further that there is no objective "law" of love "in nature" for Ivan, for love is only a fake, and a human invention (*PSS* 14:64). Ivan is convinced that humans are "wild and evil beasts" who invented God for their own sake and as a cover-up for their meanness (*PSS* 14:214). Ivan's God is a product of his split subjectivity that cannot overcome the illusion of conceiving itself as free and autonomous. By producing God, it kills God; its God has always been dead. In this sense, Ivan not only pens the *Grand Inquisitor* (*PSS* 14:224 and pages following), but he himself personifies the Grand Inquisitor.

Because God is thus a projection of the human mind, Ivan can and does accept God; but because this is a projection of a restless and unreconciled mind, he cannot understand God, since he cannot understand his own mind, misguided in its persistent reflexivity. In this respect, the idea of God is similar to that of non-Euclidean geometry, which is also a product of the human mind that accepts yet cannot understand the nonevident (*PSS* 14:214).

However, once the divided mind puts itself in a position to create the idea of God and to reflect on it as its own product, it cannot abstain from creating the idea of its other, of the devil. This other becomes the intimate self of and within Ivan's split mind, which it inevitably generates yet does not want to accept. This is evident in Ivan's conversation with the devil, the stranger whom Ivan intimately addresses as "thou" (*ty*; *PSS* 15:71–72), which is appropriate between relatives and close friends but never in talking with an unknown visitor. Ivan knows that he faces a "diabolic chaos" (*PSS* 14:209) and realizes that the devil who "philosophizes" with him is his own other and thus himself. Ivan knows that the devil does not exist (*PSS* 14:124) and is only a "fantasy," and thus he speaks to himself ("this is me speaking, not you!"; *PSS* 15:72). No wonder that the devil, who is as learned as Ivan, ironically quotes Descartes's famous "I think, therefore I am,"[34] and demands his own *annihilation* ("I . . . am demanding, simply and straightforwardly, my own annihilation"; *PSS* 15:77). And yet, Ivan's Cartesian mind is incapable of reaching out for the other and therefore *cannot get rid of* the other of and within himself. He is forever possessed by this diabolic—not reachable—other and is thus a "demon" beyond the redemption of both love and a simple conversation or dialogue with the other.

Reflective yet not fully self-transparent and not self-accessible, such thinking is "demonic." It is the thinking that creates God by elevating itself to being godlike (Ivan cannot become either one of his brothers) yet at the same time unsuccessfully annihilating or denying itself. Such thinking *is* the devil, which, however, it does not want to be. It wants to become God, which it is not. Such "demonic" thinking can only destroy itself and fall into insanity and oblivion.

One could say that the three brothers are various aspects of one integrated personality that can be never "sublated" or incorporated (literally—put in one body) into one person. Yet in fact there are four brothers, and if Alyosha and Dmitry represent the "divine" opposites, Ivan and his "brotherly other" Smerdyakov represent the "demonic" opposites. In each case, the opposites are not reconciled or bridged and thus represent two "abysses," the "divine" and the "demonic," which, as Dostoevsky writes in the preliminary notes to the novel, constitute the basis of the Karamazovs' character (*PSS* 15:363).

Ivan realizes his close connection with Smerdyakov, with whom he holds three intimate conferences (*PSS* 15:41 and pages following), which in their subtlety rise to the level of three conversations between Raskolnikov and Porfiry Petrovich in *Crime and Punishment*. As the other "demonic" figure, together with Ivan, Smerdyakov stands against the "gods," and is thus an atheist (*PSS* 15:97). Smerdyakov's very name invokes all kinds of connotations with stench (*smerdyaschiy*, which is the nickname of his mother), lackey (*smerd*, which he is), and death (*smert'*, which he brings). He lives in constant humiliation of not being recognized as an equal, which he tries to rectify by deranged and hideous means. In fact, he would have preferred not to be born at all (*PSS* 14:204). As a boy, he was hanging cats and organizing their funeral ceremonies, in which he played the priest (*PSS* 14:114). As an adult, he taught a boy to feed a dog a piece of bread with a needle hidden inside (*PSS* 14:480). Incapable of love, in which he is very similar to Ivan, Smerdyakov is despised by everyone and, in turn, despises everyone (*PSS* 14:114). His perverse mind shows itself in the incapacity to reconcile with himself and others, and is further underlined by his epilepsy (*PSS* 14:116), which in the novel becomes the sign of the demonic, in contradistinction to the "divine" epilepsy of Myshkin in the *Idiot*. At the same time, Smerdyakov is an able actor—a hypocrite—who can imitate an epileptic fit and use it for his own carefully calculated purposes (*PSS* 15:47). He even tries to imitate Ivan's learnedness, appearing as a pathetic buffoon who learns French "vocables" written in Cyrillic and reads a book while putting on glasses and assuming airs (*PSS* 15:48, 50). Among Smerdyakov's reading are Gogol's *Evenings on a Farm near Dikanka* (a literary adaptation of folk stories about demons) and the *Life of St. Isaac the Syrian* (in the genre of hagiography, which, as the Great Menaion Reader, was a favorite folk reading; *PSS* 14:115; 15:58).

Just like Ivan, Smerdyakov shows the same cunning yet self-destroying reflection (also exemplified in another "demon," Petr Verkhovensky in the *Demons*). Still, Ivan does not want to recognize Smerdyakov as his brother and a real other (which is the devil). Ivan is increasingly irritated by thoughts about Smerdyakov up to the point of hating him; he wants to beat Smerdyakov up, although does not know why, and even to kill him (*PSS* 14:242–43, 251; 15:57). The recognition of Smerdyakov as the *alter ego* is impossible for Ivan not only because of social differences, but also because he does not want to recognize Smerdyakov as the mirror reflecting his own inability to love, to be with the other, which eventually results in Ivan's desperate solitude (after the death of the father; *PSS* 15:41) and demise.

However, one's own reflection in the other remains inaccessible for the reflection of the split "demonic" mind, and Smerdyakov remains an enigma even for perspicacious Ivan. Smerdyakov not only speaks in riddles, "prophesies," and ironic allusions (*PSS* 15:46)—he also draws hints from others who are reluctant to recognize openly their own inclinations and thus comfortably remain in the safety of unuttered and unrecognized intentions. Smerdyakov understands something about Ivan that Ivan himself does not want to understand (*PSS* 15:43).

Most importantly, Smerdyakov hints that he understands that Ivan would not object to killing their father, which is the thought Ivan himself never wants or dares to recognize (*PSS* 15:53). Smerdyakov does all the carefully planned "dirty work" of killing the father, yet in the end he makes Ivan recognize that it is Ivan who is the real murderer (*PSS* 15:54–55, 63). Ivan is thus the *causa finalis* of the murder (an even more remote *causa finalis* might be Alyosha, who could make Ivan act out of bad consciousness and a feeling of guilt), whereas Smerdyakov "humbly" assumes the role of the *causa instrumentalis*. Clearly, Smerdyakov kills the father not out of a mercantile interest, because in the end he gives Fedor Pavlovich's money to Ivan, frankly relates the story of the murder in all the details (*PSS* 15:60), and then commits suicide by hanging himself, which is commonly perceived as a disgraceful and humiliating death. There is, however, a way of interpreting the murder, which is never depicted in the novel, as committed by Dmitry, so that the story of persecution in the court would be correct. This would turn Smerdyakov into a "saint" who calumniates himself in order to save Dmitry by sacrificing himself for the wrongdoing of his brothers who refuse to recognize him. Smerdyakov's reading the *Life of St. Isaac the Syrian*, then, would not have been in vain. Yet such an act would still testify to Smerdyakov's deeply split "demonic" mind. But if this is indeed so, why does Ivan have to kill the father? An evident motive is his moral revulsion against the disgrace that the father's debauchery brings on every member of the family and people around him. However, the murder of the father becomes inevitable for the "demonic" sons as the expression of their inability to reach out for their other—paradigmatically represented by the father—and to reconcile with him.

Yet there is more: Fedor Pavlovich is commonly portrayed as a buffoon (*PSS* 14:9, 21, 38) and is thus a comic character. In New Comedy, the three "generations" of actors are the children, the parents, and the servants. The initial conflict between the sons and the fathers is eventually resolved by a complex set of actions, where the shrewd and smart servant plays the leading role. Rather than being dead as at the end of a tragedy, everyone is well off at the end of a comedy. The murder of the father, then, is the symbolic murder of comedy. Both Nietzsche and Dostoevsky reject comedy as banal and "diabolic" or "demonic" and prefer tragedy to it.[35] This is why the devil in Dostoevsky casually quotes Terence's *Self-Tormentor* (*Haut.* 77) in a "diabolically perverse" way: "*Satan sum et nihil humanum a me alienum puto*" (I am Satan, and nothing human is alien to me; *PSS* 15:74). For Dostoevsky and Nietzsche, a person is better off dead than happy. In Nietzsche, however, there are no demons, because Nietzsche himself *is* Ivan, which he never wants to acknowledge.

THE MAENADS

One cannot fail to notice that Nietzsche's main philosophical categories are disguised as male gods. Only in passing does he mention the maenads, the female followers of Dionysus (*GT* 5, 44). In Dostoevsky, on the contrary, female characters not only play a crucial role in the novels, but the central female characters are disguised as maenads. Already mentioned in Homer (*Il.* 22.460–61), maenads become ubiquitous suitors of Dionysus in later times and as such find their way into drama (in Euripides's *Bacchae*). Recognized by the phallic attributes of thyrsus and snake, maenads are primarily characterized by Bacchic fury, drunken frenzy, and erotic rage (Diodorus 4.3.3).[36] Possessed by the Dionysian "life-asserting" rampage, they even become involved in an ecstatic killing. As Apollodorus tells us, Orpheus invents the Bacchic mysteries but eventually dies, being torn to pieces by the maenads (I.3.2); and Agave kills her son Pentheus, tearing him apart when mistaking him for a beast (III.5.2).

Dostoevsky's most important female characters are maenads in that, far from being meek and mild, tamed and dutiful housewives, they are primarily defined by the "heroic" or "Dionysian" passions of the "heart"—anger and rage. Such are Nastasya Filippovna and Aglaya in the *Idiot* and Grushenka and Katerina Ivanovna in the *Brothers Karamazov*. As maenads, they passionately love and enthusiastically follow their Dionysus (Rogozhin and Dmitry). After the condemnatory verdict is passed on Dmitry, the women who attended the trial seem to be in a kind of delirium and ready to revolt (*PSS* 15:178). The love rage of the maenads even unduly extends to the beautiful Apollo (Myshkin and Alyosha) whom they want to seduce, yet they eventually abandon the intention once they realize its inappropriateness.

Like the "gods," the "maenads" in Dostoevsky are characterized by a "coincidence of the opposites," by contrasting intentions, passions, and qualities, by embracing and containing "the other within," so conspicuously absent in Nietzsche. As the "gods" and "demons," the "maenads" come in pairs, in which each one is both opposed to and complements her other. In each pair, a well-educated and well-mannered maenad (Aglaya or Katerina

Ivanovna) stands opposite to a seemingly uncouth and vulgar maenad who is also perceived as "fallen" and compromised as a kept mistress (Nastasya Filippovna or Grushenka, "a provincial hetaera"; *PSS* 14:454). Yet beyond the superficial social conventions, they are very similar in that they are both spectacularly beautiful, and thus attractive—*and* unmistakably furious, and thus repulsive.

In her beauty, Grushenka appears perfectly Apollonian and is thus compared to the Venus de Milo (*PSS* 14:136–37). In his notebooks, Dostoevsky describes Grushenka as a "goddess," later adding: "GODDESS!" (*PSS* 15:287). Both Grushenka and Katerina Ivanovna attract by the way they walk, even if differently (*PSS* 14:136). Yet maenadic beauty is not serene but rather "mysterious" in its sensuousness and seduction. It is "an awful and frightening thing" (*PSS* 14:100), as Dmitry experiences it when he "goes mad" and abandons his fiancée, Katerina Ivanovna, for Grushenka, becoming both sanctified and tortured by his love. Such beauty is not only a blessing but also a curse, both for oneself and others; it is the beauty of rage and fury.

No wonder, then, that Katerina Ivanovna appears as "blistering" and a woman of "great wrath" (*PSS* 14:446; 15:121), and Grushenka is seen by others as "possessed," "proud and insolent," a "tiger," "terrible woman," and "mutinous wench" (*PSS* 14:141, 323; 15:270). Yet Grushenka's and Katerina Ivanovna's self-descriptions are surprisingly similar: each one considers and describes herself in contradictory terms, both as beautiful and worthy—and as nasty and willful, furious and amok (*PSS* 14:139, 324; 15:181). Young Lise Khokhlakova, who is an "aspiring" maenad in the novel, is an embodiment of the maenadic paradox: she claims to want not to do good but bad, not to be happy but tormented, and to love Alyosha for his letting her not love him (*PSS* 15:21–22)! The maenad is thus constituted and torn by the opposite forces, which affect both herself and everyone around her.

For each other, the maenads show opposite affects, too: mutual distrust, jealousy, and even hatred—but also human sympathy, compassion, and readiness to forgive. In fact, Grushenka clearly realizes her maenadic affinity with Katerina Ivanovna and expresses it to her in a double act of recognizing and rejecting the sister maenad ("We are wicked, you and I! We are both wicked!"; *PSS* 15:188). On the one hand, Katerina Ivanovna acknowledges that she would have "beaten up" Grushenka, yet on the other hand, she also asks Grushenka for forgiveness (*PSS* 14:141; 15:188). A quick change of mood is characteristic of maenads—from the Dionysian to the Apollonian and back, from being on the edge to being self-possessed (*PSS* 14:173). The maenads do not keep their passions to themselves; they express their feelings for each other and their Dionysus openly in public and in each other's face. Their meetings, therefore, invariably turn into a *scandal*, a "rich" spectacle bordering on farce (*PSS* 15:122; see, by way of comparison, 14:132–41;

15:187–89). The profoundly ambivalent attitude not only toward each other and others and but also toward oneself distinguishes the "divine" maenads, who harbor and cherish the Dionysian and the Apollonian much more intensely than the Dostoevskian "gods."

This same ambiguity is seen in the maenads' capacity not only for spontaneous rage but also for carefully calculated revenge, which is a motive well known in literature since the time of Aristophanes.[37] They both tear apart those whom they love—and save them by an act of unselfish sacrifice; they both ruin and destroy—and save and expiate their Dionysus (Dmitry). They ruin his life as femmes fatales by making him act in an uncontrollable delirium, yet they help him in all possible ways, by providing him with money at a crucial moment (Katerina Ivanovna) and by being willing to follow him into the "underground" world of Siberian exile. For this reason, the maenads are not "demonic," insofar as they are not overly reflective and *are* capable of action that is not only destructive but also truly generous and redeeming (*PSS* 15:266).

Most importantly, without the maenads, the interaction of the characters cannot go on and the plot cannot unfold. The power that holds all the characters together is *love*: not the brotherly love of the gods or sisterly love-hate of the maenads but erotic and ecstatic—rather than redeemed and unfulfilled—love. Love relations between heroes differ from dialogical relations in that erotic love is never reciprocal and remains unanswered. Alyosha seems to love Lise; he wants to marry her and wheel her around in a wheelchair (*PSS* 14:167). Lise, in turn, fantasizes about marrying Alyosha yet desperately falls in love with Ivan (*PSS* 15:19–20). Ivan, however, ardently loves Katerina Ivanovna (*PSS* 15:48). But Katerina Ivanovna is deeply in love with Dmitry. Dmitry cannot stop loving Grushenka. And Grushenka strives to love Alyosha and thus attempts to seduce him (she sits on his lap and wants to "swallow" him; *PSS* 14:315, 318). The chain that unrequited erotic love builds and by which it inexorably links the "gods," "demons" and maenads together, appears then as: Alyosha → Lise → Ivan → Katerina Ivanovna → Dmitry → Grushenka → Alyosha. But the erotic full circle is broken by Alyosha, who falls in love with one of the boys, Kolya Krasotkin (whose name comes from *krasotka*, or "beauty"): both blush and make a mutual declaration of love, and Kolya ardently exclaims: "I loved you, loved terribly, loved and dreamed of you!" (*PSS* 14:504). In this way, Alyosha redeems himself from the Apollonian inability to love. The line of maenadic erotic love, however, is finally interrupted by a maenad herself—by Grushenka, who turns to Dmitry in self-sacrifice (*PSS* 14:469). Yet at this moment the action stops, and all the gods, demons, and maenads return from the ongoing tragedy of the novel to the myth of the final redemption.

Thus, despite Nietzsche's quibbles about the death of tragedy, Dostoevsky keeps tragedy alive as narrative in which people face their fate, are afflicted by disasters, commit crimes, and die; in which they freely accept the guilt for what they could not do otherwise, and are saved by a *maenas ex machina*'s miraculous moral transformation in the end. In the grand tragedy of Dostoevsky's works, where the characters are interconnected through suffering, aspiration, and love, the Apollonian and the Dionysian thus turn out to be two indissoluble aspects of heroes' characters, rather than two abstract dialectical opposites as the driving forces of a historical downfall.[38]

NOTES

1. "Dostoevsky, the only psychologist . . . from whom I had something to learn . . ." Friedrich Nietzsche, *Götzen-Dämmerung*, Aph. 45, in *Kritische Studienausgabe in 15 Einzelbänden*, ed. Giorgio Colli and Mazzino Montinari (Munich: Deutscher Taschenbuch Verlag, 1988), 6:147. See also Wolfgang Gesemann, "Nietzsches Verhältnis zu Dostoevskij auf dem europäischen Hintergrund der 80er Jahre," *Die Welt der Slaven* 2 (1961): 129–56, and C. A. Miller, "Nietzsche's 'Discovery' of Dostoevsky," *Nietzsche-Studien* 2 (1973): 202–57.

2. Friedrich Nietzsche, *Philologische Schriften (1867–1873): Kritische Gesamtausgabe*, ed. Fritz Bornmann and Mario Carpitelli (Berlin–New York: De Gruyter, 1982), Division 2, 1:3–58. On the importance of philology for Nietzsche and his reinvention of antiquity, see James I. Porter, *Nietzsche and the Philology of the Future* (Stanford: Stanford University Press, 2000), 228–35.

3. Nietzsche, "Homer und die klassische Philologie," in *Philologische Schriften*, 247–69.

4. Nietzsche, *Die Geburt der Tragödie aus dem Geiste der Musik*, in *Kritische Studienausgabe*, vol. 1 (referred to as *GT* followed by section and page number). For the English translation, see Friedrich Nietzsche, *The Birth of Tragedy and the Case of Wagner*, trans. Walter Kaufmann (New York: Vintage Books, 1967).

5. Nietzsche, "Aus der Jugendzeit," "Unendlich," "Heldenklage," etc., in *The Piano Music of Friedrich Nietzsche*, played by John Bell Young (Providence, R.I.: Newport Classic, 1992).

6. G. W. F. Hegel, *Vorlesungen über die Ästhetik*, in *Werke*, ed. Eva Moldenhauer and Karl Markus Michel (Frankfurt am Main: Suhrkamp, 1986), 14:446–53; 15:462–64, 527–31. See also G. W. F. Hegel, *Aesthetics: Lectures on Fine Art*, trans. T. M. Knox (Oxford: Clarendon, 1975), 2:1199–1201.

7. Nietzsche calls Zarathustra the "Dionysian monster"; *GT, Attempt at Self-Criticism*, 7, 22.

8. August Wilhelm von Schlegel, *Sämtliche Werke*, vol. 5, *Vorlesungen über dramatische Kunst und Literatur*, part 1; vol. 6, *Vorlesungen über dramatische Kunst und Literatur*, part 2, ed. Eduard Böcking (Leipzig: Weidmannsche Buchhandlung, 1846; repr. Hildesheim-New York: Georg Olms, 1971). The English translation: August Wilhelm von Schlegel, *Course of Lectures on Dramatic Art*

197

and Literature, trans. John Black, revised according to the last German edition by A. J. W. Morrison (New York: AMS Press, 1973 [second printing; first printing 1965, repr. from the original edition, London, 1846]). Nietzsche explicitly refers to Schlegel in *GT* 7, 54.

9. Schlegel, *Course of Lectures on Dramatic Art and Literature*, 145–46.

10. Schlegel, *Course of Lectures on Dramatic Art and Literature*, 176.

11. Dmitri Nikulin, *Comedy, Seriously: A Philosophical Study* (New York: Palgrave Macmillan, 2014), 113–31.

12. Schlegel, *Course of Lectures on Dramatic Art and Literature*, 188–89.

13. Friedrich Schiller, "Naive and Sentimental Poetry," in F. Schiller, *Naive and Sentimental Poetry: On the Sublime*, trans. Julius A. Elias (New York: Frederick Ungar, 1966).

14. Friedrich Schiller, "Zwei philosophische Entwürfe," in *Sämtliche Werke in 5 Bänden*, ed. Wolfgang Riedel (Munich: Deutscher Tauschenbuch Verlag, 2004), 5:1019: "Furcht zielt auf Stillstand . . . Freude auf Fortschreitung . . . Furcht existiert in den Grenzen dessen, was da ist. Freude schafft, was nicht da ist." (Fear aims at stillness . . . Joy at progression . . . Fear exists in the limits of that which is. Joy creates that which is not.)

15. Dmitri Nikulin, *Dialectic and Dialogue* (Stanford: Stanford University Press, 2010), 58–68.

16. See, by way of comparison, Vyacheslav Ivanov, "Nietzsche and Dionysus," in V. Ivanov, *Selected Essays*, trans. Robert Bird, ed. Michael Wachtel (Evanston: Northwestern University Press, 2001), 177–88.

17. Alexander Nehamas, *Nietzsche: Life as Literature* (Cambridge, Mass.: Harvard University Press, 1985), 42–43.

18. See, by way of comparison, Archilochus, 41–44, 46, and others; West, *Iambi et elegi Graeci ante Alexandrum cantata*, ed. M. L. West, 2nd ed. (Oxford: Oxford University Press, 1989), 1:18–20. See also M. West, *Studies in Greek Elegy and Iambus* (Berlin–New York: De Gruyter, 1974), 22–39; *Die griechische Literatur in Text und Darstellung, Bd. 1: Archaische Periode*, ed. Joachim Latacz (Stuttgart: Reclam, 1991), 240–47.

19. The two instruments are even assigned to different Muses as their attributes: flute to Euterpe, and lyre to Polyhymnia or sometimes to Erato. The use of the lyre in poetry goes back at least to the Mycenaean time, as seen in one of the Pylos frescoes. Geoffrey S. Kirk, *Homer and the Oral Tradition* (Cambridge: Cambridge University Press, 1976; repr. 2010), 19.

20. Plutarch, *Moralia*, vol. VI, fasc. 3, rev. and ed. K. Ziegler and M. Pohlenz (Leipzig: Teubner, 1966), 5.10–15.

21. *Iambi et elegi Graeci*, p. 174 and pages following.

22. See, by way of comparison, F. Nietzsche, *Philologische Schriften*, 8–9.

23. M. L. Gasparov, commentary to Pindar, Bacchylides, *Carmina et fragmenta* (Moscow: Nauka, 1980), 345–46.

24. It is only much later that Walter Otto will argue for the double character of Dionysus: Walter F. Otto, *Dionysus: Myth and Cult* (Bloomington: Indiana University Press, 1995).

25. *Der Kleine Pauly: Lexikon der Antike*, ed. Konrad Ziegler and Walther Sontheimer (Munich: Deutscher Taschenbuch Verlag, 1979), vol. 1, cols. 441–48.

26. The story becomes a favorite subject of depiction both in ancient and Renaissance art. See, by way of comparison, the painting *Apollo and Marsyas* by Michelangelo Anselmi, ca. 1540, in the National Gallery in Washington.

27. See, by way of comparison, the reverse of the bronze coin of Pergamum from the time of Marcus Aurelius, SNG France 2123–25.

28. In what follows, all references are to F. M. Dostoevsky, *Polnoe sobranie sochinenii v tridtsati tomakh* (Leningrad: Nauka, 1972–76), designated as *PSS* followed by volume and page number. The notes and commentaries to *The Brothers Karamazov* are by G. M. Friedlander, V. E. Vetlovskaya, et al., in *PSS* 15:393–619.

29. Lev Shestov, "Dostoevsky and Nietzsche: The Philosophy of Tragedy," in L. Shestov, *Dostoevsky, Tolstoy, Nietzsche*, trans. Bernard Martin and Spencer Roberts (Athens: Ohio University Press, 1969), 141–322, 201–202, 219; Simona Forti, *I nuovi demoni: Ripensare oggi male e potere* (Milan: Feltrinelli, 2012), 3–67, 272–75 et passim (see also the English translation: Simona Forti, *New Demons: Rethinking Power and Evil Today*, trans. Zakiya Hanafi [Stanford, Calif.: Stanford University Press, 2015], 15–54); C. A. Miller, "Nietzsche's 'Discovery' of Dostoevsky," p. 255–56; Janko Lavrin, "A Note on Nietzsche and Dostoevsky," *Russian Review* 28 (1969): 160–70; Nel Grillaert, *What the God-Seekers Found in Nietzsche: The Reception of Nietzsche's* Übermensch *by the Philosophers of the Russian Religious Renaissance* (Amsterdam-New York: Rodopi, 2008), 37–48, 71–77, 107–37; Edith W. Clowes, *The Revolution of Moral Consciousness: Nietzsche in Russian Literature, 1890–1914* (DeKalb: Northern Illinois University Press, 1988), 95.

30. Andrei Belyi, *Petersburg* (1913–14; 2nd ed. 1920), in *Sochinenia v dvukh tomakh* (Moscow: Khudozhestvennaia literatura, 1990), 2:7–292; commentaries by S. Piskunova and V. Piskunov. Nietzsche drew Bely's attention because of Bely's interest in the problem of suffering and sacrifice, the symbol of which he saw in Dionysus. Bely even wrote an essay, "Friedrich Nietzsche," which was published in 1911 in the *Arabeski*. See Clowes, *Moral Consciousness*, 156–57. Apollo also appears in the title and on the cover of the symbolist journal *Apollo*.

31. That the Apollonian-Dionysian distinction is applicable to the description of crimes committed by Dostoevsky's characters has been noticed by Khatchadourian, who has argued that the Dionysian impulses of the "heart" define the "crimes of sensuality and eroticism," such as those of Fyodor and Dmitry Karamazov, which are less serious than the "Apollonian" crimes of Raskolnikov, Stavrogin, and Ivan Karamazov that are defined by Platonic-Aristotelian measure-oriented reason (Haig Khatchadourian, "Rational/Irrational in Dosto-

evsky, Nietzsche, and Aristotle," *Journal of the British Society for Phenomenology* 11 (1980): 107–15). However, I want to argue that the distinction is much more pervasive in Dostoevsky. In what follows, I will be mostly referring to the last and most elaborate of Dostoevsky's novels, *The Brothers Karamazov*, with occasional references to and parallels in his earlier works.

32. The Dionysian "darkness" shows itself variously in the Karamazov family (in Dmitry, through rage; in the father, through greed and lust; in Ivan, through the recognition of the "power" of the Karamazovs' "baseness" (*PSS* 14:240). Dostoevsky's careful choice of the form of the family name points to it: *kara* means "dark" in Turkic languages, so the family name would then mean "darkly painted." This derivation is rather obvious to others: one of the minor characters mistakenly calls Alyosha "Chernomazov" (*chernyi* is "black"; *PSS* 14:184), which she does intentionally, in order to avenge an offense to her husband by offending Alyosha's other, his brother Dmitry. By this fictional etymology Dostoevsky probably also tried to stress the incongruence between the family's deeds and its old nobility, suggested by the form of its name, which would be the gentry of Tatar extraction going back to the Golden Horde (compare "you, Karamazovs, feign some great and ancient nobility," "*Vy, gospoda Karamazovy, kakikh-to velikikh i drevnikh dvorian iz sebia korchite*"; *PSS* 14:77). Such is also the pedigree of the family of the Apollo and Dionysus heroes in Bely's *Petersburg*, of the father and son Ableukhov, whose name is playfully derived from that of a fictional mirza Ab-Lay with a comic ending, Ukhov, pointing to the size of the father's ears. In a sense, the name Ablai-Ukhov can be read as a parodic reference to Kara-mazov, both being a cross between a Turkic and a Russian root.

33. Mikhail Bakhtin, *Problems of Dostoevsky's Poetics*, ed. and trans. Caryl Emerson (Minneapolis–London: University of Minnesota Press, 1984), 36 and pages following.

34. René Descartes, *Discours de la méthode*, in *Oeuvres de Descartes*, ed. Charles Adam and Paul Tannery (Paris: Vrin, 1996), 6:33.

35. This is not to say that Dostoevsky's novels are lacking in humor, parody, and satire. See R. L. Busch, *Humor in the Major Novels of F. M. Dostoevsky* (Columbus: Slavica, 1987).

36. The characteristics of maenads include "frenzy, running, intrafamilial killing and destruction of the household, and lamentation for family members." Richard Seaford, "Tragedy and Dionysus," in *A Companion to Tragedy*, ed. Rebecca Bushnell (Oxford: Blackwell, 2005), 25–38; 34–37.

37. Aristophanes, *Lysistrata*; F. Schiller, "Merkwürdiges Beispiel einer weiblichen Rache," in *Sämtliche Werke*, 5:183–219.

38. I am grateful to Carol Bernstein, Caryl Emerson, Joseph Lemelin, and Lev Nikulin for their most helpful suggestions on this essay.

Contributors

Edith W. Clowes holds the Brown-Forman Chair in the Humanities and teaches Russian language, literature, and culture in the Department of Slavic Languages and Literatures at the University of Virginia. Among her recent book-length publications are an interdisciplinary work on post-Soviet Russian identity, *Russia on the Edge: Imagined Geographies and Post-Soviet Identity* (Cornell, 2011); a discursive history of Russian philosophy, *Fiction's Overcoat: Russian Literary Culture and the Question of Philosophy* (Cornell, 2004); and an editorial collaboration, *Sbornik "Vekhi" v kontekste russkoi kul'tury* (*The Landmarks Collection in Its Russian Context*; Moscow: Nauka, 2007). *Area Studies in the Global Age: Community, Place, Identity*, a multi-authored book edited with Shelly Jarrett Bromberg (Miami University), appeared in spring 2016 (Northern Illinois University Press).

Joshua Foa Dienstag is a professor of political science and law at the University of California, Los Angeles. He is the author of *Dancing in Chains: Narrative and Memory in Political Theory* (Stanford, 1997), *Pessimism: Philosophy, Ethic, Spirit* (Princeton, 2006), and other books and articles on the history of political thought, literature, and film. His new book, *Cinema, Democracy, Perfectionism: Joshua Foa Dienstag in Dialogue*, is forthcoming from Manchester.

Michael Allen Gillespie is a professor of political science and philosophy at Duke University. He works in political philosophy, with particular emphasis on modern continental theory and the history of political philosophy. He is the author of *Hegel, Heidegger, and the Ground of History*; *Nihilism before Nietzsche*; and *The Theological Origins of Modernity*. He is also coeditor of *Nietzsche's New Seas: Explorations in Philosophy, Aesthetics, and Politics*; *Ratifying the Constitution*; and *Homo Politicus, Homo Economicus*. He has published articles on Montaigne, Kant, Hegel, Nietzsche, Heidegger, existentialism, and various topics in American political thought and public philosophy, as well as on the relation of religion and politics.

Ilya Kliger is an associate professor of Russian and Slavic studies at New York University. He is author of *The Narrative Shape of Truth: Veridiction in Modern European Literature* (2011), as well as articles on the history and theory of the novel, and literary theory more broadly. He is a member of the working groups on Historical Poetics and Retroformalism. Currently, he is working on a book on the tragic social imaginary in the age of Russian Realism.

Jeff Love is a professor of German and Russian at Clemson University. He is the author of *Tolstoy: A Guide for the Perplexed* (Continuum, 2008), and *The Overcoming of History in War and Peace* (Brill-Rodopi, 2004). He has also published an annotated translation of F. W. J. Schelling's *Philosophical Investigations into the Essence of Human Freedom* (State University of New York Press, 2006) with Johannes Schmidt.

Jeffrey Metzger is an associate professor of government at Cameron University. He is the editor of *Nietzsche, Nihilism, and the Philosophy of the Future* and has published essays on Nietzsche, Dostoevsky, and Richard Rorty.

Dmitri Nikulin is a professor of philosophy at The New School for Social Research in New York. He is the author of a number of books including *Matter, Imagination, and Geometry* (2002), *On Dialogue* (2006), *Dialectic and Dialogue* (2010), *Comedy, Seriously* (2014) and the editor of *Memory: A History* (2015).

Francesca Cernia Slovin is an independent scholar. Her work published in Italian and in English includes books on Warburg, *Obsessed by Art* (1995, 2006); Rousseau, *The Last Walk* (1999, 2009); the politico-philosophical roots of the foundation of Israel, *Eretz Israel* (2003, 2011); and the novel *Paris at Night* (2012).

Geoff Waite teaches literature, philosophy, political theory, art history, and visual studies at Cornell University. He is the author of *Nietzsche's Corps/e*.

Index

Index

Dostoevsky, Fyodor: *bogatyr'* figure in,
151–55; Christ figure in, 49, 51, 53,
156, 164; female characters in, 156,
163, 194–96; man-god concept in, x,
89, 94, 97–98, 102, 107n36; melodrama in, 171n70; narrative in, 39–40,
48–53; plot in, 157–64, 170n58; statue
of, 32n71; women and, 11. *See also*
education; nationalism; Nietzsche,
Friedrich; nihilism; truth
WORKS: *The Adolescent* (*A Raw Youth*),
17–18, 23, 32n63, 48–49; "Bookishness and Literacy," 145; *The Brothers Karamazov*, xii–xiv, 13, 30n40,
30n42, 33n82, 46, 50–53, 94–101,
103, 107nn32–33, 143–44, 160, 173,
184, 185–96, 200n32; *Crime and
Punishment*, xiii, xvi, 5, 11, 28n10,
37, 50, 99, 155, 158, 161–62, 164–65,
170n66, 192; *Demons*, x–xi, xii, xiii,
3, 5, 8, 9, 11, 18–22, 26, 29n21, 40,
48–49, 93–96, 99, 107n40, 192;
L'esprit souterrain, 15–16, 24, 60,
82, 109, 118, 125, 129, 131, 141n17,
173; "The Gambler," 22, 81n2; *The
House of the Dead*, 14, 23, 25, 28n10,
92, 109, 152–53; *Humiliated and Insulted*, 16–17, 21, 34n85; *The Idiot*,
xvi, 39–40, 48–49, 109, 121, 155–57,
161, 162–64, 173, 186, 187, 194;
"The Landlady," 15–16, 24, 60, 129;
"Life of a Great Sinner," 169n42;
"The Meek One," 153–54; *Notes
from Underground*, xii–xiii, xiv–xv,
5, 15–17, 21, 24, 28n10, 41–43, 44,
46–51, 54, 56n18, 58–60, 62–63,
70–81, 82n6, 83n12, 84nn21–23,
85n27, 91, 109, 110, 117–22, 125–38,
139n2–140n3, 157, 160; "A Series of
Articles on Russian Literature," 154;
"Vlas," 151–52, 162; "White Nights,"
14–15, 16, 21, 26; *Winter Notes on
Summer Impressions*, 70–71; *A Writer's Diary*, 4–5, 151–53

education: Dostoevsky on, 145–46;
Nietzsche on, 147–49
Engels, Friedrich, 3, 5, 9
Euripides, 177, 179, 182, 194
evil, Christian concept of, ix, xiv, 38–39
existentialism, x–xi

Feuerbach, Ludwig, 107n25, 107n36, 127,
137, 140n11
finitude, xi
Flaubert, Gustave, 41
Förster-Nietzsche, Elisabeth, 8, 12
Frank, Joseph, 130, 140n2
free will, 57n42, 69, 96, 133
Freud, Sigmund, ix, 126, 132, 138
Friedlander, G. M., 189

Gadamer, Hans-Georg, x, xviin2
Garnett, Constance, 31n56
German Romanticism, 41, 155, 174,
176–79, 185
Gilbert, David, 25
Glucksmann, André, 27n4
Goethe, Johann Wolfgang von, 45, 98, 176
Gogol, Nikolay, 192
Gramsci, Antonio, 25, 32n70
Greek drama, xiv, 43, 112–15, 117, 119–20,
150–51, 154, 158, 160, 165, 170n57, 177,
182; New Comedy, 177–78, 180, 193–94
Grigoriev, Apollon, 144, 189

Habermas, Jürgen, 34n85
Hamlet, 33n73, 119
Hartmann, Eduard von, 112
Hegel, Georg Wilhelm Friedrich, 39, 93,
98, 100, 111, 151, 159, 176–77, 178–79
Heidegger, Martin, x, xviin2, 40, 45, 174
Heraclitus, 114, 115–16
Herzen, Alexander, 6, 8–9, 10, 35n99
Herzen, Natalie, 6, 8–9, 11, 13, 28n10
Hesse, Hermann, 188
Hobbes, Thomas, 126, 175
Homer, 38, 50, 174, 179, 182–83, 194
Homeric Hymns, 183–84
Hugo, Victor, 128
Humboldt, Wilhelm von, 147–48

Ilya Muromets, 154, 169n41
indeterminacy and determinacy, xii–xiii,
37–40, 42, 43, 46, 47–48, 53–54
individuality, 58, 80, 81n1, 118, 146,
150–51, 154–55, 162, 175
Ivanov, Vyacheslav, 158–59, 167n2

Jackson, Robert Louis, xviin2, 46, 82n4,
140n3
Jameson, Frederic, 35n98
Janz, Curt Paul, 105n4

Index

Index

Wagner, Richard, 6, 8, 29n15, 43, 87, 90,
    109, 148, 149–50, 166, 174, 176
Waite, Geoff, 59
Wellhausen, Julius, 20
wickedness, 44, 59, 70, 71–73, 77–78,
    80–81

Widmann, Joseph Viktor, 17–18, 19, 22
Wittgenstein, Ludwig, 33n73

Zamyatin, Yevgeny, 57n42
Zasulich, Vera, xii, 8–9, 13